# Quality Indicators for Assistive Technology

## A COMPREHENSIVE GUIDE TO ASSISTIVE TECHNOLOGY SERVICES

**THE QIAT LEADERSHIP TEAM**

Gayl Bowser | Diana Foster Carl | Kelly S. Fonner | Terry Vernon Foss
Jane Edgar Korsten | Kathleen M. Lalk | Joan Breslin Larson | Scott Marfilius
Susan R. McCloskey | Penny R. Reed | Joy Smiley Zabala

Library of Congress Control Number 2015946662
Paperback ISBN 978-0-9898674-5-0
Ebook ISBN 978-0-9898674-6-7
Library Edition ISBN 978-0-9898674-7-4

Published by
CAST Professional Publishing
an imprint of CAST, Inc.
www.castpublishing.org

CAST Professional Publishing
40 Harvard Mills Square/Suite 3/Wakefield, MA 01880

Publisher's Cataloging-In-Publication Data
(Prepared by The Donohue Group, Inc.)

Quality indicators for assistive technology : a comprehensive guide to
  assistive technology services / the QIAT Leadership Team: Gayl Bowser
  [and 10 others].

     pages ; cm

   "The QIAT Leadership Team: Gayl Bowser, Diana Foster Carl, Kelly S. Fonner, Terry Vernon Foss,
Jane Edgar Korsten, Kathleen M. Lalk, Joan Breslin Larson, Scott Marfilius, Susan R. McCloskey,
Penny R. Reed, Joy Smiley Zabala."
   Includes index.
   Issued also as an ebook.
   ISBN: 978-0-9898674-5-0 (paperback)
   ISBN: 978-0-9898674-7-4 (library edition)

   1. People with disabilities—Education.  2. Self-help devices for people with disabilities.  3. People with disabilities—Services for.  4. Special education—Technological innovations.  5. Assistive computer technology.  6. Social indicators.  I. Bowser, Gayl.  II. QIAT Leadership Team.

LC4019 .Q53 2015
371.9/043        2015946662

APA Citation: QIAT Leadership Team (2015). Quality indicators for assistive technology: A comprehensive guide to assistive technology services. Wakefield, MA: CAST Professional Publishing.

Cover and interior design by Happenstance Type-O-Rama.

Printed in the United States of America.

*To all of the dedicated individuals with and without disabilities, the families, professionals, and countless others who work hard every day to ensure that people with disabilities have the assistive technology devices and services they need to participate fully in all that life has to offer.*

# Contents

# Preface

The development of the Quality Indicators for Assistive Technology (QIAT) began in the summer of 1998 when 14 assistive technology (AT) service providers from across the nation gathered to share common concerns about the complexity of issues and processes related to AT training and service delivery. We each had a history of experience and leadership in AT in K–12 school settings. Many of us were engaged in professional development about AT and improving AT services at the local, state, or national level. Some were also parents or family members of individuals with disabilities. We were, by intention, geographically and professionally diverse. Many participants in this original core group, now known as the QIAT Leadership Team, have continued to actively guide the ongoing development of the QIAT work over the years.

Early in our discussions we recognized there were no consistent, clearly-defined descriptors of quality AT services to guide the alignment of our professional development efforts. When faced with this void, we decided to create a set of descriptors that would be widely applicable and could serve as unifying guidelines for quality AT services, regardless of geographic location or service delivery model. We realized early on that quality indicators would be most readily understood and usable if they were closely aligned to the major activities associated with the delivery of AT services in schools across the country. Based on concerns from the field, our initial focus was on AT consideration, assessment, implementation, and evaluation of effectiveness. In preparation for developing the initial drafts of the descriptors in each of these areas, we explored the standards developed by the Joint Committee on Standards for Educational Evaluation and used their format as a model for our efforts (Joint Committee on Standards, 1994).

## Expanded Input

Soon after the initial work was produced, we began engaging others in sharing, improving, and expanding the content through interactive sessions at local, state, national, and international conferences. Over the years, these sessions included over 4,000 individuals who participated in critical discussion of the Quality Indicators, and provided oral and written suggestions for the continuing development of collaborative efforts.

Throughout the development of QIAT, the ideas gained from participants at conference sessions served as the basis for revision and continued refinement of the Quality Indicators. In addition, participants assisted in determining the perceived value of QIAT, not only to conference participants but also to others with similar responsibilities and interests. Over 2,000 written responses and many hours of collegial conversations convinced us that QIAT could be useful to those concerned with the development and delivery of AT services with a variety of perspectives ranging from students and families to school staff and policy makers.

To gain even more input, we held QIAT Summits, inviting anyone interested in AT services. These three-day meetings expanded the number of people who participated in the development and writing of the quality indicators and increased the amount of time for participation. Summits were face-to-face work sessions that took place in many regions of the country, which provided an opportunity to gather information on variations in regional practices. Over the years they were held in Missouri (1999), Kansas (2001), Oregon (2003), Georgia (2005), Texas (2007), Minnesota (2009), Florida (2010), and Arkansas (2011). In a series of sessions, participants worked collaboratively in large and small groups to review, revise, refine, and expand the Quality Indicators. Over the years, this work deepened the understanding of the purpose, scope, and potential uses of the Quality Indicators and led us to develop tools that can be used to assist with the development and implementation of high-quality AT services (e.g., self-evaluation matrices for each indicator, guidance documents, and a variety of forms for specific uses).

In 2004, Joy Zabala conducted a study that sought to establish the perceived importance, validity, and utility of the first six areas of Quality Indicators to five different groups: AT users and family members, AT service providers, K–12 administrators, higher education professionals, and policy makers. (Zabala's research did not include transition or professional development.) Their input affirmed the importance, validity, and utility of the main ideas of each of the Quality Indicators across all groups (Zabala, 2007). Their suggestions for minor changes to improve clarity led us to revise the wording of several of the indicators in 2005.

## Dissemination

We began disseminating the QIAT work almost immediately after the development of the initial indicators knowing that the engagement of many people was critical to the quality and utility. Dissemination included holding face-to-face interactive conference presentations and summits, developing the QIAT website (*www.qiat.org*), establishing the QIAT electronic list, and creating publications for consumer and research journals. This four-pronged approach enabled people with varied perspectives in different parts of the country to access the Quality Indicators, contribute actively to the ongoing work, and benefit from it.

The most active methods for sharing and participating in the QIAT work have been through the QIAT electronic mail list and website. Initially the website contained working drafts of the QIAT Indicators, a historical perspective of the work, information on ways to support ongoing collegial conversations, and an invitation to join the QIAT electronic mail list. The website has evolved with the work and now includes copies of the Indicators, supporting documents, links to research related to QIAT work, and a range of resources submitted by QIAT electronic mail list participants. Readers are encouraged to sign up for the QIAT list, following links on the website.

Although we originally began the QIAT list to facilitate widespread participation in conversation about the Quality Indicators and topics related to their continued development, over the years it has grown into a highly regarded learning community about all aspects of AT that includes people from across the U.S. and abroad. Members of the QIAT list include, but are not limited to, special education teachers, speech-language pathologists, occupational therapists, AT specialists, adult AT users, parents of students using assistive technology, general education teachers, rehabilitation specialists, teacher educators in higher education, vendors, and people engaged in the development and implementation of AT related policy.

The members of QIAT discuss not only the Quality Indicators, but also a range of topics that pertain to quality AT services, such as report writing, research, staff qualifications and certification, device specifics, and state standards. The QIAT List has been recognized in the literature as a community of practice (Edyburn, 2005, 2007); and, recently Wojcik (2011) analyzed three years of conversation on the QIAT list to identify themes of AT service delivery and self-reported functions related to the school-based, AT service-delivery process.

## Publications

The Quality Indicators for Assistive Technology have been included in a wide range of publications. They were first described by Bowser, Korsten, Reed, and Zabala (1999), and soon after published in their entirety in the *Journal of Special Education Technology* (Zabala et al., 2000). Breslin-Larson, Smith, Fields, & Hill (2004) later described how they used the Quality Indicators and the self-evaluation matrices to develop and implement a state improvement effort. Zabala and Carl (2005) described their use in schools. Castellani et al. (2004) included the Quality Indicators for Consideration in a publication on Assistive Technology Consideration published by the Council for Exceptional Children. Bowser and Reed (2004) used them as a tool for program administrators wishing to evaluate the programs they supervise and to help develop consensus for the actions that need to be taken to develop or improve programs that provide assistive technology services. Reed and Bowser (2005) also highlighted the Quality Indicators for Including Assistive Technology in the Individual Educational Program (IEP) in a chapter on writing assistive technology in the IEP. The Quality Indicators frequently appear in the literature, are included in the AT guidelines of several state departments of education, and are among the most widely known guidelines for the provision of assistive technology services (Dell, Newton, & Petroff, 2008).

# Acknowledgements

The authors of this book, collectively and individually, would like to express their thanks and admiration for all of those who have contributed to this work. This includes more than 3,850 members of the QIAT list from 17 different countries, the hosts and participants in QIAT Summits, and participants at conferences and workshop sessions. We would like to thank our colleagues at the National Assistive Technology Research Institute (NATRI) and the National Assistive Technology in Education (NATE) Network for their support. We would also like to acknowledge and thank former members of the QIAT Leadership Team who have been part of this work from our earliest days, including Kim Hartsell, Sandy Nettleton, Sharon Davis, Terry Hamman, Merv Blunt, and Cheryl Deterding. Last, but certainly not least, our thanks to our families and loved ones who have supported, encouraged, cooked for, tolerated, chauffeured, and loved us.

We are delighted that you have chosen this book and are indebted to the thousands of people in the QIAT community who have been involved in some way in the development of the body of work. As the QIAT Leadership Team, it has been our professional and personal privilege to donate the time and effort to lead this initiative over the years. Through the collaboration of so many, it has led to something much more world-changing than we ever could have imagined.

## QIAT Leadership Team

Gayl Bowser, M.S., Special Education

Diana Foster Carl, M.A., L.S.S.P., School Psychology

Kelly S. Fonner, M.S., Educational Technology/Special Education

Terry Vernon Foss, M.Ed., Special Education

Jane Edgar Korsten, M.A., Speech Pathology and Audiology

Kathleen M. Lalk, M.S., A.T.P., Educational Technology

Joan Breslin Larson, M.Ed., Special Education

Scott Marfilius, M.A., Special Education

Susan R. McCloskey, M.S., CCC-SLP, Speech Pathology

Penny R. Reed, Ph.D., Special Education

Joy Smiley Zabala, Ed.D., A.T.P., Special Education

# CHAPTER 1

# Introduction to the Quality Indicators for Assistive Technology

Technology plays an increasingly diverse and important role in the lives of most people, but nowhere is it as critical as in the life of an individual with a disability. Technology can help overcome barriers imposed by disability and create access to a broad range of activities. For students with disabilities, technology can be an important tool to improve access to the curriculum and increase learning. When technology is used to increase functional capability of a student with a disability it is, by definition, assistive technology (AT). A wide variety of tools, many developed for other purposes and ranging from simple to complex, can be AT for students with disabilities.

The Quality Indicators for Assistive Technology (QIAT) describe critical elements involved in the provision of AT services. This chapter provides an overview of the

- rationale and need for QIAT,

- basic principles of QIAT, and

- structure of Quality Indicators for Assistive Technology (QIAT).

## The Rationale and Need for QIAT

*Overall, I feel that my school district does a superior job of providing an education for its students who receive special education services. Throughout the district there is a conscientious attempt to follow the letter and the intent of IDEA with the exception of one area. That area is assistive technology. This has not occurred through an intentional disregard of the law, but rather, through a lack of understanding or a misunderstanding of information about assistive technology.*

*The determinations of what assistive technology devices and services need to be provided to a student have been completed very informally and haphazardly and primarily just for the students with moderate to severe disabilities. No consistent and systematic assessment has been used in the consideration of need. This has resulted in students being under served and money being wasted. Inappropriate equipment has been ordered. Equipment has been duplicated unnecessarily. Items are strewn throughout the district with no record of what is where. Equipment is underused, unused, and inappropriately used because the proper training was not provided.*

(Special Education teacher, 1998 in Bowser and Reed, 2012, p.i)

The Individuals with Disabilities Education Improvement Act of 2004 (IDEA) notes that almost 30 years of research and experience have demonstrated that the education of children with disabilities can be made more effective by "... supporting the development and use of technology, including assistive technology devices and assistive technology services, to maximize accessibility for children with disabilities." (IDEA, 2004 [C.F.R § 601.(5)(H)34]). In addition, research has shown AT can improve outcomes in a variety of academic areas including mathematics (Maccini & Gagnon, 2005), writing (Sitko, Laine, & Sitko, 2005), reading (Strangman & Dalton, 2005), achievement of IEP goals (Watson, Ito, Smith, & Andersen, 2010), and across various types of disabilities (Ostensjo, Carlberg, & Vollestad, 2005; Stumbo, Martin, & Hedrick, 2009). In spite of the wide recognition of the benefits of AT, many students with disabilities still do not receive needed AT devices and services as part of their IEP.

In part, this is because school districts still struggle to develop and sustain programs that effectively and efficiently consider, assess, and provide AT devices and services to the students who need them. Although it's clear that a student's need for AT must be considered in the development of an IEP, no official national guidance has been provided about how to consider and determine a need for AT or how to ensure appropriate levels of service. Much is left to chance or individual discretion. School district teams commonly struggle with questions such as: "What does it mean to *consider* AT?" "Which procedural safeguards apply to the provision of AT?" "How do we know what AT devices and services are really needed for a child to participate in and benefit from a free, appropriate, public education (FAPE)?" "How do we help a child use AT and evaluate that use?"

The primary purpose of QIAT is to guide thoughtful development, provision, and evaluation of AT services for students with disabilities. The Quality Indicators, intent statements, and descriptions included in QIAT provide support for the development and delivery of AT services of consistently high quality to all students who require those services to make progress toward meeting their educational goals. Rather than proposing or supporting any particular model of AT service delivery, QIAT describes core components that should be present in some form in all AT service delivery systems of high quality.

Regardless of where services are provided or the specific model used to support service provision, the Quality Indicators apply (Zabala, 2007). Further, QIAT supports the federal requirement that the services should address not only the needs of students, but also the needs of family members and school personnel working with students who require AT devices and services to receive FAPE.

## Quality Indicator Areas

QIAT describes core components of quality AT services in eight core areas. The indicators in each area can be used as guideposts for developing effective, efficient, and ethical services. The eight Quality Indicator areas are

- Consideration of Assistive Technology Needs,

- Assessment of Assistive Technology Needs,

- Including Assistive Technology in the IEP,

- Assistive Technology Implementation,

- Evaluation of Effectiveness of Assistive Technology,

- Assistive Technology Transition,

- Professional Development and Training in Assistive Technology, and

- Administrative Support of Assistive Technology Service.

QIAT supports systemic AT decision-making and actions at all points of AT service delivery as well as guidance for effectively documenting, organizing, and monitoring AT selection, acquisition, and use by individual students. Quality Indicator Areas align to specific areas of responsibility in special-education processes that may require services to support the use of AT. The first six indicator areas guide teams through the processes necessary to determine support needed for an individual student's use of AT. *Professional Development and Training in Assistive Technology* and *Administrative Support of Assistive Technology Services* support planning and implementation of AT processes and procedures at the education agency level.

# Principles Underlying All Areas of QIAT

The complexity of identifying Quality Indicators that are useful across a wide variety of educational environments and service provision options is evident. The issues with implementing quality services in a way that supports positive student results are even more complex. There is clearly a need for people with a wide variety of perspectives and experiences as providers and consumers of AT services to participate in defining and implementing this work.

When reviewing or using QIAT, it's important to know the basic principles underlying all areas of QIAT:

- It is essential that all AT services developed and delivered by states or education agencies are legally correct according to the mandates and expectations of federal and state laws.

- AT efforts at all stages involve ongoing collaborative work by teams that include families and care givers, school personnel, and individuals from other service agencies as appropriate. These teams are referred to as "collaborative teams" throughout the text because the ability to share knowledge and work together is critical.

- All team members involved in AT processes are responsible for following the code of ethics for their respective professions; nothing being asked of them should negate that responsibility.

QIAT is designed to be specifically applicable to educational settings at all levels. The term "IEP team" will be used throughout the text, but it applies equally to early childhood services, where it would be the Individual Family Services Plan (IFSP). Therefore the term "education agency" is used throughout QIAT rather than school, district, service provider, or some other more specific term to avoid the assumption that QIAT applies to only one level or type of service provision. Though QIAT is intended for education agencies and is based on the regulations of the United States, other countries and service agencies have found that, with minor adjustments, pertinent to specific regulations and service plans, the content is valuable and useful in other settings where AT services are provided (Martin, 2013).

In order to understand the need for the Quality Indicators, it's important to understand the history of AT in educational policy, the research about the delivery of AT services, and the impact of AT on the education of students with disabilities.

## Legal Mandate for Assistive Technology in IDEA

As early as 1990, the Office of Special Education Programs (OSEP) of the United States Department of Education provided guidance requiring consideration of AT needs during the development of IEPs for children with disabilities (Schrag, 1990). This guidance indicated that the provision of FAPE for all students with disabilities must include the tools needed for the student to benefit from educational opportunities. Also, for the first time, in 1990, the Individuals with Disabilities Education Act (IDEA) (P.L. 101-476) mandated the provision of AT devices and services if students need them in order to receive FAPE, and provided definitions of AT devices and services (Individuals with Disabilities Education Act, 1990). Subsequent revisions of the law in 1997 and 2004 included the mandate that every IEP team consider each student's need for AT devices and services during the development of the IEP, and the 2004 revision stipulated that AT is considered in the development, review, and revision of the IEP (IDEA, 1997; IDEA, 2004). This addition increased awareness and scrutiny among education agencies of the procedures and practices used to plan and implement AT services.

The definition of AT was initially published in federal law in the Technology Related Assistance for Individuals with Disabilities Act of 1988 and remains consistent in all federal legislation. In IDEA, AT is defined as follows:

### 34 C.F.R. § 300.5 Assistive technology device

Assistive technology device means any item, piece of equipment, or product system, whether acquired commercially off the shelf, modified, or customized, that is used to increase, maintain, or improve the functional capabilities of a child with a disability. The term does not include a medical device that is surgically implanted, or the replacement of that device. (Authority 20 U.S.C. 1401(1))

IDEA also defines assistive technology services:

### 34 C.F.R. § 300.6 Assistive technology service

Assistive technology service means any service that directly assists a child with a disability in the selection, acquisition, or use of an assistive technology device. The term includes

a.  The evaluation of the needs of a child with a disability, including a functional evaluation of the child in the child's customary environment;

b.  Purchasing, leasing, or otherwise providing for the acquisition of assistive technology devices by children with disabilities;

c.  Selecting, designing, fitting, customizing, adapting, applying, maintaining, repairing, or replacing assistive technology devices;

d.  Coordinating and using other therapies, interventions, or services with assistive technology devices, such as those associated with existing education and rehabilitation plans and programs;

e.  Training or technical assistance for a child with a disability or, if appropriate, that child's family; and

f.  Training or technical assistance for professionals (including individuals providing education or rehabilitation services), employers, or other individuals who provide services to, employ, or are otherwise substantially involved in the major life functions of that child. (Authority: 20 U.S.C. 1401(2))

IDEA defines the responsibility of the local education agency (LEA) to provide AT devices and services. LEA is the legal term for school districts and other local K–12 education agencies. It is this mandate that heightened the awareness of AT among education agencies throughout the country and provided the impetus for the development of the Quality Indicators for Assistive Technology.

### 34 C.F.R § 300.105 Assistive technology

a.  Each public agency must ensure that assistive technology devices or assistive technology services, or both, as those terms are defined in §§ 300.5 and 300.6, respectively, are made available to a child with a disability if required as a part of the child's

    1.  special education under § 300.36;

    2.  related services under § 300.34; or

    3.  supplementary aids and services under §§ 300.38 and 300.114(a)(2)(ii).

b.  On a case-by-case basis, the use of school-purchased assistive technology devices in a child's home or in other settings is required if the child's IEP

Team determines that the child needs access to those devices in order to receive FAPE. (Authority: 20 U.S.C. 1401(2))

Unfortunately, members of IEP teams often are unprepared to implement this statute effectively and school districts often are unprepared to provide sufficient training and support in AT to members of IEP teams and others involved in AT work (Bowser & Reed, 1995; Hutinger, Johanson, & Stoneburner, 1996; Todis & Walker, 1993).

Even excellent educational practices, such as universal design for learning (UDL), can add to the confusion. UDL is a framework that guides the shift from trying to make lessons and activities accessible after the fact to a process that includes the incorporation of accessible instructional materials and barrier-free learning options at the instructional design stage (Rose & Meyer, 2002). When instruction is designed with built-in choices and access for all students including those with special education needs, it makes the teacher's job much easier. However, it does not eliminate the need to document in the IEP the specific features or AT a student needs in order to make progress in the general education curriculum. For example, a teacher might think she doesn't need to note the need for text-to-speech in an individual student's IEP because she provides a universally designed learning environment where all of the lessons in the classroom include the option of using text-to-speech when reading new material. But, if that student moves to another education agency, text-to-speech may not be commonly available. The IEP must document his need for access to text via text-to-speech, without regard to what is available for other students.

## Additional Mandates: Section 504 and the ADA

Not all students with disabilities need specially designed instruction. Students with disabilities who do not require specially designed instruction are not eligible under IDEA and will not have IEPs. These students may still need AT in order to access or participate in their education and may receive it under the provisions of Section 504 of the Rehabilitation Act of 1973 or the Americans with Disabilities Act of 1990 (Title II). Section 504 is a civil rights law that guarantees that no student with a disability will "be excluded from participation in, be denied the benefits of, or be subjected to discrimination under any program or activity receiving Federal financial assistance." (Rehabilitation Act of 1973, Section 504, 1977) Education agencies that receive federal funds must provide accommodations, including AT to students with disabilities if needed, so that they will receive an education equal to that of their peers.

There is no required schedule for the consideration or assessment of the need for AT under Section 504 or Title II. The education agency should have a procedure in place to address the need for AT for students who receive services under Section 504. The Americans with Disabilities Act (ADA) of 1990 (Title II) is also a civil rights law that prohibits discrimination on the basis of disability. Students with disabilities are covered by Title II and Section 504, regardless of their eligibility for special education and related services under the IDEA. Individuals with disabilities who qualify under Section 504 and Title II are those who: (1) have a physical or mental impairment that substantially limits one or more major life activities; (2) have a record of such an impairment; or (3) are regarded as having such an impairment. State and local education agencies have an obligation under Section 504 and Title II to ensure an equal educational opportunity to students with disabilities, including the timely provision of AT to students with disabilities who need it.

There are notable differences between IDEA and the Title II regulations (U.S. Department of Justice and U.S. Department of Education, 2014a). Title II regulations require that public schools provide appropriate auxiliary aids and services when necessary to afford an "equal opportunity" to participate in and benefit from the agency's services, programs, or activities and that communication with students with disabilities is as effective as communication with students without disabilities. (23 C.F.R. §§ 35.130 and 35.160) Title II also requires that the education agency gives "primary consideration" to a request from the student or parent for a particular auxiliary aide related to their disability when determining what is appropriate for that student. (29 C.F.R. § 35.160(b)(2)) AT may be included under this auxiliary aide designation. Under the IDEA, the child's program must be individually designed to provide meaningful educational benefit. The IDEA does not require that a district compare the effectiveness of communications for a student with a disability to the effectiveness of communications with students without disabilities, while Title II does (U.S. Department of Justice and U.S. Department of Education, 2014a, 2014b).

For a student with a disability who is covered under both laws, the education agency must ensure that both sets of legal obligations are met. For many students, the special education and related services that they receive under the IDEA will ensure that their communication is as effective as communication is with other students. In other instances, AT and other methods or strategies for providing effective communication that are provided under the IDEA, may not be sufficient to ensure that communication with the specific student is as effective as communication with other students. In this case, the Title II obligations have not been met (U.S. Department of Justice and U.S. Department of Education 2014a, 2014b).

## Need for Guidance

Approaches to the provision of AT devices and services vary across the nation. Literature reviews reveal that there is a significant and continuing gap between what is required by policy and what consistently occurs in educational settings due to: (1) absence of systematic planning for delivery of AT services; (2) insufficient opportunity for school staff and family members of students with disabilities to learn about and use the AT; and (3) differing perspectives, attitudes, knowledge, and skills for those who have a role in AT services in school settings (Bray, Brown, and Green, 2004; Hitchcock et al., 2005; Warschauer, 2007). This gap points to the continuing need for guidance in assuring that quality AT services are available on a broader scale in order to provide equity across students, schools, and agencies.

The lack of a clearly understood description of quality AT services has resulted in differences in AT practice and inconsistent educational access for students who need it. This has not occurred through an intentional disregard of the law, but rather, through a lack of or misunderstanding of information about AT. A reliable and systematic approach to the consideration and evaluation of the need for AT as well as the delivery of those devices and services continues to be needed.

Practitioners working to narrow the gap note that the ability of education agencies to develop and provide AT services of consistently high quality has been complicated by at least three realities: (a) the complexity of issues and processes related to AT; (b) large numbers of diverse individuals involved in the processes; and (c) lack of a unifying set of descriptors to aid in the development, provision, and evaluation of quality AT services (Bowser & Reed, 1995; Carl, Mataya & Zabala, 1994; Zabala, 1996; Todis, 1996; Todis & Walker, 1993).

Teachers may be knowledgeable about AT, relevant laws and procedures, and effective models for AT integration. However, current literature shows that this does not ensure that teachers will be able to identify or use AT effectively to support students with disabilities in their classrooms (Dalton, 2002).

In their research about school district processes for students who use AT, Todis and Walker (1993) concluded that beyond barriers identified in any one area of AT service provision, the most pervasive barrier was a lack of understanding of the interaction of the different factors that influence effective use of AT. In a later report based on the same study, Todis (1996) examined the differing perspectives and experiences school personnel bring to the task of determining AT devices and services needed by students, and discussed the difficulties of reaching consensus about what can and should be done. As in the previous report, Todis underscored the complexity of factors related to the provision of educational services to students with disabilities, particularly when AT is involved, and called for closer examination of both intended and unintended results of the processes used to make decisions about AT services.

AT can only be used by a student with a disability if it is made available to that student in the settings where it is needed (Bouck, 2010). Access to technology, including AT, is not equal across all education agencies. Factors such as socio-economic status and culture impact access to technology (Hitchcock et.al., 2005). Students with disabilities from lower socioeconomic areas typically have much less access to technology than their peers from better funded school districts (Bray, Brown, & Green, 2004; Warschauer, 2007). Research suggests that students from some cultures have different reactions toward using AT and may not be comfortable using it (Heur, Parette, & Scherer, 2004). In addition to access, selecting the appropriate AT devices is significant because choosing a device that is too complicated or has the wrong features can set up a student with a disability to fail (Alper & Raharin-irina, 2006).

The current federal mandate as well as research into the current state of AT services suggests that efforts must be undertaken to greatly increase the capacity of educators and family members relative to AT. The leaders of the QIAT project determined it would be helpful in this endeavor to identify the core components of AT services and develop a set of widely applicable, and generally accepted, indicators that could serve to guide the development, delivery, and evaluation of AT services of consistently high quality.

# Development of the Quality Indicators for Assistive Technology

QIAT provides a structured and research-based resource for addressing gaps in planning and learning about and aligning AT services. Beginning in 1998, a community of over 4,000 professionals, consumers, and family members has contributed to the development of QIAT. The indicators offer over-arching guidelines for the provision of AT in educational settings. *Quality Indicators for Assistive Technology (QIAT): A Comprehensive Guide to Assistive Technology Services* provides context and continuity for the use of the Quality Indicators.

The primary purpose of QIAT is to support the development, provision, and evaluation of quality AT services for students with disabilities, regardless of where the services are provided or the specific model used. Further, QIAT supports the idea that these services should address not only the needs of students, but also the needs of family members and school personnel who work with students who require AT to receive FAPE.

Initially six Quality Indicator Areas were chosen by multiple focus groups that came together as the work began. Participants brainstormed lists of areas where guidance was needed and prioritized these to, determine the areas that are the most common concerning, and foundational to, the provision of AT services. The indicator areas selected for development were chosen because they involved core services that must be undertaken during the provision of AT services. Each area applies to multiple models of AT services whether they are provided in a clinical setting by specialists or in a classroom supported by teachers and paraprofessionals. Focus groups determined that each of the areas describes an important aspect of assistive technology services in which schools and school-based service providers have significant and ongoing responsibilities and need additional guidance and information in order to consistently provide services of high quality. The six original Quality Indicator Areas also parallel the IDEA requirements for IEP teams in federal law and because of this, are required in the education program of all students with disabilities. Consideration, selection, acquisition, and training to use AT are specifically cited in IDEA, while evaluation of effectiveness (i.e., periodic review), transition planning, professional development, and administrative support are required aspects of all special education programs whether or not they include AT.

Each of the next eight chapters in *Quality Indicators for Assistive Technology (QIAT)* addresses one of the indicator areas in detail. The following is a brief description of each indicator area to clarify the scope and purpose of QIAT.

**Consideration of Assistive Technology Needs**   The Quality Indicators for Assistive Technology Consideration are specific to the consideration of AT as one of the special factors mandated by IDEA. In most instances, the Quality Indicators are also appropriate for the consideration of AT for students who qualify for services under other legislation (e.g., Section 504, ADA).

**Assessment of Assistive Technology Needs**   Quality Indicators for Assistive Technology Assessment describe a process conducted by a team, used to identify tools and strategies to address a student's specific needs. The Quality Indicators are specific to the IDEA requirement to provide a functional AT evaluation in the child's customary environment.

**Including Assistive Technology in the IEP**   Quality Indicators for Including Assistive Technology in the IEP focus on the process that takes place in the IEP meeting and the information that is included in the IEP document. The Quality Indicators for Assistive Technology in the IEP help the team describe the role of AT in the child's educational program.

**Assistive Technology Implementation**   The Quality Indicators for Assistive Technology Implementation address the ways in which AT devices and services, as included in the IEP, are provided. They emphasize the importance of people working together to support the student using AT to accomplish expected tasks necessary for active participation in customary educational environments and progress in the general education curriculum.

**Evaluation of Effectiveness of Assistive Technology**   The Quality Indicators for Evaluating the Effectiveness of Assistive Technology discuss documenting changes in student performance through collection and analysis of meaningful data.

**Assistive Technology Transition**   The Quality Indicators for Assistive Technology Transition address how the student's AT devices and services are successfully transferred from one setting to another.

**Professional Development and Training in Assistive Technology**   The Quality Indicators for Professional Development and Training in Assistive Technology point out critical aspects related to increasing educators' knowledge and skills in a variety of areas. These areas include, but are not limited to: collaborative processes; a continuum of tools, strategies, and services; resources; legal issues; action planning; and data collection and analysis.

**Administrative Support of Assistive Technology Service**   The Quality Indicators for Administrative Support for Assistive Technology Services identify factors critical to developing and maintaining effective, efficient AT services that can only be accomplished by education administrators.

## Using Quality Indicators for Assistive Technology

The next eight chapters have parallel organization. Information in each chapter is presented in this sequence:

- **the Quality Indicators for the area**—includes highlighted keywords for the indicator and a corresponding intent statement;

- **in-depth information for each indicator**—offers a more thorough exploration of the indicator with short examples and key questions for each;

- **the QIAT Self-Evaluation Matrix for the area**—serves as a companion to the Quality Indicators and provides five variations in application for each indicator from unacceptable to promising practice;

- **case studies**—illustrate how the indicators and Self-Evaluation Matrices were used by teams;

- **suggested activities**—offers opportunities for readers to deepen their understanding of the particular indicator area.

## Using the Self-Evaluation Matrices

The Self-Evaluation Matrices were developed in response to formative evaluation data indicating a need for a tool that could assist in the application of QIAT in schools (Zabala et. al, 2000). The QIAT Matrices are based on the idea that change does not happen immediately, but rather, moves toward the ideal in a series of steps that take place over time. The QIAT Matrices use an innovation configuration matrix (ICM) to identify variations from unacceptable to exemplary practice (Hall & Hord, 1985). Individuals, teams, and education agencies can use the matrices to determine where their current services fall within this range and identify areas of strength and areas of improvement.

The descriptions developed for each variation of each Quality Indicator provide illustrative examples and may not be appropriate, as written, for every setting or agency. Individuals and teams completing the QIAT Matrices may use them to get an overall picture of the intent and find within the five variations, the one that best fits their unique situation. Once a variation is selected for each indicator, the information can be transferred to the Self-Evaluation Matrices Summary Sheet to provide a quick visual chart of strengths and areas of need for improvement planning.

When an individual or team completes the self-evaluation, the results can be used to measure areas of strength and identify areas for professional development, training, or needed support. If the responses show differing perceptions across the team, the matrices provide an opportunity to discuss the factors that cause those differing perceptions. Such discussion is critical to improvement within a collaborative team. When the QIAT Matrices are used by an individual or team, however, it is important to realize that the results can reasonably reflect perceptions of the services in which only that individual or team is involved and may not reflect the typical services across the agency. The perception of an individual or small group cannot be generalized to make decisions about the needs of the entire agency.

When an education agency uses the QIAT Matrices to guide improvement efforts throughout the agency, responses are gathered from a wide array of service providers across multiple sites and levels of service. A task force or planning group then uses the information gained from this larger group of respondents to identify and guide changes that will lead to manageable and attainable improvement throughout the education agency.

Using the results of the self-evaluation, stakeholders can prioritize areas for improvement and develop appropriate action plans. The QIAT matrices can also be used to evaluate the level to which expected or planned-for changes have taken place by periodically analyzing changes in service delivery over time.

## Summary

QIAT began as a response to a need reflected in scholarly research and in the personal experiences of consumers, service providers, and staff developers. QIAT provides support for improvements in the quality and consistency of AT services at every level, as evidenced by its use to shape practice at national, state, and local levels as well as in higher education and research.

To date Quality Indicators for Assistive Technology have been included in policy documents and operational guidelines at district and state levels. Numerous groups have used the QIAT materials to systematically evaluate AT services and plan for incremental and continuous improvements. Three projects have taken the quality indicator model and developed specific indicators related to their focus. The first is the QIAT Post Secondary project (*qiat-ps.org*). The other two are projects funded by the Rehabilitation Engineering and Assistive Technology Society of North America (RESNA). The Catalyst Project developed Quality Indicators for Device Demonstration and Quality Indicators for Device Loan at *http://www.resnaprojects.org/state-wide/quality/index.html*. The Pass It On Center developed the Indicators of Quality for Assistive Technology Reuse (IQ-AT Reuse) at *http://www.passitoncenter.org/Portals/passitoncenter/uploads/IQ-AT%20Reuse%20Report%20rev%2008032010.pdf*. Many service providers have used QIAT to improve their services, to communicate the importance of the various aspects of AT services to others, and as a tool to encourage collaboration throughout service delivery processes.

QIAT can be used with confidence by each of the groups for whom they were intended–consumers of AT and their families, personnel working in early childhood special education agencies, school district and regional educational personnel involved with AT service provision, state and national AT service providers, special education faculty at institutions of higher education, and individuals involved in the development, implementation, and monitoring of AT policy (Zabala, 2007). Following are specific implications for each of these groups.

**Early Childhood and K–12 educational personnel**   QIAT provides educational personnel at building, district, regional, state, and national levels with a means to understand and explain to others that the primary purpose of AT in educational settings is to foster the educational participation and achievement of students with disabilities. QIAT also helps educational personnel at all organizational levels understand the multiple factors that influence the provision of quality AT services and the various roles and responsibilities that must be fulfilled to provide high-quality AT services on a consistent basis. Further, QIAT provides educational personnel with a framework for evaluating the current status of their own AT programs. The results of such an evaluation can be used to identify areas of strength to build upon and areas that are in need of improvement. Using QIAT in this way provides a means of planning for, and supporting, continuous improvement of AT services at all levels of educational organizations.

**Higher education faculty**    QIAT provides a guide for higher educational faculty to use in the establishment of programs that prepare personnel to participate in the development, delivery, and evaluation of AT services in educational settings. QIAT is also a useful resource in teaching others about AT and how it relates to other programs of instruction. It is a valuable tool for evaluating programs and provides a summary of important issues in AT for use in presentations.

**Policy-makers and monitors**    QIAT provides a body of information that can be used to provide a base of understanding for the development of judicious and effective policy about AT services in schools. QIAT provides people involved in policy-making and monitoring with a means for understanding the impact of policy on the many variables involved in the development, maintenance, and expansion of quality AT services. Further, policy monitors can use QIAT to determine the level to which current policies are being implemented and whether they are having the intended impact on the educational achievement of students with disabilities.

**Consumers and family members**    QIAT is a useful way for consumers and families to gain an understanding of the purpose of AT in educational settings and the importance of their roles in the development of appropriate AT services. QIAT can be a guide that provides information, knowledge, and the opportunity to identify and develop the skills needed to be active participants in all phases of AT processes, from identification of the need for AT devices and services through the selection, acquisition, and use of specific devices. QIAT can also serve as a means for consumers and family members to evaluate the AT services in which they are involved to determine what changes, if any, are needed.

There is much evidence, both research-based and practical, that underscores the importance of developing and sustaining consistent, quality AT services in educational settings. Perhaps the most compelling evidence is found in the statements of those for whom QIAT is intended. An educator involved in validation research about QIAT summarized the purpose of QIAT:

> *Having Quality Indicators is essential to effective AT service delivery. They provide a frame of reference and a way for us to measure the quality of our efforts. The better and more systematic we are at addressing AT needs, the more likely we are to improve student outcomes. (Zabala, 2007, page 38)*

## Suggested Activities

1. Go to *http://www2.ed.gov/about/offices/list/ocr/whatsnew.html*. Download and read the Dear Colleague letter from the U.S. Department of Justice and the U.S. Department of Education of November 12, 2014 and the attached frequently asked questions. How do Title II and IDEA intersect? What is different and what is similar about the two laws? How will this letter change AT services in school districts?

2. Review the resources listed on the Quality Indicators website, *www.qiat.org*. Find two that you feel are helpful in understanding AT processes and procedures. Explain why you found them useful.

3. Search the Internet for two state-issued AT manuals that include or reference the Quality Indicators for Assistive Technology. Compare and contrast how each manual used the Quality Indicators.

4. Download and review the *Assistive Technology Consideration Resource Guide*. To do so, go to the Georgia Project for Assistive Technology, *www.gpat.org*. From the menu on the right, choose Considering Assistive Technology for Students with Disabilities. Then from the Downloads menu on the right, choose to download the *Assistive Technology Consideration Resource Guide*. How could this guide be used to help general education teachers understand AT? What is the most useful aspect of the guide?

5. Review the Johns Hopkins University AT Cycle and mATchuptool: *http://marylandlearninglinks.org/matn*. What are the most useful aspects of this website? What three parts could you use to help others learn about AT?

# CHAPTER 2

# Exploring the Quality Indicators for Consideration of Assistive Technology Needs

1. Assistive technology devices and services are *considered for all students with disabilities* regardless of type or severity of disability.

2. During the development of an individualized educational program, every IEP team consistently uses a *collaborative decision-making process* that supports systematic consideration of each student's possible need for assistive technology devices and services.

3. IEP team members have the *collective knowledge and skills* needed to make informed assistive technology decisions and seek assistance when needed.

4. Decisions regarding the need for assistive technology devices and services are *based on the student's IEP goals and objectives, access to curricular and extracurricular activities, and progress in the general education curriculum.*

5. The IEP team *gathers and analyzes data* about the student, customary environments, educational goals, and tasks when considering a student's need for assistive technology devices and services.

6. When assistive technology is needed, the IEP team *explores a range* of assistive technology devices, services, and other supports that address identified needs.

7. The assistive technology consideration process and *results are documented in the IEP* and include a rationale for the decision and supporting evidence.

The requirement for each IEP team to consider a child's need for AT is mandated in IDEA as one of five special factors that each IEP team is to consider:

Consideration of special factors. The IEP Team shall-

*(i)* In the case of a child whose behavior impedes the child's learning or that of others, consider the use of positive behavioral interventions and supports, and other strategies, to address that behavior;

*(ii)* In the case of a child with limited English proficiency, consider the language needs of the child as those needs relate to the child's IEP;

*(iii)* In the case of a child who is blind or visually impaired, provide for instruction in Braille and the use of Braille unless the IEP Team determines, after an evaluation of the child's reading and writing skills, needs, and appropriate reading and writing media (including an evaluation of the child's future needs for instruction in Braille or the use of Braille), that instruction in Braille or the use of Braille is not appropriate for the child;

*(iv)* Consider the communication needs of the child, and in the case of a child who is deaf or hard of hearing, consider the child's language and communication needs, opportunities for direct communications with peers and professional personnel in the child's language and communication mode, academic level, and full range of needs, including opportunities for direct instruction in the child's language and communication mode; and

*(v)* **Consider whether the child needs assistive technology devices and services. (emphasis added)**

IDEA Sec. 614(d)(3)(B)

While the first four special factors refer to very specific areas of need or disability, the last one, which addresses AT consideration, has no such limitation. Rather, every IEP team must consider whether a child needs AT devices and services. While most education agencies have a question about AT on the IEP form in order to comply with federal law, this is often only paper implementation (Wallace, Blase, Fixsen, & Naoom, 2008). In other words, few actually implement consideration. Many education agencies across the United States continue to struggle with performance implementation (i.e., actually doing it well; Paine, Bellamy, & Wilcox, 1984). This has created an AT consideration environment fraught with inconsistencies.

The law does not define or describe what constitutes "consideration" for any of the special factors or provide any guidelines on conducting a consideration process. Best practice suggests education agencies develop their own procedures for consideration. The Quality Indicators for Consideration of Assistive Technology Needs address the core components that must be present and can provide guidance and organization to education agencies as they do so.

1. **Assistive technology devices and services are *considered for all students with disabilities* regardless of type or severity of disability.**

**Intent: Consideration of assistive technology (AT) need is required by IDEA and is based on the unique educational needs of the student. Students are not excluded from consideration of AT for any reason. (e.g., type of disability, age, administrative concerns).**

As a part of the required deliberation of the special factors in IDEA, it is the responsibility of every IEP team to consider the student's need for AT. Each team's decision about a student's need for AT in educational settings is to be based on the student's abilities and the tasks they need to accomplish across environments. The need for AT does not depend on a specific type or level of disability. As IEP teams develop goals, objectives, and benchmarks for students, AT is explored as a potential support for all areas addressed in the IEP. Perhaps the most common error in the consideration of AT need is the practice of considering it only for students with severe disabilities. IDEA very clearly states that consideration must be completed for all students who qualify for special education. Failure to do so is caused by a lack of knowledge of the legal mandates of IDEA and of the education agency's responsibilities.

*Charmaine is a fourth grade student with a specific learning disability in reading. On previous IEPs, AT was not recommended because the school district procedures did not include consideration of the AT need for students with mild disabilities. There had been no training for team members about AT and the team did not know there were AT tools that could help students like Charmaine. After attending a regional training focusing on AT, the team learned about technology that supports reading (e.g., devices with features, such as adjustable spacing, highlighting, text-to-speech) and wondered if any of this might benefit Charmaine. While talking to other teams about AT regulations, the team realized that its district practice did not comply with the law. The team members met with their special education director following the training and began to plan how to bring district procedures into compliance. In the meantime, Charmaine's team arranged trials with technology that supports reading.*

**KEY QUESTIONS**

- How does the district ensure that all IEP teams appropriately consider AT for their students?

- What training is provided for IEP team members to ensure they are aware of appropriate AT?

- What processes, including forms or other documentation, are used to guide IEP team members through an effective consideration process?

2.  **During the development of the individualized educational program, the IEP team consistently uses a *collaborative decision-making process* that supports systematic consideration of each student's possible need for assistive technology devices and services.**

    **Intent: A collaborative process that ensures that all IEP teams effectively consider the AT needs of students is defined, communicated, and consistently used throughout the agency. Processes may vary from agency to agency to most effectively address student needs under local conditions.**

    Procedures improve the decision-making ability of groups (Pavitt & Curtis, 2001). Using a formal process increases the likelihood that team members think about the same thing at the same time, helps curb powerful or overly talkative team members, and helps the team deal with conflict (Poole, 1990). Specific decision-making procedures that IEP teams use during consideration are identified at the agency level and training on those procedures is provided. Once teams are trained, the teams use the process consistently during every IEP meeting. Steps and criteria for the process are well defined and understood by all IEP team members. Teams identify critical information that the team should gather and review in order to make good decisions about AT. This information might include the tasks that are most difficult for the student, the specific problems and frustrations the student experiences, and specific accessibility features that may benefit the student. The agency may develop a form or adopt a form such as the *QIAT Planning Document: Consideration of the Need for AT* included in Appendix D to support the process. Questions such as those in Table 2.1 help to guide the discussion. The agency also defines the steps the team will take if more information is needed (e.g., observation of the student, referral for further assessment, gathering of information about strategies and tools).

**TABLE 2.1**
Discussion questions for AT consideration

- With what curriculum areas and specific tasks is the student struggling?
- What strategies, accommodations, or modifications have been tried and with what success?
- What AT has been tried and with what success?
- What assistive features are needed by the student?
- What AT tools have those features?

Team members collaborate to ensure the student's needs are thoroughly analyzed and decisions are not based on a single subject or situation. All team members, including the student and family, provide information and have input into the decision-making process so that they understand and value the decisions regarding AT.

*Teresa is a middle school student with mild cerebral palsy that impacts her ability to produce legible written work and her organization skills. She has had extensive occupational therapy and recently the occupational therapist (OT) raised the question about using AT to help Teresa cope successfully with the increased academic demands of middle school. The team had little experience with AT but were used to working together to problem solve. They used a decision-making process that focused on the student to collaboratively identify the problem and potential solutions.*

*They met briefly after the AT question was raised and decided that they needed to identify the specific tasks that were difficult for Teresa and also to learn more about AT that could help her with those tasks. They all agreed to collect data about Teresa's written work and organizational strategies for two weeks at home and at school. At the same time, one member volunteered to investigate AT tools in preparation for the IEP meeting scheduled at the end of the month. They came to the IEP meeting with a list of specific tasks that seemed to be most difficult for Teresa, including keeping track of assignments, taking notes in the two classes where the teachers lecture, and completing legible and readable written assignments. Early in the IEP meeting the resource teacher explained what AT devices and services are to Teresa and her mother. Together the team members agreed that trials were needed with several of the identified tools to help determine if any of these tools made a difference in Teresa's independence and legibility of written work. The team documented the need for AT in the IEP and planned for the trials with the identified tools.*

- How does the district define a collaborative process for AT consideration?

- How are new employees informed about the collaborative process that is used in AT consideration?

- How does the district ensure that the appropriate team members are involved in the collaborative process?

- How does the process ensure that everyone has input?

3. **IEP team members have the *collective knowledge and skills* needed to make informed assistive technology decisions and seek assistance when needed.**

   **Intent: IEP team members combine their knowledge and skills to determine if a student needs AT devices and services to remove barriers to student performance. When the AT needs are beyond the knowledge and scope of the IEP team, the team seeks out additional resources and support.**

No one person on the team knows everything needed to make informed AT decisions. The most effective teams work collaboratively to identify their strengths and deficits and to determine how to gain knowledge. Parents and students know about the student's interests, strengths, weaknesses, and long-range goals. They also know about strategies used successfully outside the school setting. Teachers who work with the student on a daily basis know about the schedule and the student's performance and preferences at school. They are also aware of the specific tasks for which supports may be needed, the times in the day that lend themselves to implementing AT use, the steps in the curriculum that will be required in the future, and many other details that are critical to sound decision-making. If team members are unsure about which AT tools to consider, additional information is gathered and support is sought from someone who has the needed knowledge and skills. It is critical to have information about the AT (e.g., stand-alone AT devices, hardware, and software) available within the agency, other AT that should be acquired, training that may be needed, and ways in which any of these AT tools may integrate with the school network. Administrative support may be needed to bring in additional resources when the student's team needs more information or training.

**EXAMPLE**

*Mary is a ninth grader who is reading at the fifth-grade level. Due to her reading level, Mary is not making adequate progress in her content area classes, all of which require extensive reading and application of information gained from text. Mary and her teacher agree that when Mary does not have to decode every word, she can successfully recall and apply the information in academic activities. Mary's parents have also noticed this and frequently help Mary with her homework by reading complex material aloud to her. Recently Mary's mother saw an ad for an e-book reader and wondered if it could help Mary become a more successful and independent student. As a first step to exploring this possibility, the team discussed the assistive features Mary may need and text-to-speech was at the top of their list. One team member had personally used the e-book reader that Mary's mother had seen on television and described its features and limitations to Mary and the rest of the team. All were disappointed that text-to-speech was not an option on this e-book reader but they knew there were other options. Another team member mentioned that he had also heard that even on devices with text-to-speech capability, not all content could be read aloud. The team thought that an e-book reader with accessible content could be really useful to Mary but they realized they did not have enough information about AT that supports reading and accessible content to make a decision. So they requested an AT consultation to learn more about e-book readers and similar technology and an appointment with the curriculum director to learn more about accessible content in the agency's curriculum.*

- How does the team gain input from all team members, including the parent and student?

- What resources do IEP team members use to increase their knowledge of AT when additional information is needed?

- If the team needs additional information, who could be contacted either inside or outside of the education agency to provide needed skills and knowledge?

4. **Decisions regarding the need for assistive technology devices and services are based on the student's IEP goals and objectives, access to curricular and extracurricular activities, and progress in the general education curriculum.**

   **Intent: As the IEP team determines the tasks a student needs to complete and develops goals and objectives, the team considers whether AT is required to accomplish those tasks.**

   After establishing the present levels of academic achievement and functional performance and developing the student's goals, the IEP team discusses and identifies tasks that may be especially difficult based on the student's past performance and any concerns the student, parents, or educators express during the consideration process. The team considers whether AT devices might be needed. Across all settings and grades, IEP teams consider a range of factors including academic, non-academic, social, and personal issues as they develop IEPs for students with disabilities. While a student's academic progress in the curriculum is the starting point, other social needs and communication (e.g., requesting, protesting, negating) are also typically discussed across environments (e.g., the lunch room, the playground, physical education classes, or sports).

   The decision to provide AT devices or services does not mean the student will not receive instruction in the area of concern. High quality instruction is always the key to continued progress in the curriculum. AT is specifically used to overcome one or more barriers to that progress. If an individual team member does not understand the role of AT or expresses concerns that its use will mean the student will stop learning new skills in the area of concern, that team member needs supportive and informed discussion about what AT can do for the student. For example, research shows that the use of augmentative communication has a positive effect on language acquisition, and does not impede natural speech production (Millar, Schlosser, and Light, 2006). The team describes in the IEP, the ways that AT may combine with effective instruction to help the student make progress in the curriculum and attain learning goals.

*Audrey has hearing loss and uses American Sign Language (ASL) as her primary means of communication. She has severe motor involvement that impacts her ability to use her hands resulting in sign approximations that are not easily understood by an unfamiliar communication partner. The team agreed that Audrey was able to communicate within her classroom at this time, but the team is aware that Audrey will be in more demanding settings in the future. As the discussion continued, Audrey's mom expressed concerns about her ability to communicate outside the classroom with unfamiliar communication partners. Audrey's mom asked about ways Audrey could communicate more effectively with her Girl Scout troop and during other afterschool activities. Discussion led to a decision to seek more information about communication needs in outside environments, potential strategies, and AT tools that might help Audrey in the wider school environment and in other settings. The team agreed to meet again in two weeks to discuss the information gathered.*

**KEY QUESTIONS**

- How does the team identify the student's curricular and extracurricular needs?

- How does the IEP team identify specific tasks for which AT may be needed?

- How does the IEP team address issues about the use of AT to support the achievement of identified IEP goals?

5. **The IEP team *gathers and analyzes data* about the student, customary environments, educational goals, and tasks when considering a student's need for assistive technology devices and services.**

    **Intent: The IEP team shares and discusses information about the student's present levels of achievement in relationship to the environments and tasks to determine if the student requires AT devices and services to participate actively, work on expected tasks, and make progress toward mastery of educational goals.**

    In preparation for the IEP meeting, the team gathers data about the student's performance from multiple environments using sources such as observations in the classroom, portfolios, test data, parent observations, rating scales, response to past interventions, student self-report, and other formal and informal sources. Data related to all primary areas of concern are gathered and brought to the IEP meeting for use in the consideration discussion. Many aspects of the environment are included (e.g., classroom arrangement, available tools and supports, lighting, noise level).

    Analysis and discussion of the data provide the team with information to identify barriers for the student and the most difficult tasks. This is the basis to determine whether AT devices and services are needed to support the student in achieving IEP goals.

*Chaz is a fifth grader with difficulty in the area of reading as evidenced by low comprehension scores. As the team developed the IEP, they looked at the effectiveness of previous intervention strategies. Performance data showed that when Chaz used a portable electronic dictionary to identify unknown words, he was slower at completing reading assignments and his comprehension did not increase. After further analyzing the data, the IEP team determined that Chaz had trouble retaining information, making connections with background knowledge, and answering comprehension questions. The team realized that, although Chaz was using AT, it was not adequate for his current needs and additional tools or strategies were needed. They decided to complete an AT assessment that would look at his abilities and needs as well as other tools and strategies with a focus on connecting to background information and expanding his vocabulary.*

**KEY QUESTIONS**

- How does the IEP team determine what data is relevant and appropriate to identify student needs?
- How does the team analyze the data?
- How do they use data to determine next steps?

6. **When assistive technology is needed, the IEP team *explores a range* of assistive technology devices, services, and other supports that address identified needs.**

   **Intent: The IEP team considers various supports and services that address the educational needs of the student and may include no-tech, low-tech, mid-tech, and high-tech solutions and devices. IEP team members do not limit their thinking to only those devices and services currently available within the district.**

   IEP teams use a process to explore a number of AT devices when they consider a student's need for AT. They understand the concept of features and use it to help them make AT decisions. Features are aspects of a device that help a student overcome barriers and are components of a product that make it particularly suited to a student's needs. Examples might be portability, device size, sound production, background to text contrast, text re-sizing, text-to-speech, range of digital voices with changeable speed or pitch.

   After identifying the needs and abilities of the student and analyzing the data they have available, the team generates a list of features that the student needs. The team then identifies devices with those features. This is called a *feature match*. Due to requirements of different learning environments, the team may need to consider creating an AT system with more than one tool. They discuss AT services and other strategies or supports that the student may need for success.

The team reviews a range of devices that have the prioritized features. Teams that are not aware of current technology contact someone outside of the team to inform and support their consideration. They know and use resources inside their agency and contract resource or assessment services when necessary. In some instances, a new device may be needed for the student. In other instances, technologies with those features may be currently available within a student's school building or agency.

The team also determines the services that will be needed to support the student's use of the identified AT. This can include coordination among staff, training for staff, student, and families, as well as other services identified in IDEA.

EXAMPLE

*Pablo, a seventh grader, has a congenital deformity of his right hand. Although he has received occupational therapy (OT) services for many years, he continues to struggle with written assignments. He tires quickly so he tends to write shorter, less complicated responses on tests, essays, and homework. His teachers report that his oral presentations are more comprehensive and complex than his written reports.*

*After exploring a range of AT, the IEP team considered a system that included a special pencil grip for short answers, as well as an audio recorder that can be used as an alternative for note taking and lengthier assignments. They will introduce both tools immediately. The team also determined that he needed a trial with a portable word processor, tablet, or computer with word processing. All three devices were available in their school and a trial with each of them was planned and written into the IEP. They discussed that he may also be a candidate for voice recognition software for some writing assignments. Since the members of the IEP team were not familiar with voice recognition technology, they requested support from a teacher in the agency who was familiar with the technology.*

**KEY QUESTIONS**

- How do IEP team members find information on AT devices that have already been considered?

- How do the IEP team members learn about AT devices with the identified features that meet the student's needs?

- How does the education agency ensure that IEP teams explore a full range of AT devices and consider a range of services and supports?

- When a student needs supports and services, how do IEP team members know who can be a resource within or outside of the school system?

7. **The assistive technology consideration process and *results are documented in the IEP* and include a rationale for the decision and supporting evidence.**

   **Intent: Even though IEP documentation may include a checkbox verifying that AT has been considered, the reasons for decisions and recommendations should also be clearly stated. Supporting evidence may include the results of AT assessments, data from device trials, differences in achievement with and without AT, student preferences for competing devices, and teacher observations, among others.**

   While a simple "yes" or "no" answer verifying consideration of AT on the IEP document may indicate that AT was considered, documentation of the rationale or process is helpful to the individuals who are implementing the IEP. Clearly explaining the tasks that were identified as most difficult and the AT devices that were considered to complete those tasks is valuable for both immediate implementation and for future IEP teams who will be looking for as much information as possible to help in their decision-making.

   There are three possible outcomes to AT consideration:

   - Yes, the student needs AT.

   - No, the student doesn't need AT.

   - We don't know if the student needs AT.

   When the IEP team determines that AT is needed, it is then written into the IEP. If the team determines that AT is not needed, there is no legal requirement that they explain why it isn't needed. However, best practice is to write a brief explanation so that future IEP teams know what was considered and why this IEP team decided it was not needed. When the IEP team realizes that they do not know whether or not AT is needed, they then refer the student for an AT assessment. Many districts use a specific form, such as the *QIAT Planning Document: Consideration of the Need for AT* in Appendix D, to help guide the discussion of the need for AT. That form is attached to the IEP to serve as documentation of the team's consideration. In other districts, the team writes a simple paragraph to explain the data and the discussion that led to the decision about the need for AT. Some states attach meeting minutes pages to the IEP. Meeting minutes also provide a logical place to document the important facts about the discussion that takes place and the decision made. When there are no minutes, an explanatory page, chart, or table can be attached to the IEP. The goal is for IEP documentation to clearly describe the team's consideration process and decisions.

*As he entered kindergarten, Ivan's team was concerned about his extensive communication, behavior, language, and learning needs. He had been identified as being on the autism spectrum. The team discussed several areas in which they thought AT devices might help him make progress in the curriculum. Research on visual strategies for students on the autism spectrum led them to consider the fact that he might need an individual visual schedule. The team also considered the need for a voice output communication device and the importance of using the same symbol system for both the visual schedule and the device.*

*The team members used the district's one-page form to guide their AT decision-making. The team documented their discussion and the specific AT Ivan would need. The form documented the identified symbol system and included examples of symbols that had been most effective. They also included on the form the voice output device that was appropriate for the symbol system and the settings and activities in which Ivan used it successfully.*

**KEY QUESTIONS**

- How is the AT consideration process documented in the IEP?

- What guidance does the district provide to ensure consideration is documented?

- What guidance is provided to ensure that the documentation includes reasons for decisions and that recommendations are clearly stated?

## Exploring the Quality Indicators for Consideration of Assistive Technology Needs with the QIAT Self-Evaluation Matrix

The Self-Evaluation Matrix for Consideration of AT Needs focuses on how to conduct and document the consideration process. The matrix provides descriptive steps for each of the Quality Indicators for Consideration of AT Needs through variations from "unacceptable" to "best practice." The matrix

- provides a tool for analyzing current AT consideration practice,

- highlights key factors in quality AT consideration, and

- provides a scaffold for improving AT consideration practices across IEP teams.

The first Quality Indicator for Consideration of AT Needs helps determine if any specific populations are being overlooked in the district's typical consideration practices. The next four indicators assess collaboration, knowledge of AT, connection to the curriculum, and use of data during the consideration process. The last two indicators address whether the IEP team explores a range of AT and how the process is documented in the IEP.

The following case study provides an example of an IEP team using the Quality Indicators for Consideration of AT Needs and the Self-Evaluation Matrix to improve their practices. In the case study you will see how Misha's IEP team effectively worked together to consider his need for augmentative communication.

# Quality Indicators for *Consideration* of Assistive Technology Needs

| QUALITY INDICATOR | UNACCEPTABLE | | |
|---|---|---|---|
| **1. Assistive technology (AT) devices and services are *considered for all students with disabilities* regardless of type or severity of disability.** | 1<br>AT is not considered for students with disabilities. | 2<br>AT is considered only for students with severe disabilities or students in specific disability categories. | |
| **2. During the development of the individualized educational program (IEP), every IEP team consistently uses a *collaborative decision-making process* that supports systematic consideration of each student's possible need for AT devices and services.** | 1<br>No process is established for IEP teams to use to make AT decisions. | 2<br>A process is established for IEP teams to use to make AT decisions but it is not collaborative. | |
| **3. IEP team members have the *collective knowledge and skills* needed to make informed AT decisions and seek assistance when needed.** | 1<br>The team does not have the knowledge or skills needed to make informed AT decisions. The team does not seek help when needed. | 2<br>Individual team members have some of the knowledge and skills needed to make informed AT decisions. The team does not seek help when needed. | |
| **4. Decisions regarding the need for AT devices and services are based on the student's IEP goals and objectives, access to curricular and extracurricular activities, and progress in the general education curriculum.** | 1<br>Decisions about a student's need for AT are not connected to IEP goals or the general curriculum. | 2<br>Decisions about a student's need for AT are based on either access to the curriculum/IEP goals or the general curriculum, not both. | |
| **5. The IEP team gathers and analyzes data about the student, customary environments, educational goals, and tasks when considering a student's need for AT devices and services.** | 1<br>The IEP team does not gather and analyze data to consider a student's need for AT devices and services. | 2<br>The IEP team gathers and analyzes data about the student, customary environments, educational goals, or tasks, but not all, when considering a student's need for AT devices and services. | |
| **6. When AT is needed, the IEP team *explores a range* of AT devices, services, and other supports that address identified needs.** | 1<br>The IEP team does not explore a range of AT devices, services, and other supports to address identified needs. | 2<br>The IEP team considers a limited set of AT devices, services, and other supports. | |
| **7. The AT consideration process and *results are documented in the IEP* and include a rationale for the decision and supporting evidence.** | 1<br>The consideration process and results are not documented in the IEP. | 2<br>The consideration process and results are documented in the IEP but do not include a rationale for the decision and supporting evidence. | |

| VARIATIONS | | PROMISING PRACTICES |
|---|---|---|
| 3<br>AT is considered for all students with disabilities but the consideration is inconsistently based on the unique educational needs of the student. | 4<br>AT is considered for all students with disabilities and the consideration is generally based on the unique educational needs of the student. | 5<br>AT is considered for all students with disabilities and the consideration is consistently based on the unique educational needs of the student. |
| 3<br>A collaborative process is established but not generally used by IEP teams to make AT decisions. | 4<br>A collaborative process is established and generally used by IEP teams to make AT decisions. | 5<br>A collaborative process is established and consistently used by IEP teams to make AT decisions. |
| 3<br>Team members sometimes combine knowledge and skills to make informed AT decisions. The team does not always seek help when needed. | 4<br>Team members generally combine their knowledge and skills to make informed AT decisions. The team seeks help when needed. | 5<br>The team consistently uses collective knowledge and skills to make informed AT decisions. The team seeks help when needed. |
| 3<br>Decisions about a student's need for AT sometimes are based on both the student's IEP goals and general education curricular tasks. | 4<br>Decisions about a student's need for AT generally are based on both the student's IEP goals and general education curricular tasks. | 5<br>Decisions about a student's need for AT consistently are based on both the student's IEP goals and general education curricular tasks. |
| 3<br>The IEP team sometimes gathers and analyzes data about the student, customary environments, educational goals, and tasks when considering a student's need for AT devices and services. | 4<br>The IEP team generally gathers and analyzes data about the student, customary environments, educational goals, and tasks when considering a student's need for AT devices and services. | 5<br>The IEP team consistently gathers and analyzes data about the student, customary environments, educational goals, and tasks when considering a student's need for AT devices and services. |
| 3<br>The IEP team sometimes explores a range of AT devices, services, and other supports. | 4<br>The IEP team generally explores a range of AT devices, services, and other supports. | 5<br>The IEP team always explores a range of AT devices, services, and other supports to address identified needs. |
| 3<br>The consideration process and results are documented in the IEP and sometimes include a rationale for the decision and supporting evidence. | 4<br>The consideration process and results are documented in the IEP and generally include a rationale for the decision and supporting evidence. | 5<br>The consideration process and results are documented in the IEP and consistently include a rationale for the decision and supporting evidence. |

# Exploring the Quality Indicators for Consideration of Assistive Technology Needs Through Misha's Case Study

Misha is 13 years old and attends middle school in his home district. He spends most of the day in a self-contained classroom where the curricular focus is on life skills, social skills, and communication. He also participates in social studies and art class. Misha has a diagnosis of autism and a secondary diagnosis of intellectual disability.

Misha is able to speak a few words and is developing beginning expressive communication skills. He understands much of what is said to him and follows verbal directions, but he rarely uses his voice. Because he can speak a few words and make sounds, his IEP teams over the years have focused their efforts on oral communication and receptive language development.

Before Misha's annual IEP meeting, his father and his teacher talked a lot about his communication needs. Misha's need for expressive communication was growing as he developed and matured. He was experiencing more and more frustration when he was unable to tell people what he wanted. Because he had few social communication skills, he had trouble getting the attention he wanted and was limited in his participation in school activities. The only way his parents knew what happened at school was if someone wrote in the notebook he carried in his backpack. It was of growing concern that when Misha did not like or want to do something, his only strategy for refusal was to hit, kick, or drop to the floor and flail.

Misha's father and teacher discussed whether he might need AT for communication. The agency had augmentative and alternative communication (AAC) equipment that included a few basic communication devices that would allow him to access up to 50 pre-recorded messages. They agreed that the teacher would try one or more of the devices with Misha before the next IEP meeting and bring the data from that informal trial to the IEP meeting.

Goals for communication established during the IEP meeting included: developing more conventional refusal skills, using communication strategies to initiate an interaction with peers, increasing social communication during his daily work routines in the school cafeteria, and responding appropriately to teacher questions in general education classes.

After his annual IEP goals were set, the teacher gave a brief report about Misha's experiences with AAC devices and the reasons for the trials. She reported that Misha was very interested in trying the AAC device and expressed a lot of excitement when he was allowed to use it. Classroom staff provided him with vocabulary that allowed him to participate more actively in morning meeting discussions and he had an entire page of questions and responses specific to that activity. Even though the trial period was only two weeks long, Misha learned all of the vocabulary choices on the vocabulary page during the second week of the trial and used them with only an environmental or verbal prompt at least five times during each class. His teacher documented his positive interactions using the device and his rapid acquisition of the vocabulary. The data showed that he understood why he might use the AAC device, had a desire to communicate in new ways, and could use the device in at least two different settings for several communicative functions. The team reviewed the two weeks of data that described the number of words and phrases he used spontaneously as well as the number he used when prompted in two different settings. This data was compelling enough that Misha's team was confident that his use of AT would help him achieve social and behavioral goals as well as expressive language goals that were a part of his IEP. The IEP team included the report from the trial period prior to the IEP meeting as an addendum to the IEP to support the team decision.

As the IEP team considered Misha's need for AT, several team members expressed concerns. One team member advised caution in moving to an AAC device, stating that he still had the potential to use his speech for expressive communication. She wanted to be sure that they all still worked on his speech in addition to the use of an AAC device. Another thought that he might destroy an AAC device if he became angry. On the other hand, Misha's dad was very excited about it and expressed concern that Misha would soon need more communication options than the devices being discussed offered. He suggested that a tablet computer with communication apps might be needed instead, and asked that it be specifically mentioned in the IEP. Even though some team members had seen tablet devices used by other students, no one knew whether Misha could use one at his level of communication. The team decided to further investigate the use of tablet computers for beginning expressive communication, and Misha's speech and language clinician took responsibility for contacting the education agency's AT consultant.

After their discussions, the IEP team decided that Misha did need an AAC device for expressive language. The IEP team then proceeded to identify necessary features, potential devices, and ways to evaluate each device's effectiveness in meeting Misha's specific needs.

## Application of the QIAT Self-Evaluation Matrix for Consideration of Assistive Technology Needs by Misha's Team

Misha's IEP team members wanted to improve their process for AT consideration. They had participated in a short training session about the Quality Indicators and decided to use them to evaluate and discuss their processes.

1. **Assistive technology devices and services are *considered for all students with disabilities* regardless of type or severity of disability.**

   **Discussion:** From the time Misha began his educational program in preschool until he reached the age of 13, the teams that had worked with him were convinced that he would be able to develop speech. Even though he did begin to speak a few words in elementary school, the IEP team agreed that his speech was not meeting his communication needs as he matured. At this point, the team reconsidered the use of AT in the form of an AAC device and included it in the IEP. The team realized that more complete consideration of Misha's AAC needs should have been done earlier and rated their performance a 3 for this indicator.

| 1 | 2 | 3 | 4 | 5 |
|---|---|---|---|---|
| AT is not considered for students with disabilities. | AT is considered only for students with severe disabilities or students in specific disability categories. | **AT is considered for all students with disabilities but the consideration is inconsistently based on the unique educational needs of the student.** | AT is considered for all students with disabilities and the consideration is generally based on the unique educational needs of the student. | AT is considered for all students with disabilities and the consideration is consistently based on the unique educational needs of the student. |

2. **During the development of the individualized educational program, every IEP team consistently uses a *collaborative decision-making process* that supports systematic consideration of each student's possible need for assistive technology devices and services.**

   **Discussion:** Misha's father and teacher began their collaboration before the IEP meeting by talking about the kinds of AAC that might help Misha express himself more clearly and more appropriately. Other team members joined the collaborative discussion during the IEP meeting as they contributed to the development of Misha's goals for communication. The data and information that was brought to the IEP team meeting was complete enough for the team to make a determination that Misha needed AT in the form of AAC. Team members contributed by making suggestions about next steps even though they did not complete a formal assessment in this case. The team felt their current consideration of Misha's AAC needs was collaborative and would result in the information they needed. They rated their performance on this indicator a 4.

| 1 | 2 | 3 | 4 | 5 |
|---|---|---|---|---|
| No process is established for IEP teams to use to make AT decisions. | A process is established for IEP teams to use to make AT decisions but it is not collaborative. | A collaborative process is established but not generally used by IEP teams to make AT decisions. | **A collaborative process is established and generally used by IEP teams to make AT decisions.** | A collaborative process is established and consistently used by IEP teams to make AT decisions. |

3. **IEP team members have the *collective knowledge and skills* needed to make informed assistive technology decisions and seek assistance when needed.**

   **Discussion:** When some members of the team began to think about AT use for Misha, they had enough knowledge and access to some devices to begin their investigation into whether he could benefit from AAC devices. When his father raised the question about the use of a tablet for communication, the team realized that they did not have enough information about apps that could be useful to Misha and asked for help from an AT consultant who sometimes worked for the school district. The team rated their consideration activities for Misha a 4 in this area since, once they decided to really look at his AT needs, they were careful to share knowledge and get more information when they needed it.

| 1 | 2 | 3 | 4 | 5 |
|---|---|---|---|---|
| The team does not have the knowledge or skills needed to make informed AT decisions. The team does not seek help when needed. | Individual team members have some of the knowledge and skills needed to make informed AT decisions. The team does not seek help when needed. | Team members sometimes combine knowledge and skills to make informed AT decisions. The team does not always seek help when needed. | **Team members generally combine their knowledge and skills to make informed AT decisions. The team seeks help when needed.** | The team consistently uses collective knowledge and skills to make informed AT decisions. The team seeks help when needed. |

4. **Decisions regarding the need for assistive technology devices and services are *based on the student's IEP goals and objectives, access to curricular and extracurricular activities, and progress in the general education curriculum.***

   **Discussion:** Misha's team did not initially consider AT for expressive language even though he clearly understood what people said to him and had more to say than his speech would allow. When the team reviewed annual goals for Misha in prior IEPs, they discovered that focus had been solely on speech development and did not consider AT options. It was only at the point when it became clear that Misha's inability to request, protest, socialize, and share information was beginning to have an impact on his behavior that the team began to consider

AT options. His team gave themselves a 2 because they realized that earlier consideration of his AAC and AT needs might have resulted in increased goal attainment.

| 1 | 2 | 3 | 4 | 5 |
|---|---|---|---|---|
| Decisions about a student's need for AT are not connected to IEP goals or the general curriculum. | **Decisions about a student's need for AT are based on either access to the curriculum/IEP goals or the general curriculum, not both.** | Decisions about a student's need for AT sometimes are based on both the student's IEP goals and general education curricular tasks. | Decisions about a student's need for AT generally are based on both the student's IEP goals and general education curricular tasks. | Decisions about a student's need for AT consistently are based on both the student's IEP goals and general education curricular tasks. |

5. **The IEP team** *gathers and analyzes data* **about the student, customary environments, and educational goals and tasks when considering a student's need for assistive technology devices and services.**

**Discussion:** One difficulty that members of Misha's team frequently encountered as they talked about his needs for AT was that he had many challenges in his educational program. In addition to his need for a tool to support participation in academic settings, he needed a way to express frustration and interact socially. Team members found it difficult to consider only one area at a time when they talked about his need for AT. Eventually, one team member developed a table that listed all the tasks for which they were considering AT across the top row and the tools they were considering down the left column. Team members were able to refer to this list as they collected their data about his performance on each task and record that data in the appropriate box on the table. This helped them identify AT solutions that had the most functionality for Misha. The team gave themselves a 4 in this area.

| 1 | 2 | 3 | 4 | 5 |
|---|---|---|---|---|
| The IEP team does not gather and analyze data to consider a student's need for AT devices and services. | The IEP team gathers and analyzes data about the student, customary environments, educational goals or tasks, but not all, when considering a student's need for AT devices and services. | The IEP team sometimes gathers and analyzes data about the student, customary environments, educational goals and tasks when considering a student's need for AT devices and services. | **The IEP team generally gathers and analyzes data about the student, customary environments, educational goals and tasks when considering a student's need for AT devices and services.** | The IEP team consistently gathers and analyzes data about the student, customary environments, educational goals and tasks when considering a student's need for AT devices and services. |

6. **When assistive technology is needed, the IEP team *explores a range* of assistive technology devices, services, and other supports that address identified needs.**

   **Discussion:** Misha's team rated their performance as a 2 for this item. They actually felt they had done a good job of considering the options they had available, but realized they needed to access more AT for trial periods from the agency or regional AT library.

| 1 | 2 | 3 | 4 | 5 |
|---|---|---|---|---|
| The IEP team does not explore a range of AT devices, services, and other supports to address identified needs. | **The IEP team considers a limited set of AT devices, services, and other supports.** | The IEP team sometimes explores a range of AT devices, services, and other supports. | The IEP team generally explores a range of AT devices, services, and other supports. | The IEP team always explores a range of AT devices, services, and other supports to address identified needs. |

7. **The assistive technology consideration process and *results are documented in the IEP* and include a rationale for the decision and supporting evidence.**

   **Discussion:** In previous IEP meetings, the consideration of Misha's need for AAC had been superficial. Since the team had a primary goal that he would develop speech, they simply stated on the IEP that AT was not needed. They also did not consider his need for AT in any other area and did no further documentation of their discussions.

   Misha's team rated their consideration work as a 3 in this area. They talked about the idea that more complete documentation in previous years' IEPs might have resulted in earlier use of AAC as a strategy for him.

| 1 | 2 | 3 | 4 | 5 |
|---|---|---|---|---|
| The consideration process and results are not documented in the IEP. | The consideration process and results are documented in the IEP but do not include a rationale for the decision and supporting evidence. | **The consideration process and results are documented in the IEP and sometimes include a rationale for the decision and supporting evidence.** | The consideration process and results are documented in the IEP and generally include a rationale for the decision and supporting evidence. | The consideration process and results are documented in the IEP and consistently include a rationale for the decision and supporting evidence. |

## Summary

The case study illustrates the outcome of consideration of the need for AT. In Misha's case, the IEP team was able to determine Misha needed an AAC device written into the IEP and implemented immediately. At the same time, they planned to explore a more complex tool to determine if it would offer better long-term options for him.

Chapter 3 describes the core components of quality AT assessment.

## Suggested Activities

1. Complete the Self-Evaluation Matrix for Consideration of Assistive Technology Needs reflecting on your own past experiences. If you have never participated in an IEP meeting, use the Self-Evaluation Matrix to interview a special education teacher about the practices in his or her school.

2. Think of a student with disabilities. Using the questions in Table 2.1, answer them in regard to that student.

3. Go to *www.atinternet.org/modules* and complete the module titled "Assistive technology consideration in the IEP process" provided by the Ohio Center for Autism and Low Incidence. How does the information in the module compare to the Quality Indicators for Assistive Technology Consideration?

4. Search the Internet using "Assistive Technology Consideration form." Select at least two different AT Consideration forms and evaluate them to see which features you find useful. What do you like about the form you chose and why? How do you think it will help IEP teams?

5. View the two webinars on AT Consideration at Ablenet University. *https://www.ablenetinc.com/resources/recorded_webinars/*. Sign in and search the list of recorded videos on AT. View *Consideration for Assistive Technology* by Kirk Behnke and *QIAT Session 2: Consideration of AT Needs* by Penny Reed and Kathy Lalk. Compare and contrast the information you got from each webinar. How do they differ? What do they have in common? How can one or both of them help you in the future?

# Exploring the Quality Indicators for Assessment of Assistive Technology Needs

1. *Procedures* for all aspects of assistive technology assessment are clearly defined and consistently applied.

2. Assistive technology assessments are conducted by a *team with the collective knowledge and skills needed* to determine possible assistive technology solutions that address the needs and abilities of the student, demands of the customary environments, educational goals, and related activities.

3. All assistive technology assessments include a functional assessment in the student's *customary environments*, such as the classroom, lunchroom, playground, home, community setting, or work place.

4. Assistive technology assessments, including needed trials, are completed within *reasonable time lines*.

5. Recommendations from assistive technology assessments are *based on data* about the student, environments, and tasks.

6. The assessment provides the IEP team with clearly *documented recommendations* that guide decisions about the selection, acquisition, and use of assistive technology devices and services.

7. Assistive technology needs are *reassessed* any time changes in the student, the environments, and/or the tasks result in the student's needs not being met with current devices and/or services.

AT devices and AT services are defined in IDEA. The first service listed in the definition of AT services is " the evaluation of the needs of a child with a disability, including a functional evaluation of the child in the child's customary environment." (Authority: 20 U.S.C. 1401(2)(a)) The use of the term "functional evaluation" is not accidental; Congress wanted to convey the importance of gathering authentic information based on the child's performance while completing meaningful tasks as part of familiar routines and activities. Completing a functional evaluation yields more contextually relevant information about a child's strengths and needs than conventional, standardized assessments (Bagnato, Neisworth, & Pretti-Frontczak, 2010). The information gained during a functional evaluation is also more culturally sensitive and more authentic. Authenticity is critical, because as the more realistic the task, the more applicable the results will be to every day routines and activities (Delaney, 1999). Another critical term in the definition is "customary environment." This, too, is not to be ignored because it has implications to education agencies, families, and independent third party evaluators.

The use of the terms "assessment" and "evaluation" varies across disciplines, geographic areas, and agencies. In IDEA, the term "evaluation" is used. However, this document uses the term "assessment" to refer to a formative, ongoing process for determining a child's unique need for AT.

1. **Procedures for all aspects of assistive technology assessment are clearly defined and consistently applied.**

   **Intent: Throughout the education agency, personnel are well informed and trained about assessment procedures and how to initiate them. There is consistency throughout the agency in conducting AT assessments. Procedures may include, but are not limited to, initiating an assessment, observing, planning, and conducting an assessment, conducting trials, gathering data, reporting results, and resolving conflicts.**

   While AT assessment is not a standardized process, there are essential steps and a variety of free and commercial assessment packages (e.g., Wisconsin Assistive Technology Initiative Assessment Packet, 2009; Functional Evaluation of Assistive Technology, 2002; SETT Scaffolds, 1999) that suggest a scope and sequence of tasks to teams in a variety of settings. Utilizing procedures, such as the ones outlined in Table 3.1 and in the *Assistive Technology Assessment Process Planner* in Appendix D, will guide the process and help ensure useful outcomes.

   Consistency throughout an agency occurs when there are clearly defined procedures, and staff is trained on how to implement those procedures. To be effective, procedures for all aspects of the AT assessment process are written and readily available in a manner that is accessible to all in the education agency. Procedures might include: observing the student completing meaningful tasks as part of familiar routines in customary environments, reviewing student records, interviewing the student and family, and conducting formal or informal tests needed to obtain essential information. Individual team members might use informal assessment tools like Every Move Counts (Korsten, Foss & Berry,

2007), the Communication Matrix, (Rowland, 2004), the Protocol for Assessment in Reading (DeCoste, D. & Wilson, L. B. (2012), or the Written Productivity Profile, (DeCoste, D., 2006) to help determine specific student skills.

| | |
|---|---|
| *Complete an AT assessment by a collaborative team sharing responsibilities*<br>    Determine team members | **TABLE 3.1** Suggested steps in an AT assessment (from Assistive Technology Assessment Planner, Appendix D). |
| *Create a written AT assessment plan including:*<br>    Determine the assessment questions<br>    Identify expected results and outcomes *(e.g,. Student will be able to____)*<br>    Determine what will be measured (e.g., speed, quantity, quality, rate, accuracy, endurance)<br>    Assign responsibilities<br>    Set a timeline | |
| *Gather information from multiple sources including previous information (e.g., educational reports, assessments, background interviews, and other records)*<br>    Student's strengths<br>    Student's needs<br>    Environmental expectations<br>    Tasks (e.g., required curricular work, testing, homework, projects, in-class work, materials, statewide testing, and other school functions)<br>    Current levels of performance for identified tasks (baseline data)<br>    Barriers to participation and independence | |
| *Analyze information to identify tools and strategies for the trials*<br>    Determine the features needed<br>    Choose tools with appropriate features<br>    Determine source of trials from demos, loaners, and rental programs<br>    Set timelines<br>    Prepare recording method and strategies for data to be collected | |
| *Conduct the trials with identified tools*<br>    Have student use tools and strategies in customary environment for identified tasks<br>    Collect data | |
| *Analyze Data*<br>    Report the results of the trials<br>    Revisit the assessment questions to determine the outcomes<br>    Determine the most appropriate tools and strategies or if additional trials are necessary | |
| *Document recommendations in written form following district AT procedural guidelines*<br>    Summarize student performance while using AT tools, including tools that were and were not successful<br>    Document appropriate tools and potential impact on student achievement<br>    If needed, include specific language for procurement of AT, and possible funding sources | |
| *Document required tools and strategies in student's plan (e.g., IEP, 504 Plan)*<br>    Develop Implementation Plan<br>    Describe instructional/access areas which were explored during the trial<br>    Create summary of specific skills assessed<br>    Write action plan including team member roles and responsibilities | |

The procedures also describe a decision-making process to ensure collaborative assessment, and all staff members are made aware of the AT assessment process and their role in it. AT assessment procedures are included with all other agency procedures in regular, ongoing updates. The importance of having locally developed, well-defined procedures is discussed more fully in Chapter 8.

*The South Washington County School District recently hired a new director of technology who assumed responsibility for technology with both general education and special education students. As he took over the role, it became evident that there were no defined procedures for AT assessment. While current practice for IEP teams was to ask colleagues for help in determining AT needs, this lacked consistency from team to team and from building to building.*

*After realizing this lack of consistency, an AT task force was developed to create consistent procedures, based on best practices. Some of the tools they used were in the Indicator and Resource sections of the QIAT website (www.qiat.org). The task force clearly defined the district's AT assessment processes: conducting assessments, evaluating related data, identifying device features to support student needs, and conducting trials with the AT in students' customary environments.*

*Once the procedures for assessment were established, staff was provided Internet access to the guidelines as well as training to support their use. After further reflection, the AT task force decided to focus their future work on the area of implementation.*

**KEY QUESTIONS**

- Where are AT assessment procedures located and how does the staff access them?

- How is the staff made aware of the procedures, how often are they reviewed, and what is the review process?

- What aspects of the AT assessment process are addressed in the written procedures?

- What training do staff members need in order to follow AT assessment procedures?

- How does the agency ensure that the AT assessment procedures are consistently applied?

2. **Assistive technology assessments are conducted by a *team with the collective knowledge and skills needed* to determine possible assistive technology solutions that address the needs and abilities of the student, demands of the customary environments, educational goals, and related activities.**

   **Intent: Team membership is flexible and varies according to the knowledge and skills needed to address student needs. The student and family are active team members. Various team members bring different information and strengths to the assessment process.**

   Effective teams that conduct AT assessments include individuals who have knowledge about the student's strengths and needs, the tasks required of the student, and the demands placed on the student in customary settings. The team also includes at least one person who has knowledge about appropriate AT options. Team members, depending upon individual student needs, may include general and special education teachers; parents; the student, when appropriate; therapists, such as occupational therapists (OT), physical therapists (PT), and speech-language pathologists (SLP); curriculum specialists; technology specialists; and others with unique information to contribute, such as a job coach. For example, if communication is an area of deficit, the SLP would be a necessary team member. If the student has a hearing loss, an audiologist or a teacher of students with hearing impairments would be a critical member.

   The important factor is that no one individual knows or needs to know everything about the student, the environment, the routine tasks, or the potential AT tools, rather each team member contributes important information to create the knowledge base necessary for good decisions. The synergy that occurs as a result of involving the team that works with the student on a daily basis is critical. Team members who participate in decision-making and then implement their own decisions are knowledgeable and empowered. They have a vision of what they want to accomplish through the use of AT.

---

EXAMPLE

*Maria is a first-grade student in the general education instructional setting. She has developmentally appropriate communication skills, however she uses a wheelchair for mobility and exhibits fine motor difficulties. She has a visual impairment and fatigues easily when asked to complete reading assignments. In addition to her core team of the general education teacher, resource teacher, and family, the team conducting the AT assessment also includes an OT, PT, and her teacher of students with visual impairments. It was noted that Maria can understand text when it is read to her, but she is not making adequate progress in reading independently. An AT specialist and reading specialist were requested to help explore specialized formats for print instructional materials. She is also experiencing fine motor challenges, causing difficulty with the production of written output. The team will explore alternative ways for her to complete written assignments.*

---

- What team members are needed to address individual student needs?

- What knowledge and skills does each team member bring to the process?

- How is information communicated to all team members?

- What processes are used to ensure team collaboration?

3. **All assistive technology assessments include a functional assessment in the student's *customary environments*, such as the classroom, lunchroom, playground, home, community setting, or work place.**

   **Intent: The assessment process includes activities that occur in the student's current or anticipated environments because characteristics and demands in each may vary. Team members work together to gather specific data and relevant information in identified environments to contribute to assessment decisions.**

   The team begins the assessment process by identifying the student's unique strengths and needs, the typical environments in which the student participates, and the tasks the student needs to accomplish. The team gathers and reviews assessment data about the student, the environment, and the tasks before suggesting AT tools and strategies. Observation in the classroom and other routine environments will be part of the information gathering and will yield valuable data about critical elements in the environments (e.g., lighting, sound, location of teacher, location of student, type of instructional activity, distractions, and typical behavior during routine tasks and activities).

   Once the team identifies AT tools that may meet the student's needs, the student uses them during trial periods established by the team. Then they evaluate the extent to which these tools support student success. They collect data across environments in case the need for AT supports may differ in different settings.

   While results of assessments conducted outside the customary environments may contain useful information and can contribute to the overall picture, such assessments may not accurately capture information necessary to identify the specific AT tools and services needed in the customary home, school, and community environments. Such assessments may not include input from IEP team members knowledgeable about tasks the student needs to accomplish or characteristics and demands of daily activities and routines in specific customary environments.

*Jose is a kindergarten student with severe dysarthria and spastic quadriplegia who uses a wheelchair for mobility. His family members are not native English speakers. He participates with his peers in general education settings and attends classes in art, music, and physical education. The team collaboratively planned a functional assessment in multiple, environments including his home, to identify Jose's skills and abilities and required tasks and demands in each environment. They assigned themselves specific data collection tasks including identifying messages needed for class participation and peer interaction. They will work together to collect data on his communication attempts in various environments and the type of messages he needs to communicate with peers, teachers, and family members. His team will consider the need for AT including communication systems and strategies to meet the identified needs, physical access, mounting, and positioning. They will analyze both the nature and content of his communication attempts and the needs of his communication partners to determine if his communication system will need to be bilingual. The team's assessment will include analysis of how much his communication needs vary across environments and what the features of an effective communication system will need to be. Trials will be carried out in customary environments with one or more standalone AAC devices, a tablet with AAC apps, or a combination of these before anything is purchased.*

**KEY QUESTIONS**

- How do teams determine the customary environments in which functional assessments will be completed?

- How are the tasks identified within each environment to determine which features might be needed to support student achievement?

- How might AT assessment processes vary across environments?

- What strategies do team members use to ensure that no critical aspect of the AT assessment is overlooked?

4. **Assistive technology assessments, including needed trials, are completed within *reasonable timelines*.**

   **Intent: Assessments are initiated in a timely fashion and completed within a timeline that is reasonable as determined by the IEP team. The timeline complies with applicable state and agency requirements.**

   This Quality Indicator uses the phrase "within reasonable timelines" and the intent statement says "in a timely fashion." These terms are used because there can be a great deal of variance in what may be considered an acceptable timeline to complete an AT assessment. Part of that variance is due to the fact that, based on IDEA, the timeline for an initial evaluation for eligibility for special education can vary in each state. Therefore, if the AT assessment is part of the initial evaluation, the time requirement will be whatever has been set by that state.

However, the question of AT typically arises after the student has already qualified for special education services as a child with a disability. A new request for assessment of AT (if it has never been provided to the child as part of his or her special education services or never addressed in previous evaluations) may, in some states, trigger a comprehensive reevaluation. The timeline for reevaluation is not specified in IDEA. In this instance, the IEP team determines an appropriate timeline within state or local education agency guidelines or policies.

If the student already has AT, but an assessment is needed to identify new or additional AT, it does not generally trigger a comprehensive reevaluation and therefore there may not be any timeline specified by the state or the local education agency. In addition, there are other factors that may affect the timeline such as the age of the student, the complexity of needs, and the amount of time needed for trials. It is the responsibility of the IEP team to set a time frame within local and state guidelines that is reasonable to determine what AT the student may need.

The length of a trial period is set to provide sufficient opportunity for the student to use the tools and for the impact of the tools on the student's achievement to be determined. In some cases that may become apparent in a few days, in others a student may require longer to become sufficiently familiar with the device and demonstrate proficiency. Data gathered during the trial period will influence the selection of specific AT.

**EXAMPLE**

*Brian has been identified as a student on the autism spectrum. He primarily responds verbally to spoken requests with one to two words. He does respond in writing using a pencil and a small note pad with five to seven words. He rarely initiates verbal interactions with anyone but he occasionally indicates choices through gestures. When he transferred to Harbor Hills School District, his parents provided reports from two previous AT evaluations focused on increasing his expressive output: one completed by his former school district and one conducted by an outside agency that the parents had chosen. The previous school personnel recommended a portable word processor. The outside agency recommended a laptop computer with text-to-speech. However, neither written report included evidence of data from trial use of either AT tool.*

*In the absence of data from trial use, Brian's team decided to conduct an AT assessment with trial periods of both devices. The team felt these trial periods could support Brian's expressive language goal. His current IEP did not include any reference to AT. Under state guidelines, the AT assessment would be part of a comprehensive reevaluation to address his needs. They had 45 school days to complete it within their state's guidelines.*

*Brian's team identified current needs related to expressive language in his customary environments and established a timeline that would allow trial use of more than one tool. It was agreed that the portable word processor recommended by his previous school offered potential support for Brian and was selected as the first tool for trial use. Data from this first trial period provided information about features he preferred and that resulted in increased length of responses. The team selected a different portable word processor that had the text-to-speech feature that had been recommended by the outside agency and an additional trial period was provided. The data from the two AT device trials was analyzed in order to complete the assessment and make recommendations to the IEP team within the timeline that had been set. They recommended the provision of the portable word processor with text-to-speech.*

---

**KEY QUESTIONS**

- What is your state's specific timeline for initial evaluation and reevaluation?

- Does your education agency follow the state requirement or does it have a more restrictive policy?

- How are timelines for trial periods of potential AT solutions determined in your agency?

5. **Recommendations from assistive technology assessments are *based on data* about the student, environments, and tasks.**

   **Intent: The assessment includes information about the student's needs and abilities, demands of various environments, educational tasks, and objectives. Data may be gathered from sources such as student performance records, results of experimental trials, direct observation, interviews with students or significant others, and anecdotal records.**

   During the assessment process, information is collected about the student, the tasks the student needs to be able to do, and the demands of the environments in which the student will do the identified tasks. AT assessment may include both formal and informal testing, if needed, to provide critical information. For example, if the team questions the student's receptive language level, a formal test of receptive language ability may be conducted. If the team finds highly variable data about reading rate when reviewing his portfolio, an informal reading test may be conducted. The assessment activities are selected to yield data about the specific needs and potential effectiveness of AT use.

Opportunities to try out the potential AT are a critical part of the AT assessment process. The specific data from any trial periods that are part of the assessment is analyzed to determine whether using the AT was effective in helping the student meet the target outcomes. This analysis helps the team identify key features needed on any proposed AT device as well as any additional instruction or services that the student will need. If the analysis does not provide enough information to clearly identify specific AT tools that have potential to help the student with important tasks, additional assessment activities or trials are completed. Following identification of necessary features and analysis of data available from trial periods, recommendations are developed and submitted to the IEP team.

**EXAMPLE**

*An AT assessment was initiated because Jamie exhibited behavior outbursts in specific environments. Her team thought her behavior might be related to an inability to communicate and actively participate in activities. Jamie was using a paper picture-based communication system, but observation and further evaluation showed it was only used as a visual scheduling strategy to show her what was going to happen next (receptive language). Jamie had no independent access to the picture-based system and did not have a way to express herself except through behavior.*

*The team decided to give Jamie her own copy of the picture-based system and encouraged her to use the pictures for expressive communication. Data showed that Jamie understood the expressive use of the pictures almost immediately. She began to use the pictures to communicate her preferred activities, and her behavior outbursts decreased.*

*Jamie experienced so much success with independent access to the picture-based system that the team decided to also try an AAC device. Observation data indicated that Jamie's use of expressive language with the AAC device increased and outbursts decreased even more. The key features that Jamie needed were picture-based vocabulary, recorded speech, no more than 12 pictures at a time, and multiple levels to be used in various activities. The assessment team made a recommendation to the IEP team to consider a device with these features.*

**KEY QUESTIONS**

- How does the team identify expected outcomes of the AT assessment?
- How is progress toward these outcomes evaluated?
- What data is used to determine that the student has had ample opportunity to try the AT device(s)?
- How does the data support the recommendations?

6. **The assessment provides the IEP team with clearly *documented recommendations* that guide decisions about the selection, acquisition, and use of assistive technology devices and services.**

    **Intent: A written rationale is provided for any recommendations that are made. Recommendations may include assessment activities and results, suggested AT devices and alternative ways of addressing needs, AT services required by the student and others, and suggested strategies for implementation and use.**

    Recommendations to the IEP team resulting from AT assessment activities need to include information about what was done and what was found. Suggested information to be included is in Table 3.2

**TABLE 3.2** Suggested information in an AT assessment report

| |
| --- |
| Reason for the Assessment |
|   A list of the tasks that need to be accomplished by the student in customary environments |
|   Current barriers to performance |
|   Information regarding AT currently in use and how it is working, if applicable |
| Process for the Assessment |
|   Specific tasks conducted by the assessment team |
|   Location where the assessment was conducted |
|   Length and conditions under which the assessment was done |
|   Accommodations, interventions, and strategies, including features of the AT used during the assessment |
| Results of the Assessment |
|   Changes in the student's performance when using the AT |
|   Specific features of AT tools identified as important |
|   Recommended accommodations, interventions, and strategies, including any AT devices |

The AT assessment report provides recommendations to the IEP team. The IEP team is empowered by IDEA to make all decisions about the students IEP including decisions about AT. When writing recommendations, it is important to include as much information as possible so the IEP team has clear and complete documentation on which to base their decision. The AT assessment report may include the names of the specific AT devices or tools used during the assessment, but must include a list of critical features that enabled the student to be successful. The inclusion of specific features is important because the IEP team will need that information in writing the IEP document.

EXAMPLE

*Jonah is a middle school student who has difficulty generating more than a simple sentence when composing written assignments. The IEP team requested an AT assessment asking for voice recognition technology. The general education teacher provided five writing samples in various genres (narrative, poem, etc.). The AT assessment team observed Jonah in his educational settings. They noted that during class Jonah contributed actively to discussion and group work. His verbal contributions were thoughtful and robust.*

*However, his written work consisted of single sentences with multiple misspellings. Teachers confirmed that this was typical in all settings.*

*The assessment team demonstrated the use of voice recognition technology in a quiet room. Jonah immediately asked how he would be able to use this technology in a noisy classroom. The assessment team then showed him word prediction software, which Jonah also liked.*

*Jonah used voice recognition software and word prediction software for three weeks at home and at school. The data showed that Jonah's written production increased dramatically using each technology. Jonah preferred voice recognition software because it was so fast, but he did not like leaving his classroom in order to use it. He expressed a preference for using word prediction software in school.*

*The IEP team was able to make a well-informed decision because the report described the features Jonah needed. The recommendation from the assessment team to the IEP team was that Jonah would have access to voice recognition at home to complete homework and access to word prediction at school. It listed the important features in each of these options that Jonah would need to be successful.*

**KEY QUESTIONS**

- How do reports describe the accommodations, interventions, and strategies, including AT, that were used during the assessment?

- What data are included in reports to support recommendations?

- How do reports explain features of AT that are identified as needed by the student?

7. **Assistive technology needs are *reassessed* any time changes in the student, the environments, and/or the tasks result in the student's needs not being met with current devices, and/or services.**

   **Intent: An AT assessment is available any time it is needed due to changes that have affected the student. The assessment can be requested by the parent or any other member of the IEP team.**

   Over time, the AT a student uses may no longer meet his or her needs effectively because of changes in the student's skills, environments, tasks, or curricular demands. Additionally, the team may become aware of new technology or updates that have the potential to help the student complete tasks with increased proficiency. A reassessment may also be appropriate when past assessments did not indicate a need for AT, but conditions have changed that would suggest a possible current need.

Any IEP team member may request a reassessment to identify new AT that will better address changing student needs. Reassessment may include typical classroom assessments to determine effectiveness of current AT and/or the need for adjustments/modifications/changes. Reassessments may be requested during the annual IEP meeting or at any time when new information is needed.

EXAMPLE

*Gus went to camp during the summer after his third grade year. The camp he attended was for kids who had difficulty reading and writing, and his parents hoped the camp would help him overcome his difficulties in school. Before camp, Gus read at the pre-kindergarten level. Due to weak muscles in his hands, he was able to write three words per minute with poor legibility when he used a pencil. The school provided a standard word processor for longer writing tasks.*

*While he was at camp, in every activity, there were interesting things to do to help kids improve their literacy skills at the same time they were having fun. For example, when they built birdhouses, they read the directions and wrote a paragraph about the birds that would live in it.*

*During camp, Gus showed remarkable progress in reading when he was introduced to a new instructional approach that included word attack skills. To address his difficulty with writing, the camp staff introduced him to software that included word prediction with auditory preview and electronic word banks. At the end of camp, camp staff wrote a report for parents about what they had tried and what they noted about Gus's performance.*

*During their fall meeting the team reviewed the AT for writing that Gus used at school and his parents shared information about the software he used at camp with the IEP team. The team wondered whether Gus might use AT similar to what he used at camp to increase his writing skills. An AT assessment was initiated to help answer this question.*

**KEY QUESTIONS**

- What changes in student performance have occurred since the previous assessment?

- What changes in the environment, tasks, or demands on the student have occurred?

- Which student needs are not currently addressed?

- What does data show about how the current AT supports student performance?

- What questions will be answered through assessment?

# Exploring the Quality Indicators for Assessment of Assistive Technology Needs with the QIAT Self-Evaluation Matrix

The Self-Evaluation Matrix for Assessment of Assistive Technology Needs focuses on the development of quality AT assessment services in an education agency. The matrix provides descriptive steps ranging from the unacceptable to promising practices for each of the Quality Indicators for Assessment of AT Needs. Through its variations from "unacceptable" to "best practice," the matrix

- helps identify characteristics of quality AT assessment services,

- provides a means to measure areas of strength and areas in need of improvement,

- supports identification of variations in AT assessment practice across sites, and

- offers a scaffold for improving AT assessment practices across the agency.

Quality Indicators 1, 2, 3, 4, and 7 in the area of AT assessment are about team processes. The first quality indicator concerns procedures—and which individuals within the agency are aware of them and use them. The second indicator is about the practice of conducting the assessments and the use of a team with the necessary knowledge and skills. The third indicator focuses on providing a functional assessment in the student's customary environment. The fourth inquires about the length of time generally taken to complete an AT assessment. The seventh indicator addresses how the AT needs of students are monitored and reassessed.

Quality Indicators 5 and 6 are about the recommendations an AT assessment team makes. These two indicators focus on the use of data in making recommendations (Indicator 5) and the documentation of those recommendations (Indicator 6).

When the collaborative AT team members and any other individuals who are involved in AT assessments have completed the matrix, their results can be used to analyze AT assessment procedures and determine where efforts might be focused in order to improve practice across the education agency.

While the language of the Self-Evaluation Matrix for Assessment of AT Needs specifically addresses collaborative teams, the matrix may be used in several different ways, either by a building or agency team, a local education agency, or a state education agency as a self-assessment or survey. The team may use the self-evaluation tool to review a student's services as well as to evaluate how the team functions in their interactions with several students. Furthermore, a school district or state agency might use the matrix as a survey and request that other key players provide the team with a perspective on how services are perceived across the agency.

Regardless of how the matrix is utilized, the information obtained can be applied to guide continuous improvement planning.

The case study following the Self-Evaluation Matrix for AT Assessment provides an example of a team that struggled with a lack of clear procedures and how they moved forward to meet their student's needs.

# Quality Indicators for *Assessment* of Assistive Technology Needs

| QUALITY INDICATOR | UNACCEPTABLE | | |
|---|---|---|---|
| **1. *Procedures* for all aspects of AT assessment are clearly defined and consistently applied.** | 1<br>No procedures are defined. | 2<br>Some assessment procedures are defined, but not generally used. | |
| **2. AT assessments are conducted by a *team with the collective knowledge and skills needed* to determine possible AT solutions that address the needs and abilities of the student, demands of the customary environments, educational goals, and related activities.** | 1<br>A designated individual with no prior knowledge of the student's needs or technology conducts assessments. | 2<br>A designated person or group conducts assessments but lacks either knowledge of AT or of the student's needs, environments, or tasks. | |
| **3. All AT assessments include a functional assessment in the student's *customary environments*, such as the classroom, lunchroom, playground, home, community setting, or work place.** | 1<br>No component of the AT assessment is conducted in any of the student's customary environments. | 2<br>No component of the AT assessment is conducted in any of the customary environments, however, data about the customary environments are sought. | |
| **4. AT assessments, including needed trials, are completed within *reasonable timelines*.** | 1<br>AT assessments are not completed within agency timelines. | 2<br>AT assessments are frequently out of compliance with timelines. | |
| **5. Recommendations from AT assessments are *based on data* about the student, environments and tasks.** | 1<br>Recommendations are not data based. | 2<br>Recommendations are based on incomplete data from limited sources. | |
| **6. The assessment provides the IEP team with clearly *documented recommendations* that guide decisions about the selection, acquisition, and use of AT devices and services.** | 1<br>Recommendations are not documented. | 2<br>Documented recommendations include only devices. Recommendations about services are not documented. | |
| **7. AT needs are *reassessed* any time changes in the student, the environments and/or the tasks result in the student's needs not being met with current devices or services.** | 1<br>AT needs are not reassessed. | 2<br>AT needs are only reassessed when requested. Reassessment is done formally and no ongoing AT assessment takes place. | |

| 3 | 4 | 5 |
|---|---|---|
| Procedures are defined and used only by specialized personnel. | Procedures are clearly defined and generally used in both special and general education. | Clearly defined procedures are used by everyone involved in the assessment process. |
| A team conducts assessments with limited input from individuals who have knowledge of AT or of the student's needs, environments, and tasks. | A collaborative team whose members have direct knowledge of the student's needs, environments, and tasks, and knowledge of AT generally conducts assessments. | A collaborative, flexible team formed on the basis of knowledge of the individual student's needs, environments, and tasks, and expertise in AT consistently conducts assessments. |
| Functional components of AT assessments are sometimes conducted in the student's customary environments. | Functional components of AT assessments are generally conducted in the student's customary environments. | Functional components of AT assessments are consistently conducted in the student's customary environments. |
| AT assessments are completed within a reasonable timeline and may or may not include initial trials. | AT assessments are completed within a reasonable timeline and include at least initial trials. | AT assessments are conducted in a timely manner and include a plan for ongoing assessment and trials in customary environments. |
| Recommendations are sometimes based on data about student performance on typical tasks in customary environments. | Recommendations are generally based on data about student performance on typical tasks in customary environments. | Recommendations are consistently based on data about student performance on typical tasks in customary environments. |
| Documented recommendations may or may not include sufficient information about devices and services to guide decision-making and program development. | Documented recommendations generally include sufficient information about devices and services to guide decision-making and program development. | Documented recommendations consistently include sufficient information about devices and services to guide decision-making and program development. |
| AT needs are reassessed on an annual basis or upon request. Reassessment may include some ongoing and formal assessment strategies. | AT use is frequently monitored. AT needs are generally reassessed if current tools and strategies are ineffective. Reassessment generally includes ongoing assessment strategies and includes formal assessment, if indicated. | AT use is frequently monitored. AT needs are generally reassessed if current tools and strategies are ineffective. Reassessment generally includes ongoing assessment strategies and includes formal assessment, if indicated. |

# Exploring the Quality Indicators for Assessment of Assistive Technology Needs Through Mark's Case Study

Mark is a fourth grader who is served in special education under the category of Other Health Impairment due to a medical diagnosis of Attention Deficit Hyperactivity Disorder (ADHD). He has difficulty with fine motor skills and his handwriting is not legible. Pencil-to-paper tasks are very difficult for him and result in behavior outbursts. Several prompts may be needed for Mark to respond with an answer to a question that is posed to him verbally. It consistently takes several minutes for him to express even short answers in writing.

Mark receives instruction in general education classes and 60 minutes daily in a resource room to support reading, writing, and social skills. He receives direct service weekly from the OT, PT, and SLP. The OT is working on fine motor skills and also sensory support. The use of pencil grips for writing activities was in Mark's IEP and he had used several, but the pencil grips did not decrease his writing frustration or increase his legibility. The physical therapist is working on postural control. The speech and language pathologist is working on conversational skills and vocabulary development. A paraprofessional is assigned to work with him on a full-time basis in general education classes to encourage on-task behavior, reinforce social skills, and encourage interactions in his environment.

The fourth-grade curriculum requires written assignments in all content areas and Mark often has missing or incomplete assignments. Assignments requiring hand-written responses often lead to behavior outbursts even though he is able to verbally produce the answer. Mark's fourth-grade teacher is unsure if she should accept a different format of response than what is expected from other fourth graders. When his difficulties with independent written work were discussed during an IEP meeting, the team was unsure how to help him complete his work.

Mark's elementary school is in a rural area. AT assessments are conducted for students with physical and cognitive involvement but there is no formal AT assessment system for students with mild disabilities. For these students, informal assessments are conducted as needed by the special education staff. As a part of one of those informal trials of AT, the OT collaborated with Mark's special education teacher and determined that he was able to use a touch screen accurately. His mom pointed out that he uses a tablet computer for recreation at home and shows aptitude and interest in anything electronic. The special education department had access to a set of tablet computers that were loaded with word processing apps. The OT and the special education teacher decided to try providing a tablet as writing support for all of Mark's assignments.

Initially, she taught Mark how to use the tablet to write about his favorite topic, super heroes. Once he was comfortable creating text, he began using the tablet for structured responses in all content areas. This made a significant difference in Mark's attitude toward writing. He could complete written assignments at grade level and used the tablet to respond to test questions. He used his AT throughout the day and once his mother was provided training on his new writing apps he took it home as needed. His mother has been extremely supportive and has also learned how to assist Mark with his written homework assignments.

When Mark began to use the device in additional classes where writing was expected, he was successful in some classes and not successful in others. There were several incidents of frustrated behavior from Mark. As the team looked at the characteristics of each environment and each writing task, they realized that Mark had more difficulty with writing tasks that involved creativity rather than factual answers. They suspected that he needed additional instruction in creative writing and this instruction was added to what he received in the resource room. They modified his program to use alternative writing strategies like dictation for some tasks while he continued to use the tablet for tasks at his independent instructional level. The recommendations about AT and the ways Mark used it were documented in the IEP meeting minutes as well as in the OT's end-of-the-year service report.

# Application of the QIAT Self-Evaluation Matrix for Assessment of AT Needs by Mark's Team

1. **Procedures for all aspects of assistive technology assessment are clearly defined and consistently applied.**

   **Discussion:** This district did not have defined assessment procedures for students with mild disabilities; however, special education staff did consistently consider students' need for AT. Even though the special education teacher and the occupational therapist had some experience and information regarding assessing the need for AT for writing, the team members gave themselves a 1 on this indicator. They felt that everyone would benefit from development of consistent AT assessment procedures for all students and district-wide training.

| 1 | 2 | 3 | 4 | 5 |
|---|---|---|---|---|
| **No procedures are defined.** | Some assessment procedures are defined, but not generally used. | Procedures are defined and used only by specialized personnel. | Procedures are clearly defined and generally used in both special and general education. | Clearly defined procedures are used by everyone involved in the assessment process. |

2. **Assistive technology assessments are conducted by a *team with the collective knowledge and skills needed* to determine possible assistive technology solutions that address the needs and abilities of the student, demands of the customary environments, educational goals, and related activities.**

   **Discussion:** There were only three members of the IEP team—the OT, the special education teacher, and Mark's mother—involved in the conversation about Mark's AT. Collectively, they knew the student, conducted the assessment informally in one of the student's educational environments, and provided training for the student and parent. They agreed involving additional team members, especially the general education teacher with whom he spends most of his day, would increase the team's effectiveness. They gave themselves a rating of 3, deciding that it was not a perfect description, but was the best fit.

| 1 | 2 | 3 | 4 | 5 |
|---|---|---|---|---|
| A designated individual with no prior knowledge of the student's needs or technology conducts assessments. | A designated person or group conducts assessments but lacks either knowledge of AT or of the student's needs, environments, or tasks. | **A team conducts assessments with limited input from individuals who have knowledge of AT or of the student's needs, environments, and tasks.** | A collaborative team whose members have direct knowledge of the student's needs, environments, and tasks, and knowledge of AT generally conducts assessments. | A collaborative, flexible team formed on the basis of knowledge of the individual student's needs, environments, and tasks, and expertise in AT consistently conducts assessments. |

3.  **All assistive technology assessments include a functional assessment in the student's *customary environments*, such as the classroom, lunchroom, playground, home, community setting, or work place.**

    **Discussion:** Mark's special education teacher and OT, with input from his mother, conducted an informal functional assessment. Mark initially tried the tablet for writing in the resource room and then in additional classes. The team gave themselves a rating of 3 because they realized they had only assessed his use of the tablet in two settings before they asked him to use it in every class.

| 1 | 2 | 3 | 4 | 5 |
|---|---|---|---|---|
| No component of the AT assessment is conducted in any of the student's customary environments. | No component of the AT assessment is conducted in any of the customary environments; however, data about the customary environments are sought. | **Functional components of AT assessments are sometimes conducted in the student's customary environments.** | Functional components of AT assessments are generally conducted in the student's customary environments. | Functional components of AT assessments are consistently conducted in the student's customary environments. |

4.  **Assistive technology assessments, including needed trials, are completed within *reasonable time lines*.**

    **Discussion:** Mark's district did not have operating guidelines or procedures for AT assessments for students whose educational program was delivered in the general educational setting. As the team discussed this indicator, the program administrator decided to check with the state education agency's Department of Special Education Services. The state AT specialist assured him that the same timelines apply to AT assessments as those that apply to any other kind of formal assessment. However, since Mark's AT assessment had been done informally while he was already receiving specially designed instruction, the official timeline did not apply. The team rated their performance a 2 on this indicator because, while they had actually not been out of compliance for Mark's AT assessment, the agency did not have defined timelines for AT assessments.

| 1 | 2 | 3 | 4 | 5 |
|---|---|---|---|---|
| AT assessments are not completed within agency timelines. | **AT assessments are frequently out of compliance with timelines.** | AT assessments are completed within a reasonable timeline and may or may not include initial trials. | AT assessments are completed within a reasonable timeline and include at least initial trials. | AT assessments are conducted in a timely manner and include a plan for ongoing assessment and trials in customary environments. |

5. Recommendations from assistive technology assessments are *based on data about the student, environments, and tasks.*

**Discussion:** While the team identified several indicator areas in need of improvement during this self-assessment, they focused a lot of attention on improving their performance on this indicator because they felt it was so important for Mark. They realized that once they had found an AT tool that seemed to work for Mark, they jumped very quickly from the resource room trial period to full implementation in multiple settings and for multiple writing tasks. The lack of data and information about each writing environment resulted in several incidents of frustration for Mark. As they adjusted the program, the team came to understand that Mark's behavior was very closely tied to his frustration with writing tasks he found difficult. They rated their initial performance on this indicator a 2.

| 1 | 2 | 3 | 4 | 5 |
|---|---|---|---|---|
| Recommendations are not data based. | **Recommendations are based on incomplete data from limited sources.** | Recommendations are sometimes based on data about student performance on typical tasks in customary environments. | Recommendations are generally based on data about student performance on typical tasks in customary environments. | Recommendations are consistently based on data about student performance on typical tasks in customary environments. |

6. The assessment provides the IEP team with clearly *documented recommendations* that guide decisions about the selection, acquisition, and use of assistive technology devices and services.

**Discussion:** While the AT assessment for Mark was an informal one, it included most of the essential elements of an effective AT assessment. The recommendations about AT and the ways Mark used it were documented in the IEP meeting minutes. The team discussed the need to identify a more consistent strategy for documenting the strategies they tried and AT they provided so future teams would know what Mark had used in the past and for continuity in his educational program over time. They gave themselves a rating of 3.

| 1 | 2 | 3 | 4 | 5 |
|---|---|---|---|---|
| Recommendations are not documented. | Documented recommendations include only devices. Recommendations about services are not documented. | **Documented recommendations may or may not include sufficient information about devices and services to guide decision-making and program development.** | Documented recommendations generally include sufficient information about devices and services to guide decision-making and program development. | Documented recommendations consistently include sufficient information about devices and services to guide decision-making and program development. |

7. **Assistive technology needs are *reassessed* any time changes in the student, the environments, and/or the tasks result in the student's needs not being met with current devices and/or services.**

**Discussion:** As soon as Mark began to show signs of frustration with writing in some of his classes, the team began to analyze those environments to determine how they were different than classes where he was writing independently and with great satisfaction. They monitored each class and adjusted the program so that Mark could use different strategies for creating written products depending on the nature of the task. They gave themselves a 4 instead of a 5 for this indicator only because they had not planned to assess each environment until Mark's frustration became evident.

| 1 | 2 | 3 | 4 | 5 |
|---|---|---|---|---|
| AT needs are not reassessed. | AT needs are only reassessed when requested. Reassessment is done formally and no ongoing AT assessment takes place. | AT needs are reassessed on an annual basis or upon request. Reassessment may include some ongoing and formal assessment strategies. | **AT use is frequently monitored. AT needs are generally reassessed if current tools and strategies are ineffective. Reassessment generally includes ongoing assessment strategies and includes formal assessment, if indicated.** | AT use is frequently monitored. AT needs are consistently reassessed if current tools and strategies are ineffective. Reassessment consistently includes ongoing assessment strategies and includes formal assessment, if indicated. |

## Summary

This case study highlights the need for an AT assessment procedure. While it can be challenging to answer the many questions related to AT use in a short period of time, it is important to complete the assessment within the state approved timelines. The most important component to complete within the timeline is to answer the question, "Does this student need AT?" If the answer is yes, but the specific brand or model is not yet known, trials can be completed after the commitment to provide AT is documented in the IEP. All AT assessments need to be completed within a reasonable amount of time, no matter what the specifics of the case. Nothing in this chapter should be construed to mean that months of delay are ever acceptable.

In the next chapter, core components for effectively documenting AT in the IEP will be discussed.

## Suggested Activities

1. Go to the Wisconsin Assistive Technology Initiative website—*www.wati.org*. Download the AT Assessment packet. Critique these forms and suggest how they could be used to complete an AT assessment.

2. Go to the Education Tech Points website at *www.educationtechpoints.org*. Download and review "Hey! Can I Try That?" Write a two-page paper about the importance of user input into the AT assessment process and how the content of this booklet could help in gathering that information.

3. Go to Ablenet University, *https://www.ablenetinc.com/resources/recorded_webinars/*. Sign in and search the list of recorded videos on AT. Watch *QIAT Session 3: Assessment of AT Needs* by Penny Reed and Kathy Lalk. Review one or more resources recommended in the webinar. Write a short paper suggesting how the resource(s) you chose might be used.

4. Go to either the Communication Matrix—*www.communicationmatrix.org* or the Tech Matrix: Assistive Technology Tools and Resources for Learning—*www.techmatrix.org*. Write a short paper explaining how the one you chose could be useful to you in participating in an assessment of a child's need for AT.

5. Go to the Ohio Center for Autism and Low Incidence's resource at *www.atinternetmodules.org* and complete the module titled "AT Assessment Process in the School Environment." How does this information fit with what you've learned in this chapter?

# CHAPTER 4

# Exploring the Quality Indicators for Including Assistive Technology in the IEP

1. The education agency has *guidelines for documenting* assistive technology needs in the IEP and requires their consistent application.

2. All *services* that the IEP team determines are needed to support the selection, acquisition, and use of assistive technology devices are designated in the IEP.

3. The IEP illustrates that assistive technology is a *tool to support achievement of goals* and progress in the general curriculum by establishing a clear relationship between student need, assistive technology devices and services, and the student's goals and objectives.

4. IEP content regarding assistive technology use is written in language that describes how assistive technology contributes to achievement of *measurable and observable outcomes.*

5. Assistive technology is included in the IEP in a manner that provides a *clear and complete description* of the devices and services to be provided and is used to address student needs and achieve expected results.

In both developing and reviewing IEPs, the regulations for IDEA require the IEP team to consider the special factors explained in Chapter 2, which includes the consideration of the need for AT. If, in considering the special factors, the IEP team determines that a child needs an AT device or service (including an intervention, accommodation, or other program modification) to receive FAPE, the IEP team documents that need in the child's IEP.

The law does not specify that AT be addressed in any other specific section of the IEP. Rather it says that it can be part of special education, related services, or supplementary aids and services (Authority: 20 U.S.C. 1412(a)(1), 1412(a)(12)(B)(i)). The job of the IEP team is to describe the use of AT wherever it makes the most sense. There are many ways to do it well. This chapter will provide examples of the many places and ways that AT can be included in a student's IEP.

The IEP team is empowered by IDEA to make all decisions about a student's individual program, including all decisions about the need for and use of AT. Part of this responsibility is the decision about the need to use the AT device in other settings. IDEA states: "On a case-by-case basis, the use of school-purchased AT devices in a child's home or in other settings is required if the child's IEP Team determines the child needs access to those devices in order to receive FAPE" (Authority: 20 U.S.C. 1412(a)(1), 1412(a)(12)(B)(i)). As part of their deliberations about AT, IEP teams must determine whether any AT devices purchased by the school need to be sent home with the student.

As an IEP team develops the IEP and considers the student's need for AT, questions such as those in Table 4.1 from the QIAT Planning Document: Assistive Technology in the IEP Planner can be helpful in determining where in the IEP it will be important to document the AT devices or services that will be provided

| **TABLE 4.1** Documenting AT in the IEP | ▨ Does the student currently use AT devices to participate and make progress in the general education curriculum? *Document in Present Levels* |
|---|---|
| | ▨ Does the student need AT devices and/or services to accomplish annual goals? *Document in Annual Goals* |
| | ▨ Does the student need AT devices and/or services to accomplish benchmarks and/or short-term objectives? *Document in Objectives/Benchmarks* |
| | ▨ Does the student need AT devices and/or services to participate and progress in the curriculum or to benefit from specially designed instruction? *Document in Special Factors* |
| | ▨ Does the student need AT devices and/or services to benefit from special education? *Document in Related Services* |
| | ▨ Does the student need AT devices and/or services to participate in general education classes with children without disabilities? *Document in Supplementary Aids and Services* |

- Do the school personnel working with the student need any AT related training or supports? *Document in Supports for School Personnel*

- Does the student need AT to participate in state-wide and district assessments? *Document in Accommodations for Participation in State and District-wide Assessments*

- Does the student need AT devices and/or services as a part of transition to post-school environments? *Document in Transition Services*

---

AT is provided to support or "assist" the student in meeting IEP goals and making progress in the curriculum. And yet, sometimes when reviewing an IEP, it is difficult to tell how AT will be used to help meet the student's goals. In effective IEPs the type of AT that the student requires and the manner in which it will be used is clearly described so that all participants in the IEP, including parents, have a clear understanding of the AT and how it will be used. Describing the services is a critical part of this. Focusing only on the devices and failing to document AT services or expected outcomes are common errors that can lead to very poor results for the student. The IEP is the vehicle that communicates exactly what the agency will provide and the measurable or observable results that are expected.

The IEP is the document that ensures a student will receive the services needed and must clearly describe every aspect of the planned individualized program. The Quality Indicators for Including Assistive Technology in the IEP guide the team in writing IEPs that communicate how, when, and where AT will be provided and used by the student.

1. **The education agency has *guidelines for documenting* assistive technology needs in the IEP and requires their consistent application.**

   **Intent: The education agency provides guidance to IEP teams about how to effectively document assistive technology needs, devices, and services as a part of specially designed instruction, related services, or supplementary aids and services.**

   IDEA does not describe how or specify where AT is to be included in the IEP. Review of effective practice indicates that successful state and local education agencies provide specific guidance and ensure consistent application. Comprehensive agency guidelines address the inclusion of AT in development, review, and revision of the IEP. It is important to clearly document the AT devices and services that will be provided so any team member implementing the IEP can clearly understand what AT is required as well as when, where, and the purpose for which it is to be used.

   The rapid adoption of universal design for learning (UDL) principles has created an unanticipated situation where errors can occur. The use of UDL in developing curriculum and preparing instructional materials can make the teacher's job much easier when a student requires accessible educational materials (AEM) and/or AT due to a disability. However, it does not change the IEP team's mandate to document any needed specially designed instruction, adaptations, accommodations, or AT in the student's IEP. For instance, if a student needs to hear text read aloud in order to comprehend the meaning, it must be documented in the IEP whether readily available in a UDL environment or provided by the acquisition of new scan-and-read software that no other students are using. The IEP is the document that ensures that a student will receive the services needed and must clearly describe every aspect of the planned individualized program.

**EXAMPLE**

*Simone is just starting her first year of teaching in Elderburg School District. She is preparing for the first IEP meeting for one of her students who has shown significant improvement in her writing assignments since tablet computers became available throughout the school. Simone knows that use of the tablet to complete writing assignments is AT when it is used by this student. She is not sure how to include it in the IEP. She went to the district website and searched the district's operating guidelines, where she found this statement:*

*DOCUMENTATION OF A CHILD'S NEED FOR ASSISTIVE TECHNOLOGY*

*IEP teams must specify the type of AT device the student needs (e.g., tablet computers, scheduling apps, word processing with spell checking, augmentative and alternative communication (AAC) system). The IEP team should not include specific brand names unless a device has particular characteristics that require the child to learn operational skills that are unique to the specific device provided or the child has become accustomed to a feature or style that would make it detrimental to change to a different product.*

*Simone decided that stating, "tablet computer with word processing app" would be the best description to recommend and went to the IEP meeting ready to share her data.*

**KEY QUESTIONS**

- What are the agency's guidelines for documenting AT in the IEP?

- How do district personnel access the guidelines?

- What process is used to disseminate the guidelines?

- What supports are in place to ensure that the guidelines are consistently implemented?

2. **All *services* that the IEP team determines are needed to support the selection, acquisition, and use of assistive technology devices are designated in the IEP.**

   **Intent: The provision of AT services is critical to the effective use of AT devices. It is important that the IEP describes the AT services that are needed for student success. Such services may include evaluation/assessment, customization or maintenance of devices, coordination of services, and training for the student, family, and professionals, among others.**

   Under federal law AT may be provided as a part of a student's special education, related services, or supplementary aids and services. As a result, AT may be documented in any of those areas. There is no right or wrong place to document AT needs. Each area is equally powerful. The task of the IEP team is to document AT in the places in the IEP that are the most appropriate to the device and services provided. The most important factor is that the documentation makes sense to individuals who must implement the student's individualized program. The sections of the IEP addressed below include special education, related services, supplementary aids and services, accommodations, and supports for school personnel.

   A. **Special Education**: When AT devices or services are provided as part of a student's specially designed instruction, documentation is found in the annual goals. When developing annual goals, the IEP team determines whether or not the student needs AT in order to accomplish them. First the goals are developed and then the need for AT is addressed. In most cases, AT is not the goal; rather, it is the means to achieving the goal.

   ................................................................................................................    ........................................................

   EXAMPLE

   *Bianca will express basic wants and needs in 90% of the opportunities using single word utterances or a voice output AAC device when longer utterances are needed.*

   ................................................................................................................

   On occasion, if the student does not have skills to use the AT that is needed to achieve other goals, a goal may be written to address those operational skills. For example, if a student has goals in her IEP about written productivity and the team determines that she needs voice recognition software to accomplish those goals, they may include instructional goals on the operation of the voice recognition software until she is able to use it functionally.

   In IDEA there is no requirement for benchmarks and short-term objectives for students with disabilities who are participating in the general education curriculum. They are only required for students participating in assessments aligned to alternate achievement standards. However, some states still require benchmarks and objectives for all students receiving special education. If short-term objectives or benchmarks are required, a student may have objectives to learn to use a specific AT device. The training the student needs is an AT service, and both will be documented in the IEP.

*When provided with a digital braille notetaker and instruction on its use, Scott will demonstrate proficiency to produce and publish two or more pages of text with fewer than five errors.*

*When provided with braille science and social studies textbooks at the fifth grade level, Scott will read them with fewer than two errors per page.*

B.  **Related Services:** When AT is provided as a part of a related service, it is documented in the IEP form's listing of related services. In this case, the anticipated duration, location, and frequency of the service must be documented. If AT is listed in the IEP form's Related Services section, it is important to remember that additional information may need to be added in other sections of the IEP to clarify the types of AT that will be used, the environments in which the AT will be used, and the staff responsible for supporting the use of the AT.

| RELATED SERVICES | FREQUENCY | DURATION | LOCATION |
|---|---|---|---|
| Speech-Language Therapy (including training to use a voice output communication device) | 1 hour weekly | 10-5 to 6-2 | Across multiple school environments |
| Occupational Therapy to increase targeting accuracy and maintain range of motion | 1 hour weekly | 10-5 to 6-2 | Special education classroom |
| AT Specialist Support for access to classroom computers | 3 hours each month | 10-5 to 6-2 | General education classroom |

FIGURE 4.2  Sample Related Services section of IEP

C.  **Supplementary Aids and Services:** Assistive technology may also be addressed in the Supplementary Aids and Services component of the IEP. AT is often provided as a supplementary aid and service when required for a student to participate in general education classes or other education-related activities among children without disabilities. Although federal law does not require the provider of supplementary aids and services be identified specifically in the IEP, some state and local IEP forms do ask for this information. It's recommended that IEP teams identify the providers during their discussions even if it's not required.

| SUPPLEMENTARY AIDS AND SERVICES | FREQUENCY | DURATION | LOCATION |
|---|---|---|---|
| Tablet computer with spell checking | All note-taking | 9-15 to 5-18 | General education classes |
| Acquisition of instructional materials in accessible formats by case manager | For all core instructional materials | 9-15 to 5-18 | In all core curriculum classes |

**FIGURE 4.3** Sample Supplementary Aids and Services section of IEP

D. **Accommodations Needed for Participation in State and Local Assessments:** The IEP team must determine the accommodations the student requires in order to participate in state and local assessments. For some students with disabilities, AT may be a required accommodation. The key factor is that the use of AT as an accommodation cannot invalidate the construct being tested. For example, the use of text-to-speech on a test of decoding skill would invalidate the test construct. An accommodation does not change the construct being tested, but allows an alternative mode of gaining or demonstrating knowledge. For example, a student who is blind is provided with braille materials and is allowed to provide written answers with a braille notetaker.

Students who use AT in their daily educational program may need the same technology in order to participate in state and local assessments. If a team determines that a student needs AT for participation in an assessment, it is important to review state and local guidelines for testing accommodations to determine if the use of the student's AT device is an allowable accommodation in testing.

The IEP should never indicate that a student will use AT to complete a state assessment if the student does not use the same AT regularly for participation in educational activities. At the same time, if the AT device is needed for access to the curriculum, the student should have it provided, even if it cannot be used in state assessments.

- *Marcus's team has determined he needs his auditory trainer to optimize his ability to listen to verbal directions. There are verbal directions provided by the examiner during state assessments. This is an allowable accommodation in his state. Marcus will use his auditory trainer during state assessments.*

- *Due to her severe visual impairment, Shantae requires that all testing materials, including directions and answer sheets, if appropriate, be provided to her in braille. This is an allowable accommodation in her state.*

- *In order to complete classroom written work longer than one paragraph, Stephen uses his portable word processor. The team planned to explore whether this was an allowable accommodation on his state's writing assessment. If not, Stephen's team has determined that he will receive instruction on the use of a scribe and dictate his writing assessment to a qualified scribe.*

**E. Supports for School Personnel:** The IEP team should address the supports the school staff needs to effectively provide AT devices and services to the student.

- *The AT resource person will work with Paul and his teachers in the special education classroom for one hour weekly for six weeks. Training will include programming, operation, and implementation of his augmentative communication device. All team members will participate in ongoing identification of needed vocabulary.*

- *Kelly's special education and general education teachers will be provided with follow-up training and technical assistance to aid them in integrating the use of her AT (word prediction software) into her school curriculum. Training will occur in the classroom during three one-hour sessions before November.*

- *The paraprofessional for the fourth grade pod will scan daily worksheets from the social studies workbook into the computer for use with Dyson's scan-and-read program.*

**KEY QUESTIONS**

- How is AT use documented when a student needs it for specially designed instruction (e.g., existing goal, a new goal, an objective or benchmark under a goal)?

- How are AT devices or services documented when the student needs them as part of related services in order to receive FAPE or to benefit from special education?

- How are AT supports and services documented when the student needs them in order to participate and achieve in the general education classroom and other educational settings?

- How do the IEPs communicate how, when, where, and by whom the aids and services are provided?

- How is AT documented when the student needs it to participate in state and local assessments?

- What is the process for checking which AT devices are allowable accommodations under state guidelines?

- How does the IEP document the training, technical assistance, or support that school personnel need to implement the students' AT programs?

3.  **The IEP illustrates that assistive technology is a *tool to support achievement of goals* and progress in the general curriculum by establishing a clear relationship between the student's needs, assistive technology devices and services, and the student's goals and objectives.**

    **Intent: Most goals are developed before decisions about AT are made. However, this does not preclude the development of additional goals, especially those related specifically to the appropriate use of AT.**

    AT is one of the special factors that must be considered in the development, review, and revision of each student's IEP. The team's primary responsibility during consideration is to think about whether the student needs AT devices and/or services to participate and make progress in the general education curriculum or to benefit from specially designed instruction. (See Chapter 2.)

    Although minimal compliance for considering AT may be simply checking *yes* or *no* to the consideration question, best practice is for IEP teams to use a systematic process for considering a student's AT needs and to document the outcomes of the consideration in the IEP. In most instances, it's just as important to document when a student does not require AT as when a student does require it. Documentation of the issues that were addressed during AT consideration can be especially helpful to future IEP teams.

There are many places in the IEP where tools to support achievement of goals may be documented (e.g., consideration, accommodations, present levels of academic achievement, minutes).

EXAMPLES:

*Does the student require assistive technology devices or services?*

__X__ Yes   _____ No

*Describe: Paula needs to use assistive technology (prone stander, wedge) for seating and positioning in her classes in order to access educational materials and participate in her educational program.*

*Does the student require assistive technology devices or services?*

__X__ Yes   _____ No

*Describe: Karen uses an eight location augmentative communication device with speech output to supplement her current communication skills. See present levels of academic achievement and functional performance and annual goals and objectives for additional information.*

*Does the student require assistive technology devices or services?*

_____ Yes   __X__ No

*Describe: Eduardo is struggling with completing writing assignments. We discussed the need for assistive technology but decided his problem relates more to attention. Positive behavior supports are being used to address the issues at this time.*

**KEY QUESTIONS**

- How would a person reading the IEP be able to determine what AT devices and services were considered and the basis of the decisions that were made?

- How does the AT discussed in the process of consideration relate to the student's identified educational needs?

- Does the student's use of AT assist in the achievement of individualized goals?

4. **IEP content regarding assistive technology use is written in language that describes how assistive technology contributes to achievement of *measurable and observable outcomes*.**

   **Intent: Content that describes measurable and observable outcomes for AT use enables the IEP team to review the student's progress and determine whether the AT has had the expected impact on student participation and achievement.**

   The team writes a clear description of the change in student performance that is expected as a result of the student's use of AT. This statement will include a description of success, how it will be measured, and the criteria that will indicate mastery.

   Criteria will vary with

   - type of task (e.g., crossing the street, which of course must be 100%, versus requesting a snack),

   - student's abilities (e.g., has never completed the task versus currently completes the task 50% of the time), and

   - situation (e.g., being asked to choose food items when known to be hungry versus when state of hunger isn't known).

EXAMPLES

*John will compose a paragraph of three or more sentences with less than two spelling errors on 90% of assignments, when using a spellchecker.*

*Yadira has two interrelated goals. The first includes her functional use of speech recognition software. In the second goal, her ability to operate the AT is addressed. The use of her speech recognition software may also be described in other areas of the IEP, (most commonly in supplementary aids and services).*

   *Based on the general education grading rubric, Yadira will satisfactorily complete 100% of written assignments of more than one paragraph when using speech recognition software.*

   *Yadira will demonstrate competency using speech recognition software to create, edit, and revise three paragraphs of 90 words with fewer than five errors.*

How do the IEPs describe the expected changes in achievement?

What objective ways have been defined to measure changes in student achievement related to a goal?

How are meaningful criteria for success determined?

5. **Assistive Technology is included in the IEP in a manner that provides a *clear and complete* description of the devices and services to be provided and is used to address student needs and achieve expected results.**

   **Intent: IEPs are written so that participants in the IEP meeting and others who use the information to implement the student's program understand what AT is to be available, how it is to be used, and under what circumstances. Jargon and acronyms should be avoided.**

   When IEPs are well written, everyone who uses the information to implement the student's program understands what AT is to be available, how it is to be used, and under what circumstances. There is no need to be redundant or repetitive when including AT in the IEP. If a device or service is clearly described in one place, the identical information does not need to be repeated in other sections. However, the IEP as a whole should provide a full, clear description of the AT devices and services that a student is receiving. When including AT in the IEP, it's generally preferable to describe the necessary features of the AT rather than naming a specific product. This is important for several reasons: multiple products may offer the needed features, specific products change over time, and new products are created.

   Present level of academic achievement and functional performance (PLAAFP), goals and objectives, notes or minutes of an IEP, and transition planning are places where clear and complete description is critical. State or local education agencies may specify additional places where AT can be described.

   A. **Documenting assistive technology in PLAAFP**: In this section, the IEP team addresses the student's strengths and weaknesses in academic and functional areas. It provides a natural place to document AT currently being used, and how it is used to compensate for barriers to achievement, participation, and independence. When documenting AT in the present levels of academic achievement and functional performance, the specific types of technology provided, as well as the manner in which they are used, should be described.

- *Jeff has been successfully using an "XYZ Communicator" to communicate his wants, needs, and other information. For the last two years, Jeff has been creating novel utterances of five to seven words as well as retrieving pre-stored familiar messages frequently and spontaneously throughout the day and across environments and listeners.*

- *Due to her significant visual impairment, Taylor is not able to access standard print instructional materials, such as textbooks, worksheets, and written tests. She requires that all print copies be enlarged to 24-point font, whether they are obtained through the Accessible Educational Materials (AEM) process, enlarged with a photocopier or computer, or viewed using a closed circuit television system.*

B. **Documenting AT in the minutes of the IEP meeting:** Some states and districts include minutes of the IEP meeting as part of the IEP document. The need for AT devices and services may also be addressed in these minutes. This provides a place to clearly describe information that may be important not only now but also in the future when planning and implementing a student's IEP. It's required to include the AT in the actual IEP document if the team has determined AT is needed. The minutes serve to clarify and expand on the information about AT that is included in the IEP document.

*The team considered Tim's need for AT in the area of reading. It was determined that due to significant gains in the last semester, Tim was making adequate educational progress without the need for any additional accommodations or modifications, including AT.*

C. **Documenting AT in Transition Services:** Another place where a clear description is important is in the section describing planned transitions. When addressing transition services for a student who needs AT, it's important to address the AT devices and services currently used by the student and those that may be required in the new environment.

*The case manager from the Department of Human Services will contact public and private agencies to assist in obtaining funding for the AAC device for Colin before the team's November meeting. By January the speech and language pathologist will identify potential sources of technical support after he leaves high school.*

**KEY QUESTIONS**

- How does the IEP communicate what AT the student is currently using to increase participation or make progress in the general education curriculum?

- How does the IEP show how AT helps in completing required tasks?

- Where in the IEP are the current AT services described?

- How are the activities of the transition planning team documented in transition IEPs?

## Exploring the Quality Indicators for Including Assistive Technology in the IEP with the QIAT Self-Evaluation Matrix

The Self-Evaluation Matrix for Including Assistive Technology in the IEP has two main components. The first is about the provision of written guidelines by the education agency and the second is about the documentation within the IEP. Through its variations from "unacceptable" to "best practice" the matrix

- highlights aspects of quality documentation of AT devices and services in the IEP;

- provides a means to identify areas of strength and areas in need of improvement when including AT in the IEP;

- helps identify variations in how AT is documented in IEPs across sites; and

- provides a scaffold for improvement of how AT is written into the IEP throughout the agency.

The first Quality Indicator addresses the provision of written guidelines for including AT in the IEP by the education agency. The second is about ensuring that needed AT services are not overlooked. The third indicator asks the reader to look for the connection between the AT and the achievement of IEP goals and progress in the general education curriculum. Each of the remaining two indicators is about the clarity of the statements about the provision of AT devices and services in the IEP. Indicator 4 asks the reader to determine if the statements are related to observable and measurable outcomes. Indicator 5 focuses on the overall IEP and how clearly it explains and describes the AT devices and services being provided.

# Quality Indicators for Including Assistive Technology in the IEP

| QUALITY INDICATOR | UNACCEPTABLE | |
|---|---|---|
| 1. The education agency has *guidelines for documenting* AT needs in the IEP and requires their consistent application. | 1<br>The agency does not have guidelines for documenting AT in the IEP. | 2<br>The agency has guidelines for documenting AT in the IEP but team members are not aware of them. |
| 2. All *services* that the IEP team determines are needed to support the selection, acquisition, and use of AT devices are designated in the IEP. | 1<br>AT devices and services are not documented in the IEP. | 2<br>Some AT devices and services are minimally documented. Documentation does not include sufficient information to support effective implementation. |
| 3. The IEP illustrates that AT is a *tool to support achievement of goals* and progress in the general curriculum by establishing a clear relationship between the student's needs, AT devices and services, and the student's goals and objectives. | 1<br>AT use is not linked to IEP goals and objectives or participation and progress in the general curriculum. | 2<br>AT use is sometimes linked to IEP goals and objectives but not linked to the general curriculum. |
| 4. IEP content regarding AT use is written in language that describes how AT contributes to achievement of *measurable and observable outcomes.* | 1<br>The IEP does not describe outcomes to be achieved through AT use. | 2<br>The IEP describes outcomes to be achieved through AT use, but they are not measurable. |
| 5. AT is included in the IEP in a manner that provides a *clear and complete* description of the devices and services to be provided and is used to address student needs and achieve expected results. | 1<br>Devices and services needed to support AT use are not documented. | 2<br>Some devices and services are documented but they do not adequately support AT use. |

| 3 | 4 | 5 |
|---|---|---|
| The agency has guidelines for documenting AT in the IEP and members of some teams are aware of them. | The agency has guidelines for documenting AT in the IEP and members of most teams are aware of them. | The agency has guidelines for documenting AT in the IEP and members of all teams are aware of them. |
| 3 | 4 | 5 |
| Required AT devices and services are documented. Documentation sometimes includes sufficient information to support effective implementation. | Required AT devices and services are documented. Documentation generally includes sufficient information to support effective implementation. | Required AT devices and services are documented. Documentation consistently includes sufficient information to support effective implementation. |
| 3 | 4 | 5 |
| AT use is linked to IEP goals and objectives and sometimes linked to the general curriculum. | AT is linked to IEP goals and objectives and is generally linked to the general curriculum. | AT is linked to the IEP goals and objectives and is consistently linked to the general curriculum. |
| 3 | 4 | 5 |
| The IEP describes outcomes to be achieved through AT use, but only some are measurable. | The IEP generally describes observable, measurable outcomes to be achieved through AT use. | The IEP consistently describes observable, measurable outcomes to be achieved through AT use. |
| 3 | 4 | 5 |
| Devices and services are documented and are sometimes adequate to support AT use. | Devices and services are documented and are generally adequate to support AT use. | Devices and services are documented and are consistently adequate to support AT use. |

# Exploring the Quality Indicators for Including Assistive Technology in the IEP through Jolene's Case Study

Jolene has been blind since birth and has used uncontracted braille for reading and writing since the second grade. Throughout elementary school she received daily services from the vision specialist and the assistance of a classroom paraprofessional who was trained in braille transcription. She used a manual braille writer, had access to audio books, and the paraprofessional. As she moved from elementary school to middle school, one of Jolene's goals was to become more independent in her ability to complete academic assignments. Jolene's personal goal is to attend college after high school and she plans to take college prep courses in her high school program. Her IEP team looked at the results of current assessment data and current performance levels and decided that Jolene needed an electronic braille notetaker in order to benefit from her Individualized Educational Program. The IEP team listed the braille notetaker on her IEP under the Supplementary Aids and Services section and listed weekly services of the vision specialist under related services. The District Representative agreed that the agency would purchase a braille notetaker for Jolene. No other discussion of the AT took place during this IEP meeting. The team did not include any supporting goals or objectives, any plan for support for school personnel or any timelines for that support to occur. Jolene's team made the common error of addressing the device, but not the needed services.

Two weeks after the IEP meeting, the braille notetaker arrived at the school. The school secretary sent it to the resource room where Jolene spent one period every day. Since the vision specialist wasn't due to come to that school again until the following week, the notetaker sat in the box awaiting her arrival. When the vision specialist did come to see Jolene, the paraprofessional forgot to tell her the notetaker had arrived so it sat for another week. When the vision specialist finally did receive the notetaker, she took it with her so that she could learn how to operate it. She had much difficulty transferring files from the notetaker to a computer and thought she might need another cable to do that. She submitted a purchase order for the cable but when it came three weeks later, it didn't help with the problem. In frustration, the vision specialist contacted a colleague in another city who was familiar with the device. They began a correspondence that lasted over several weeks.

When Jolene had not begun to use the braille notetaker by the beginning of December, her mother asked the IEP team to reconvene to try to figure out what the problem was. The team identified the following issues that were keeping her from accessing her AT.

1. The vision specialist was familiar with some kinds of braille notetakers but did not know how to operate the specific device that had been purchased for Jolene.

2. Jolene needed initial training in the basic operation of the device.

3. Jolene needed additional training in the use of the device to take notes and read them back.

4.  No one on the team understood the function of the device or knew for which tasks Jolene was specifically using the device, so they did not remind her to use it.

5.  Because a new paraprofessional was assigned to this school, no one except the vision specialist knew of the expectations for Jolene's use of the device.

6.  When the vision specialist wasn't there, there was no one able to help Jolene when she had problems.

At the second meeting of Jolene's IEP team, these items were addressed in her IEP with help from the district representative who guided the process of making the additions. An IEP goal to increase her independence in taking notes was developed.

*Jolene will use uncontracted braille to create three paragraphs of text with 85% accuracy on three opportunities within a one-week period.*

A timeline for implementation was discussed and Jolene was encouraged to focus on the use of the device during one academic period. Short-term objectives were written for her to take braille notes in an English class first and then in other classes such as science and math that required more skill with the device.

Time in her schedule was identified for the actual learning of the device operations. Another goal was added for Jolene to learn the specific operations and functions of the device that had been provided for her.

*Jolene will read back a text file on the braille notetaker to edit the text on 100% of opportunities within a one-week period.*

Short term objectives included learning skills such as reading back her own files, transferring files to a computer, and printing from the notetaker to a braille embosser.

Under Supports for School Personnel the team included training for the vision specialist, as well as other staff in the school environment.

By January, Jolene had begun to use her device during one academic period each day and was spending half of her resource period on practicing the new device operation skills she required for successful implementation.

Jolene's team learned about providing accessible educational materials (AEM) and how to develop properly formatted documents for her notetaker that were more helpful.

The district representative's guidance at the second IEP meeting went far to help the team describe Jolene's AT use more clearly. With a clear plan that took potential problems into account, the team was able to support Jolene's use of her AT in a much more effective manner. Her IEP team could have avoided some delays and frustrations if they had used the Quality Indicators for Including Assistive Technology in IEPs. They particularly failed to focus on two of the quality indicators in their development of the IEP.

# Application of the QIAT Self-Evaluation Matrix for Including Assistive Technology in the IEP by Jolene's Team

1. **The education agency has *guidelines for documenting* assistive technology needs in the IEP and requires their consistent application.**

   **Discussion:** The AT device to be purchased by the district was noted under the Supplementary Aids and Services section; however there was no description of services to support the implementation of the new technology. This situation was remedied in a follow-up meeting. Reflecting on the first meeting, the team rated their performance a 2.

| 1 | 2 | 3 | 4 | 5 |
|---|---|---|---|---|
| The agency does not have guidelines for documenting AT in the IEP. | **The agency has guidelines for documenting AT in the IEP but team members are not aware of them.** | The agency has guidelines for documenting AT in the IEP and members of some teams are aware of them. | The agency has guidelines for documenting AT in the IEP and members of most teams are aware of them. | The agency has guidelines for documenting AT in the IEP and members of all teams are aware of them. |

2. **All *services* that the IEP team determines are needed to support the selection, acquisition, and use of assistive technology devices are designated in the IEP.**

   **Discussion:** The services provided by the vision specialist, now on a weekly basis, were the only services listed on the IEP. The team had a great need for supports and training for the staff because they were unfamiliar with the particular AT that had been provided to Jolene. The vision specialist needed additional training and technical assistance. Other people in the school also needed training in the basic operation of the device. There was also a need for coordination between the many people who worked with Jolene on a daily basis. Because there was no discussion about how the device would be introduced, there was no documentation of the training needed for Jolene and the staff who supported her, or the timeline for that support. Reflecting on the first IEP team meeting, the team rated it as a 2.

| 1 | 2 | 3 | 4 | 5 |
|---|---|---|---|---|
| AT devices and services are not documented in the IEP. | **Some AT devices and services are minimally documented. Documentation does not include sufficient information to support effective implementation.** | Required AT devices and services are documented. Documentation sometimes includes sufficient information to support effective implementation. | Required AT devices and services are documented. Documentation generally includes sufficient information to support effective implementation. | Required AT devices and services are documented. Documentation consistently includes sufficient information to support effective implementation. |

3. **The IEP illustrates that assistive technology is a *tool to support achievement of goals* and progress in the general curriculum by establishing a clear relationship between the student's needs, assistive technology devices and services, and the student's goals and objectives.**

   **Discussion:** After the first IEP meeting, Jolene's team would have given themselves a 1. At the second IEP team meeting, the team realized the need to develop additional goals and objectives to specifically support the use of the AT. After adding the device competency goals and the training information the team rated themselves a 4.

| 1 | 2 | 3 | 4 | 5 |
|---|---|---|---|---|
| AT use is not linked to IEP goals and objectives or participation and progress in the general curriculum. | AT use is sometimes linked to IEP goals and objectives but not linked to the general curriculum. | AT use is linked to IEP goals and objectives and sometimes linked to the general curriculum. | **AT is linked to IEP goals and objectives and is generally linked to the general curriculum.** | AT is linked to the IEP goals and objectives and is consistently linked to the general curriculum. |

4. **IEP content regarding assistive technology use is written in language that describes how assistive technology contributes to achievement of *measurable and observable outcomes*.**

   **Discussion:** A common error made by IEP teams is the omission of measurable goals and objectives that link the use of the AT to achievement in the general curriculum. Initially the IEP team had not addressed this at all. The follow-up IEP team meeting was held to discuss implementation concerns, and at that time, the team discussed specific device features and operations that Jolene needed to learn, specific times during the day when she would be able to devote time to this instruction, and specific times during the day when she would be expected to actually utilize the device to accomplish academic tasks independently. The team wrote a goal using appropriate language so that it was observable and measureable. This allowed the team to rate their actions a 4 after the second meeting.

| 1 | 2 | 3 | 4 | 5 |
|---|---|---|---|---|
| The IEP does not describe outcomes to be achieved through AT use. | The IEP describes outcomes to be achieved through AT use, but they are not measurable. | The IEP describes outcomes to be achieved through AT use, but only some are measurable. | **The IEP generally describes observable, measurable outcomes to be achieved through AT use.** | The IEP consistently describes observable, measurable outcomes to be achieved through AT use. |

5. **Assistive technology is included in the IEP in a manner that provides a *clear and complete description* of the devices and services to be provided and used to address student needs and achieve expected results.**

   **Discussion:** The IEP document that resulted from the second meeting contained sufficient information for the family, staff, and Jolene to have reasonable expectations that she would be able to use the braille note taking device to complete assignments. When classroom-based staff are uninformed about the expected results of the device use, they can't be expected to support the student's use of it. After the second meeting, Jolene's team rated their performance a 4.

| 1 | 2 | 3 | 4 | 5 |
|---|---|---|---|---|
| Devices and services needed to support AT use are not documented. | Some devices and services are documented but they do not adequately support AT use. | Devices and services are documented and are sometimes adequate to support AT use. | **Devices and services are documented and are generally adequate to support AT use.** | Devices and services are documented and are consistently adequate to support AT use. |

## Summary

This chapter provided numerous examples of strategies for documenting AT in the IEP document. The purpose for specifically including the intended provision of AT devices and services is to clearly communicate the decisions of the IEP team and to provide a document that will be a resource in subsequent years. There are many ways to do it "right." The goal when including AT in the IEP is to ensure that the reader can find out when, where, and for what purpose the student is using AT.

In the next chapter we'll explore the many components of successfully implementing the use of AT.

## Suggested Activities

1. Go to Ablenet University, *https://www.ablenetinc.com/resources/recorded_webinars/*. Search the list of recorded videos on AT by QIAT. Watch the webinar *QIAT Session 4: Including Assistive Technology in the IEP* by Terry Foss and Sue McCloskey. Review one or more resources recommended in the webinar, suggesting how it might be used.

2. Go to the Texas AT Network module on AT Consideration *www.texasat.net/default.aspx?name=trainmod.consideration*. Review the materials on this website, including the video of William. How could you use these materials to train others? What changes, if any, would you make?

3. Go to *www.atinternetmodules.org* and complete the module "Assistive technology and the IEP process," provided by the Ohio Center for Autism and Low

Incidence. List three critical points about including AT in the IEP. Identify any questions you still have.

4. Using a student from one of the case studies in the previous two chapters, develop an IEP for the student using any IEP form available to you or one from Wright's Law, *www.wrightslaw.com/idea/osep.statute.htm.*

5. Review the IEP developed in #4. How would a person reading the IEP be able to determine what AT devices and services the team considered, and identify the basis of their decisions? How does the AT discussed in the process of consideration relate to the student's identified educational needs.

# CHAPTER 5

# Exploring the Quality Indicators for Assistive Technology Implementation

1. Assistive technology implementation proceeds according to a *collaboratively developed plan*.

2. Assistive technology is *integrated* into the curriculum and daily activities of the student across environments.

3. Persons supporting the student across all environments in which the assistive technology is expected to be used *share responsibility* for implementation of the plan.

4. Persons supporting the student provide opportunities for the student to use a *variety of strategies—including assistive technology*—and to learn which strategies are most effective for particular circumstances and tasks.

5. *Learning opportunities* for the student, family, and staff are an integral part of implementation.

6. Assistive technology implementation is initially based on assessment *data* and is adjusted based on performance data.

7. Assistive technology implementation includes *management and maintenance of equipment* and materials.

mplementation of the use of the AT devices is the next critical step in supporting student achievement. The teamwork that takes place during consideration and assessment and the collaborative planning to clearly describe the planned outcomes in the IEP all lead to implementing the use of the AT by the student. More than half of the following required services in IDEA involve implementation.

> Assistive technology service means any service that directly assists a child with a disability in the selection, acquisition, or use of an assistive technology device. The term includes:
>
> > *a.* The evaluation of the needs of a child with a disability, including a functional evaluation of the child in the child's customary environment;
> >
> > *b.* Purchasing, leasing, or otherwise providing for the acquisition of assistive technology devices by children with disabilities;
> >
> > *c.* Selecting, designing, **fitting, customizing, adapting, applying, maintaining, repairing, or replacing assistive technology devices;**
> >
> > *d.* **Coordinating and using other therapies, interventions, or services** with assistive technology devices, such as those associated with existing education and rehabilitation plans and programs;
> >
> > *e.* **Training or technical assistance for a child with a disability or, if appropriate, that child's family**; and
> >
> > *f.* **Training or technical assistance for professionals** (including individuals providing education or rehabilitation services), employers, or other individuals who provide services to, employ, or are otherwise substantially involved in the major life functions of that child.
>
> (emphasis added) Authority: 20 U.S.C. 1401(2)

The Quality Indicators for Implementation of Assistive Technology guide teams to thoughtful development of implementation plans. A well-thought-out implementation plan allows educators, students, and families to understand what must happen for a student's successful AT use. Table 5.1 highlights the key elements of an implementation plan. You can find The *Implementation of Assistive Technology Planner* with formatted content in Appendix D. Using a form such as the Implementation Planner guides the team through the process.

---

**TABLE 5.1** Key elements of an implementation plan

1. The team uses assessment data to identify student needs and the tasks to be completed.

2. The team develops an implementation plan that addresses clearly identified tasks.

3. The plan includes a variety of strategies to accomplish the tasks.

4. The AT use is integrated into activities across environments.

5. Frequent opportunities to use the strategies are determined.

6. The expected change in performance is well defined and understood by all team members.

7. The team has identified potential changes in the implementation plan that may be needed in response to performance data.

8. Plans for collecting data regarding the expected change in performance are developed and included in the implementation plan.

9. Primary implementers are identified and understand their roles.

10. The plan includes opportunities for initial and ongoing training.

11. Training is provided for all team members, including the student.

12. The plan addresses management and maintenance of equipment and materials.

---

One of the most common errors in providing AT services is the failure to plan adequately for implementation by assuming that everyone understands what needs to happen and their role in the implementation process. Another error occurs if only one member of the team develops the plan and tries to carry it out. That person may be thorough and knowledgeable, but all team members must have input and a role in implementation if a plan is to be comprehensive and effective.

The Quality Indicators address the many aspects of successful AT implementation. AT implementation involves people working together to support the student using AT to accomplish expected tasks that are necessary for active participation and progress in customary educational environments. The Quality Indicators for Assistive Technology Implementation provide the core components from which those responsible for implementing the AT can develop a thoughtful implementation plan.

1. **Assistive technology implementation proceeds according to a *collaboratively developed plan*.**

   **Intent: Following IEP development, all those involved in implementation work together to develop a written action plan that provides detailed information about how the assistive technology will be used in specific educational settings, what will be done, and who will do it.**

   In order for teams to effectively support a student's use of AT, an action plan is collaboratively developed. The AT implementation plan may be developed within the context of an IEP meeting or may require a separate meeting. A written AT implementation plan may be a separate document, referenced in the IEP, or part of the IEP document itself. Participation in the planning from as many team members as possible helps to ensure that it is comprehensive and collaborative. To ensure successful integration of AT into the curriculum and daily activities, the implementation plan includes input from the classroom teacher and other direct and related service providers. Individuals who are not typically members of the IEP team may have valuable input in the development of the implementation plan. These individuals might include paraprofessionals, instructional technology (IT) staff, and others who will play a role in making implementation work throughout the student's daily program.

To facilitate effective participation in the development of an AT implementation plan, information about AT devices and services may be shared prior to the planning meeting with any team members who are not knowledgeable about AT.

The plan is based on the student's IEP goals and is written in specific terms. To ensure effective progress, a procedure for collecting and using data about the student's AT use is included in the plan. AT implementation plans include

- the specific devices or strategies to be implemented,

- the relationship of AT use to IEP goals and access to the curriculum,

- action steps, including identification of:

  - *skills* the student needs to acquire in order to use the device or strategies, and who will teach new skills to the student,

  - *specific times* and *ways* the device/strategy will be used including how often and how long (e.g. daily during reading activity for 30 minutes or more),

  - *training* needed, persons who need training, persons who will provide training, when training will be provided, and what follow up will be needed,

  - *plans* for unexpected events that effect AT use,

  - *data* to be collected: its purpose, frequency, desired outcome, and relationship to IEP goals, and

  - *team meeting* schedule: When the team will meet to follow up, monitor progress, and develop subsequent steps.

**EXAMPLE**

*Shareen began using a portable e-book reader at the end of the last school year when the school purchased several and made them available to her classroom. Her teacher soon recognized that its use with text-to-speech significantly improved Shareen's understanding of complex text. Because of that, it was added to her IEP during AT consideration at her next IEP meeting. The team wrote a plan to ensure that the e-book reader would be available to her in science, language arts, and social studies. The plan identified who would acquire and load the digital content and when, where, and by whom the device would be charged and stored. After the first report card period the team realized that Shareen also needed to use the e-book reader in physical education when new games were introduced and printed rules were distributed. They met briefly to decide how to best meet that need and update their plan to address it.*

- Who, in addition to IEP team members, needs to participate in the development of the implementation plan in order to address all areas critical to the student's progress?

- What additional information, if any, is needed to develop the plan?

- What specific tasks and assignments need to be included in the plan?

2. **Assistive technology is *integrated* into the curriculum and daily activities of the student across environments.**

   **Intent: AT is used when and where it is needed to facilitate the student's access to, and mastery of, the curriculum. AT may facilitate active participation in educational activities, assessments, extracurricular activities, and typical routines.**

   In order to integrate AT use into daily activities, everyone involved with the student needs to know the purpose of the device as well as when and how it can and will be used. AT is not a separate, add-on item to be used only in isolated practice. Rather, it is a tool that allows a student to overcome or bypass some aspect of a disability to better learn new skills or more effectively demonstrate existing knowledge. It becomes a useful and effective tool when a student uses it regularly to complete meaningful tasks during typical activities. For example, a device may be expected to increase the student's productivity, participation, or independence. Using the device, the student may demonstrate improved quality and quantity of work as well as personal satisfaction.

   There are many services and arrangements to address when introducing a new AT device, including training, management, and maintenance. AT implementation addresses all of these in order for AT use to be effectively integrated into the student's daily activities across environments. When appropriate, the use of the AT device may be introduced in priority environments and be expanded across environments and activities in response to student success or needs.

*Mohammed was having difficulty meeting his written expression goals. Due to limited fine motor abilities, his handwriting was slow, tedious, and difficult to read. Mohammed had learned to keyboard the previous year and the IEP team determined that a portable word processor might help him meet his writing goals. Following training by the occupational therapist (OT), the teacher and paraprofessional supported the use of the device in language arts class. Even though the initial plan was to last six weeks, he was so successful after four weeks that the team met and planned to expand the use of the tool to other classes. Teachers from social studies and science joined the team to ensure that they knew what was expected and how to integrate its use into their classes. The science teacher was especially concerned because he typically had students move from their desks to the lab tables. His concerns included the need for an electrical outlet, the danger of breaking the word processor when moving it, and its inability to withstand moisture and spills. The team was able to address his concerns by sharing information and experiences from knowledge of the AT device and its use in language arts.*

KEY QUESTIONS

- In what ways will the AT use relate to the course objectives, daily activities, and critical elements of the curriculum for this student?

- Is AT being functionally integrated in the environments where tasks for which it is needed occur?

- Are additional AT tools or strategies needed?

3.  **Persons supporting the student across all environments in which the assistive technology is expected to be used, *share responsibility* for implementation of the plan.**

    **Intent: All persons who work with the student know their roles and responsibilities, are able to support the student using AT, and are expected to do so.**

    Classroom teachers have a critical role in determining the most effective times and activities for the student to use the AT in each unique environment. Other service providers may be responsible for training, physical setup, maintenance, repair, or other aspects of AT use. Each role is important and directly impacts the student's ability to use the AT. While one person may be assigned as the AT contact or coordinator for a student, all team members share a responsibility to monitor progress and communicate with each other regarding all aspects of implementation.

    No one team member should be expected to provide all the supports needed by a student in all environments where AT is needed. Each member of the team has the responsibility to provide support and guidance for the use of the AT when teaching or supervising the student. The role of each team member is included in the implementation plan. All team members understand that every role is critical to effective implementation and each member takes responsibility for fulfilling defined roles and tasks.

    Team members are also expected to support each other. They can use a variety of strategies, including team meetings, periodic email reminders, sharing of data, and progress monitoring. Frequent and regularly scheduled team updates are essential to keeping team members on track and accountable for supporting student achievement and independence.

    During implementation, team members may find they need more information, practice, and training in order to fulfill their roles. It is their responsibility to identify that need and access appropriate resources.

Administrators share in the responsibility for effective AT implementation. Essential aspects of administrative support include

- ensuring that responsibility is shared,

- holding high expectations for each team member's participation,

- monitoring performance, and

- providing needed resources (time, funds, etc.).

EXAMPLE

*As specified in Kelia's implementation plan, her teacher took responsibility for anticipating opportunities during the day when Kelia would be expected to use a tablet computer with a word processing app to accomplish the writing tasks for which AT was needed. The resource specialist helped the teacher identify opportunities where Kelia could use the tablet and the paraprofessional arranged the materials and AT while Kelia was learning how to use it. The AT facilitator trained Kelia, her parents, and her teachers how to use the AT and keep it working well.*

*The team decided that they needed to communicate via email weekly and meet monthly to review Kelia's progress, monitor their responsibilities, and determine needed changes. The administrator arranged duty schedules so that all team members were available at the designated time. The instructional technologist arranged for the implementation plan and data collection instruments to be placed on the network so that all team members could access them regardless of time and place.*

**KEY QUESTIONS**

- How will responsibilities for AT be shared among team members?

- How will the AT implementation plan be made available to all team members?

- What strategies will the team members use to communicate success, challenges and the need for possible changes?

- How will each team member be held accountable for appropriately supporting the student's use of AT?

4. **Persons supporting the student provide opportunities for the student to use a *variety of strategies—including assistive technology*—and learn which strategies are most effective for particular circumstances and tasks.**

   **Intent: When and where appropriate, students are encouraged to consider and use alternative strategies to remove barriers to participation or performance.**

**Strategies may include the student's natural abilities, use of AT, other supports, or modifications to the curriculum, task, or environment.**

No single AT device or strategy is effective and efficient for every setting or task. The opportunity to use a variety of tools and strategies enables the student to develop the strategic skills needed to understand what option best matches each task and environment. For example, a student who uses a portable word processor may also use a pencil for short answers, a computer while in the lab, and, occasionally, may dictate to a scribe. In addition, that same student may need extra time for longer assignments, the use of a study carrel at the side of the classroom for difficult writing tasks, or a handheld electronic thesaurus for some creative writing assignments.

Educators teach strategic decision-making and independence to students by providing opportunities for them to explore a variety of devices and strategies and guiding them to make effective selections. Strategies for completing tasks may include minor changes to the way that the task is completed, such as allowing more time, reducing the length of the assignment, or a change in learning environment where the task is completed.

**EXAMPLE**

*Bonita uses a complex dynamic display augmentative and alternative communication (AAC) device for communication and productivity but needs other tools and strategies in specific environments and activities. She uses a waterproof picture board at the swimming pool and a marker and dry erase board for brief messages to family members. She frequently uses the communication strategies of pointing, eye gaze, and vocalization, especially at meal times.*

**KEY QUESTIONS**

- What tools and strategies will be available for the student to use?

- How will the environment be structured so that the student has opportunities to use a variety of strategies, including AT?

- How will the team determine which AT tools the student will use for specific tasks?

- How will the student be taught to independently choose an appropriate AT tool or strategy for a specific setting or activity?

5. *Training* for the student, family, and staff are an integral part of implementation.

   Intent: Determination of the training needs of the student, staff, and family is based on how the AT will be used in each unique environment. Training and

**technical assistance are planned and implemented as ongoing processes based on current and changing needs.**

Training and technical assistance is an ongoing process based on current and changing student, staff, and family needs, guided by how, when, and where the AT will be used. The team identifies individuals who need to receive training and how much training each will require based on their background knowledge and specific responsibilities during implementation. Finally, the team makes plans for how the training will be phased in or layered for each team member, so the student's progress is not held back due to lack of skill or knowledge on the part of team members.

The team addresses the provider of the training, the scheduling of the training, the length of training (both initial and follow up), the location, and the content. A part of ongoing training may be the use of technical assistance. The team identifies how each team member will get answers to questions, get assistance with problem solving, and obtain additional training. The effectiveness and efficiency of the training is measured so that improvements can be made where needed.

*Due to Michael's illegible handwriting the IEP team determined that he needed to use a portable word processor in English, Social Studies, and Science. His special education resource teacher was the only person on the team with knowledge in the use and implementation of portable word processors. The team decided that the resource teacher would train the student and the three core class teachers in device use and implementation in a one-hour after school training. The initial training was to take place within two weeks of the IEP start date. Staff members would ask questions via email and request additional training if needed.*

*Michael would receive training during three study hall periods and then teach his parents how the device is used. His parents would contact the resource teacher if they had further questions. Michael would receive answers to questions, problem solving advice, and additional training, if needed, during study hall. Training consisted of device basics and device and training resources. The team identified data collection plans and how effectiveness of the AT implementation would be measured.*

**KEY QUESTIONS**

- Who needs to receive training and how much training will they need?

- When and where will the training occur?

- What will the training cover?

- How will follow-up, need for technical assistance, and effectiveness of training be addressed?

6. **Assistive technology implementation is initially based on assessment *data* and is adjusted based on performance data.**

   **Intent: Formal and informal assessment data guide initial decision-making and planning for AT implementation. As the plan is carried out, student performance is monitored and implementation is adjusted in a timely manner to support student progress.**

   Implementation actually begins with assessment. During an assessment of AT needs, the team determines the task that the student needs to be able to do and the student's current level of performance. Initial assessment data are used to plan for implementation of AT use and serve as the baseline or starting point for measuring student progress and improved ability to complete the identified tasks. Assessment data may include the student's ability to use the AT device and the benefits of the device's use for improving performance.

   Data collected during the AT implementation phase provides information to the team about whether the plan is working as anticipated and whether the AT device is providing the student with the expected benefits. Implementation data provides the evidence about the effectiveness of the strategy or tool. Some students make more progress than the team initially anticipated while other students fail to make the expected progress. In either case, the plan for AT use is adjusted with a focus on increasing the student's ability to perform the identified tasks.

   If the student is not making the expected progress, it is not necessarily an indication that the AT device should be changed or modified. A thoughtful analysis of implementation data may show that changes are needed in training, schedule, planning, or the specificity of the defined purpose for AT use. When data are reviewed as scheduled, the team is able to adjust the implementation to ensure that the use of AT is effectively supporting student achievement.

EXAMPLE

*Following Dillon's AT assessment, which focused on his use of an AAC device, his team identified the tasks he would need to be able to do and his current levels of performance on those tasks. They developed an implementation plan to ensure that the device would be used as intended.*

*When his team met the next quarter to review progress, they were surprised to find that while he demonstrated increases in communication in some settings, he had not made the expected progress across all environments. The team realized that the implementation plan they had developed did not address his ability to functionally use the device, decide when to use it, and to use it independently across communication partners and environments. Further analysis revealed that he was dependent on staff to provide his device and did not always have the vocabulary necessary to participate in different activities.*

*The team responded to this data by adjusting his implementation plan. They worked with Dillon to develop a list of factors that would guide him in identifying for himself when he needed his device and when the activity provided ways for him to respond without his device. They developed an overlay that allowed him to communicate his needs in each environment. Staff agreed to identify in advance new vocabulary required for activities and assigned responsibility to program the vocabulary so that it would be available. In addition, the team appointed someone to meet with Dillon twice a month to discuss any obstacles he was experiencing in his device use and make any needed adjustments in his implementation plan.*

7. **Assistive technology implementation includes *management and maintenance of equipment* and materials.**

   **Intent: For technology to be useful it is important that equipment management responsibilities are clearly defined and assigned. Though specifics may differ based on the technology, some general areas may include organization of equipment and materials; responsibility for acquisition, set-up, repair, and replacement in a timely fashion; and assurance that equipment is operational.**

   Management and maintenance of AT devices is assigned to an individual or individuals who are available to the student and the educational team on a regular basis. This individual is responsible for doing regular checks to make sure the device is working properly and functioning as expected. A back-up person is identified in the event that the individual with primary responsibility is not available. Those responsible for management and maintenance of equipment are clearly identified in the written AT implementation plan.

   Addressing management and maintenance of equipment ensures that implementation will run as smoothly as possible. Planning for management and maintenance answers questions such as:

   - Who is the primary contact for management and maintenance of equipment?

   - Who is responsible for ensuring that the AT is maintained?

- What is the contingency plan if a team member changes jobs or moves?

- Who will pay for needed materials such as batteries, ink cartridges, and paper?

- What is the contingency plan if an AT device is damaged or lost?

- What back up will be used when an AT device is unavailable?

- What additional information and resources are needed?

Changes in the student's program may result in a need for changes in tools or strategies. Applications, software, or devices may need to be upgraded. Additional AT may be needed after transitions from semester to semester, teacher to teacher, or school to school. For example, the student may need additional access to the school's server that requires coordination between the student's team and those who manage the IT system.

Difficulties can arise when responsibility for the care and maintenance of the AT device has not been clearly assigned; the AT may not be available or working when it is needed. Contingency plans for dealing with broken or lost equipment need to be made in advance. If contingency plans are not made, a student may be without the use of an AT device that is written into the IEP. This leaves the education agency out of compliance with the law and the student without the needed tool. These problems are much less likely to occur if all team members are involved in planning from the beginning and understand their individual responsibilities.

If the IEP team has determined that AT is educationally necessary at home in order to provide FAPE, the implementation plan will address the specific arrangements. If the district owns the AT device, specific responsibilities are identified for sending the AT home. The team may develop a list of expectations and agreements about AT used by the student at home. If the family and child own the AT device, the agreement will define the district's obligation and responsibility for management, maintenance, or replacement if necessary.

**EXAMPLE**

*When Kelly got her new portable word processor, she completed many assignments in the resource room with support from her teacher and a paraprofessional. Once she had learned how to operate the device, she began to take it with her to an English composition class. Quarterly reports indicated that Kelly was not turning in her assignments. In response, the team talked with Kelly and discovered that they had not planned for Kelly to print and turn in assignments when she was working in her general education classrooms. They discussed several options and determined the best solution was to attach an extra printer cable to a computer in each of Kelly's general education classes. Before Kelly left the room, she could print what she wrote and turn it in at the same time as other students. After this adjustment, Kelly consistently turned in her assignments.*

- What regular management and maintenance tasks are required for the AT device?

- Who will be responsible for AT device management and maintenance?

- What does each person need to know about how the AT will be managed and maintained (e.g., steps to take if the AT device is not operating correctly, person responsible for charging the AT device every night)?

- Who has the financial responsibility for AT equipment repairs and supplies?

## Exploring the Quality Indicators for Assistive Technology Implementation with the QIAT Self-Evaluation Matrix

The Self-Evaluation Matrix for Assistive Technology Implementation focuses on identifying strengths and weaknesses of AT use in the student's daily educational program. Through its variations from "unacceptable" to "best practice" the matrix

- provides a scaffold for ongoing improvement of AT implementation,

- guides the integration of the AT into the curriculum and daily activities,

- helps identify strengths and areas of need, and

- facilitates the identification of action items and barriers to effective integration of AT into the student's program.

The first three implementation indicators assess collaboration, curriculum integration, and shared responsibility during the implementation phase. The fourth indicator addresses the use of a variety of strategies to support the student AT use. The provision of training is the focus of indicator five. Use of data and the management and maintenance of equipment are addressed in the final two AT implementation indicators.

The following case study gives examples of ways in which the Quality Indicators for Assistive Technology Implementation can impact the implementation process.

# Quality Indicators for Assistive Technology *Implementation*

| QUALITY INDICATOR | UNACCEPTABLE | | |
|---|---|---|---|
| **1. AT implementation proceeds according to a *collaboratively developed plan*.** | 1<br>There is no implementation plan. | 2<br>Individual team members may develop AT implementation plans independently. | |
| **2. AT is *integrated* into the curriculum and daily activities of the student across environments.** | 1<br>AT included in the IEP is rarely used. | 2<br>AT is used in isolation with no links to the student's curriculum and/or daily activities. | |
| **3. Persons supporting the student across all environments in which the AT is expected to be used *share responsibility* for implementation of the plan.** | 1<br>Responsibility for implementation is not accepted by any team member. | 2<br>Responsibility for implementation is assigned to one team member. | |
| **4. Persons supporting the student provide opportunities for the student to use *a variety of strategies—including AT*—and to learn which strategies are most effective for particular circumstances and tasks.** | 1<br>No strategies are provided to support the accomplishment of tasks. | 2<br>Only one strategy is provided to support the accomplishment of tasks. | |
| **5. *Learning opportunities* for the student, family, and staff is an integral part of implementation.** | 1<br>AT needs for learning opportunities have not been determined. | 2<br>AT learning opportunity needs are initially identified for student, family, and staff, but no training has been provided. | |
| **6. AT implementation is initially based on assessment *data* and is adjusted based on performance data.** | 1<br>AT implementation is based on equipment availability and limited knowledge of team members, not on student data. | 2<br>AT implementation is loosely based on initial assessment data and rarely adjusted. | |
| **7. AT implementation includes management and *maintenance of equipment* and materials.** | 1<br>Equipment and materials are not managed or maintained. Students rarely have access to the equipment and materials they require. | 2<br>Equipment and materials are managed and maintained on a crisis basis. Students frequently do not have access to the equipment and materials they require. | |

| VARIATIONS | | PROMISING PRACTICES |
|---|---|---|
| **3**<br>Some team members collaborate in the development of an AT implementation plan. | **4**<br>Most team members collaborate in the development of AT implementation plan. | **5**<br>All team members collaborate in the development of a comprehensive AT implementation plan. |
| **3**<br>AT is sometimes integrated into the student's curriculum and daily activities. | **4**<br>AT is generally integrated into the student's curriculum and daily activities. | **5**<br>AT is fully integrated into the student's curriculum and daily activities. |
| **3**<br>Responsibility for implementation is shared by some team members in some environments. | **4**<br>Responsibility for implementation is generally shared by most team members in most environments. | **5**<br>Responsibility for implementation is consistently shared among team members across all environments. |
| **3**<br>Multiple strategies are provided. Students are sometimes encouraged to select and use the most appropriate strategy for each task. | **4**<br>Multiple strategies are provided. Students are generally encouraged to select and use the most appropriate strategy for each task. | **5**<br>Multiple strategies are provided. Students are consistently encouraged to select and use the most appropriate strategy for each task. |
| **3**<br>Initial AT learning opportunities are sometimes provided to student, family, and staff. | **4**<br>Initial and follow-up AT learning opportunities are generally provided to student, family, and staff | **5**<br>Ongoing AT learning opportunities are provided to student, family, and staff as needed, based on changing needs. |
| **3**<br>AT implementation is based on initial assessment data and is sometimes adjusted as needed based on student progress. | **4**<br>AT implementation is based on initial assessment data and is generally adjusted as needed based on student progress. | **5**<br>AT implementation is based on initial assessment data and is consistently adjusted as needed based on student progress. |
| **3**<br>Equipment and materials are managed and maintained so that students sometimes have access to the equipment and materials they require. | **4**<br>Equipment and materials are managed and maintained so that students generally have access to the equipment and materials they require. | **5**<br>Equipment and materials are effectively managed and maintained so that students consistently have access to the equipment and materials they require. |

# Exploring the Quality Indicators for Assistive Technology Implementation Through Gordon's Case Study

Gordon has severe athetoid cerebral palsy and is unable to walk. His speech is difficult to understand, and he has developed a sophisticated eye gaze and facial expression system to communicate with his family members and close friends. He used a variety of augmentative and alternative communication (AAC) devices over time, including some single-message, switch-activated AAC devices. During kindergarten and first grade Gordon's placement was in a regular education setting with the full time support of a paraprofessional. He also received services from the speech and language pathologist (SLP) who worked on communication, the OT whose focus was fine motor and switch use, the PT who worked on positioning and mobility, and the resource teacher who supported academics. Gordon often missed instructional activities in the classroom to go to OT, PT, and speech therapy.

In preparation for Gordon's entry into second grade a planning meeting was held. During this meeting it was evident that Gordon's first grade teacher didn't really have much information about Gordon's achievements or progress. She stated that including Gordon in activities in the classroom was difficult because he did not have the needed vocabulary and the AAC device was rarely used in the classroom. She also deferred most questions about Gordon to the paraprofessional. It appeared that Gordon had been segregated from typical classroom activities in favor of isolated, independent work with the paraprofessional and resource room teacher. The appropriateness of this regular education classroom placement was questioned.

However, according to the resource room teacher, his reading scores on adapted measures and the alternate state assessment are at the first grade level. His math scores are pre-first grade level. The state assessment data were consistent with his performance on math tasks and timed assessments from classroom software that he used in the resource room. He had used a name stamp, adapted pencil holders, magnetic letters and dictation for his writing tasks in the resource room and had many no-tech or low-tech effective communication strategies for expressive communication.

The team agreed that, while academic instruction could be provided for Gordon in a variety of settings, his communication and socialization needs could best be met in a general education environment. However, they realized that without some changes in the way implementation plans were made, it was possible that in future classroom placements Gordon would again be present but not really included. They used the Quality Indicators for Assistive Technology Implementation to examine Gordon's first grade program, to identify barriers, and make changes in the plan that would help him be a more active participant in second grade.

To expand the amount of vocabulary he could use, Gordon's SLP requested a trial of a switch-activated AAC device with visual scanning and found that Gordon was able to use it quite well. She worked with the OT on device and switch placement. The OT and PT researched switches and found one that allowed him to operate both the AAC device and the wheel chair, through a switch mounted to his wheelchair headrest.

He was able to use a wireless connection between the AAC device and a computer so that he could send written text directly through the AAC device.

When the second grade teacher saw what Gordon could do with the switch, she was determined to increase his participation in activities. She worked to get vocabulary to the SLP in the time frame needed to ensure programming. The SLP began training the paraprofessional to program the AAC device. With the new switch, Gordon was able to get himself to the appropriate place at the correct time. His increase in independent mobility reduced his need for the paraprofessional. Because of his communication skills and his determination to be understood, Gordon was able to successfully attend general education classes with co-teaching from the resource teacher and minimal support from the paraprofessional in the second grade classroom. The therapists worked together to reduce the time Gordon needed to be out of the classroom so that he would not miss critical instructional time.

# Application of the QIAT Self-Evaluation Matrix for Implementation by Gordon's Team

1. **Assistive technology implementation proceeds according to a *collaboratively developed plan.***

   **Discussion:** In reflecting on first grade, the team realized that the focus of Gordon's AT use had been isolated tasks that differed from what the rest of the students were doing. Gordon often missed classroom instruction to go to therapy. Each individual therapist had been focused on his or her own discipline without a plan for communication and coordination in the general education environment. They rated their performance a 2. As they revised the implementation plan, effort was taken to see that all team members were involved in the collaborative process.

| 1 | 2 | 3 | 4 | 5 |
|---|---|---|---|---|
| There is no implementation plan. | **Individual team members may develop AT implementation plans independently.** | Some team members collaborate in the development of an AT implementation plan. | Most team members collaborate in the development of AT implementation plan. | All team members collaborate in the development of a comprehensive AT implementation plan. |

2. **Assistive technology is *integrated* into the curriculum and daily activities of the student across environments.**

   **Discussion:** Gordon's team rated themselves a 3 on this indicator. They acknowledged that although Gordon used his computer on a daily basis for instruction and for production of written work, in first grade his communication device was rarely programmed with the vocabulary he needed during classroom instruction. In response to their discussion, the teacher began to identify needed vocabulary and give it to the paraprofessional in time for Gordon to participate in activities using his device.

| 1 | 2 | 3 | 4 | 5 |
|---|---|---|---|---|
| AT included in the IEP is rarely used. | AT is used in isolation with no links to the student's curriculum and/or daily activities. | **AT is sometimes integrated into the student's curriculum and daily activities.** | AT is generally integrated into the student's curriculum and daily activities. | AT is fully integrated into the student's curriculum and daily activities. |

3. **Persons supporting the student across all environments in which the assistive technology is expected to be used *share responsibility* for implementation of the plan.**

   **Discussion:** In their evaluation of shared responsibility, the team realized that in first grade they had not really shared responsibility for Gordon's AT use. The paraprofessional had been solely responsible for Gordon's computer use and the SLP had been solely responsible for programming Gordon's AAC device. In second grade they were making progress. The team rated themselves with a 3 on this indicator and agreed to ensure that they share the responsibilities.

| 1 | 2 | 3 | 4 | 5 |
|---|---|---|---|---|
| Responsibility for implementation is not accepted by any team member. | Responsibility for implementation is assigned to one team member. | **Responsibility for implementation is shared by some team members in some environments.** | Responsibility for implementation is generally shared by most team members in most environments. | Responsibility for implementation is consistently shared among team members across all environments. |

4. **Persons supporting the student provide opportunities for the student to use *a variety of strategies—including assistive technology*—and to learn which strategies are most effective for particular circumstances and tasks.**

   **Discussion:** It was exciting for the team to come to this indicator and realize that, aside from the use of a high tech AAC device, they felt that they had done a good job of identifying multiple strategies for Gordon's task performance. They rated their performance a 4. The implementation plans for the following year included strategies for helping Gordon learn to recognize and request the AT most appropriate for the task.

| 1 | 2 | 3 | 4 | 5 |
|---|---|---|---|---|
| No strategies are provided to support the accomplishment of tasks. | Only one strategy is provided to support the accomplishment of tasks. | Multiple strategies are provided. Students are sometimes encouraged to select and use the most appropriate strategy for each task. | **Multiple strategies are provided. Students are generally encouraged to select and use the most appropriate strategy for each task.** | Multiple strategies are provided. Students are consistently encouraged to select and use the most appropriate strategy for each task. |

5. *Training* for the student, family, and staff is an integral part of implementation.

**Discussion:** Team discussion centered around the belief that hands-on training for Gordon in the use of his AT devices was not sufficient. They agreed that this, in addition to development of a comprehensive implementation plan, had been lacking during Gordon's first grade year. They rated their performance for the previous year a 1 because they felt they had missed many staff and family training needs and opportunities. They determined that hands-on AT instruction should be paired with instruction for all team members about how Gordon's AT use could be integrated into his daily instructional programs.

| 1 | 2 | 3 | 4 | 5 |
|---|---|---|---|---|
| **AT needs for learning opportunities have not been determined.** | AT learning opportunity needs are initially identified for student, family, and staff, but no training has been provided. | Initial AT learning opportunities are sometimes provided to student, family, and staff. | Initial and follow-up AT learning opportunities are generally provided to student, family, and staff. | Ongoing AT learning opportunities are provided to student, family, and staff as needed, based on changing needs. |

6. **Assistive technology implementation is initially based on assessment *data* and is adjusted based on performance data.**

**Discussion:** When Gordon started first grade, the team had a variety of performance data about his AT use that justified the initial acquisition of the devices. However, once the devices had been purchased, they recognized that they had not collected additional performance data regarding his daily use of the devices in the first grade classroom. This had given everyone the impression that things were going well and that he was making adequate progress, even though this was not the case. They rated themselves a 2 for his first grade year. The team identified the data needed and developed a systematic approach to collecting it.

| 1 | 2 | 3 | 4 | 5 |
|---|---|---|---|---|
| AT implementation is based on equipment availability and limited knowledge of team members, not on student data. | **AT implementation is loosely based on initial assessment data and rarely adjusted.** | AT implementation is based on initial assessment data and is sometimes adjusted as needed based on student progress. | AT implementation is based on initial assessment data and is generally adjusted as needed based on student progress. | AT implementation is based on initial assessment data and is consistently adjusted as needed based on student progress. |

7. **Assistive technology implementation includes management and *maintenance of equipment* and materials.**

   **Discussion:** Ironically, the team felt they had done an excellent job of making sure Gordon's AT was available and working. Every time the team discovered a technical problem or encountered an incompatibility with the network or some other technology application, they had addressed it directly and found a solution. They rated their performance a 4 because Gordon did not have adequate vocabulary available to him in first grade, but agreed their strategies for AT troubleshooting were working and they would continue to use them.

| 1 | 2 | 3 | 4 | 5 |
|---|---|---|---|---|
| Equipment and materials are not managed or maintained. Students rarely have access to the equipment and materials they require. | Equipment and materials are managed and maintained on a crisis basis. Students frequently do not have access to the equipment and materials they require. | Equipment and materials are managed and maintained so that students sometimes have access to the equipment and materials they require. | **Equipment and materials are managed and maintained so that students generally have access to the equipment and materials they require.** | Equipment and materials are effectively managed and maintained so that students consistently have access to the equipment and materials they require. |

## Summary

In this case study, it's possible to recognize the role of evaluation of effectiveness and data collection in determining whether the implementation process is working and if use of the AT is critical to success. The interconnectedness of the Implementation and Evaluation of Effectiveness areas is important to note. The role of evaluation of effectiveness in the AT process is discussed in the following chapter.

## Suggested Activities

1. Go to Ablenet University at *https://www.ablenetinc.com/resources/recorded_webinars/*. Sign in and search the list of recorded videos on AT for *Assistive Technology Implementation: The Basics* by Kirk Behnke and *QIAT Session 5: AT Implementation* by Jane Korsten and Gayl Bowser. Watch these two webinars. What three big ideas did you get from the webinars? How will you incorporate one or more of them into your practice?

2. Go to *www.atinternetmodules.org* and complete the module titled "Assistive technology implementation," provided by the Ohio Center for Autism and Low Incidence.

3. Download the *Assistive Technology Implementation Plan* from *http://www .educationtechpoints.org/helpdesk/at-resources/POhp/*. Complete the plan using a student with whom you are familiar or one of the case studies from the previous three chapters. Feel free to make up any additional facts that you need, as long as they are not in conflict with the information in the case study.

4. Answer the following questions about the plan you developed in Activity 3:

   - Where does the implementation plan address identified tasks?

   - What strategies are included to accomplish the tasks?

   - How is AT integrated into activities across environments?

   - How is the expected change in performance defined?

   - What are the plans for collecting data regarding the expected change in performance?

   - How have primary implementers been identified and communicated with about their roles?

   - What initial and ongoing training is included in the plan?

   - How does the plan address management and maintenance of equipment and materials?

5. Complete the Self-Evaluation Matrix for AT Implementation by thinking about how AT implementation is done in a district with which you are familiar. What are three things that you might do to improve it?

# CHAPTER 6

# Exploring the Quality Indicators for Evaluation of Effectiveness of Assistive Technology

1.  Team members share *clearly defined responsibilities* to ensure that data are collected, evaluated, and interpreted by capable and credible team members.

2.  Data are collected on specific student achievement that has been identified by the team and is *related to one or more goals*.

3.  Evaluation of effectiveness includes the *quantitative and qualitative measurement of changes* in the student's performance and achievement.

4.  Effectiveness is evaluated *across environments* during naturally occurring and structured activities.

5.  Data are collected to provide teams with a means for *analyzing student achievement and identifying supports and barriers* that influence assistive technology use to determine what changes, if any, are needed.

6.  *Changes are made* in the student's assistive technology services and educational program when evaluation data indicate that such changes are needed to improve student achievement.

7.  Evaluation of effectiveness is a dynamic, responsive, *ongoing process* that is reviewed periodically.

Evaluation of effectiveness of AT use is a two-part process. It includes systematically recording data about a child's performance and then reviewing that data to determine if the child's learning is progressing at an acceptable level. IDEA contains no specific legal requirements about method or frequency of data collection for AT nor does it mention evaluating the effectiveness of AT use as a required AT service. The need to evaluate what is being done, however, is inherent in the provision of any intervention. In the development of QIAT, the evaluation of effectiveness was found to be a critical component of quality AT services (Zabala, 2004).

However, IDEA does address the schedule for reviewing a student's overall progress in two ways: during the preparation for the annual IEP; and, in reporting a child's progress to the parents at least as often as parents of typically developing children are informed of progress (34 CFR §300.347(a)(7)(ii)). For parents of typically developing children, reporting is generally in the form of regularly scheduled (e.g., once per quarter or semester) report cards and conferences. However, this scheduled review of data about how a child is progressing when AT is being used, or being used in a new way or new environment, may not allow the team to efficiently and effectively make any needed changes in the intervention.

Gordon's case study in Chapter 5 provides an example of what can happen when the evaluation of the effectiveness of AT use is not addressed until time for the annual review of the IEP. Incorporating the core components of evaluation of effectiveness can prevent the loss of valuable learning opportunities. The following discussion looks at each of the Evaluation of Effectiveness indicators in more depth.

1. **Team members share *clearly defined responsibilities* to ensure that data are collected, evaluated, and interpreted by capable and credible team members.**

   **Intent: Each team member is accountable for ensuring that the data collection process determined by the team is implemented. Individual roles in the collection and review of the data are assigned by the team. Tasks such as data collection, evaluation, and interpretation are led by persons with relevant training and knowledge, and it can be appropriate for different individual team members to conduct these tasks.**

   Evaluating the effectiveness of AT use is a process shared by all team members rather than the responsibility of any one individual serving a student. It requires clearly defining the goals of using the AT and specifying the change in performance expected. Based on the anticipated change, the team determines how progress toward the goals will be measured, as well as when, where, and by whom data will be collected. Evaluating effectiveness of AT use also requires that data are analyzed in a timely manner, shared with the team, and reviewed to identify implications for additional interventions or continuance of the current plan. As part of evaluating effectiveness of the AT, a schedule for reviewing the student's progress is set for the year.

   Regularly reviewing data has become much more prevalent in education agencies since IDEA 2004 included the requirement for early intervening services and response to intervention (RTI) (*www.interventioncentral.org*). RTI programs review student progress data on a weekly or bi-weekly schedule using it to initiate or adjust interventions to keep student's progress on track. If the student is in an education agency that has implemented RTI, the AT team can work with the RTI program to coordinate data collection and review. The RTI program may also offer a possible source of information and training.

Generally, responsibilities are not determined by job title nor is it expected that any individual team member assumes responsibility for all tasks related to evaluation of effectiveness. Rather, responsibilities are clarified and designated by the team, or a team leader, in order to move forward effectively and collaboratively. As team members reflect on their knowledge of the tasks included in evaluating the effectiveness of the AT, they may realize they do not have prior knowledge related to all aspects of the evaluation of effectiveness process. If their knowledge is not sufficient, they seek additional information or assistance. Data is recorded for all relevant tasks across the environments in which the AT use is targeted.

EXAMPLE

*Chafic's team decided he was a good candidate for voice recognition software. His plan stated that training with the software would be provided at school until competency was established. After the initial training, Chafic would use voice recognition software in the resource room for assignments longer than two paragraphs. Chafic would also continue to dictate to a designated scribe in selected classes. The school team shared a data collection tool with the parents so they could also collect data at home. During the six-week training period, his special education teacher and his parents agreed to collect data on accuracy, time on task, and number of words dictated per minute each time he used voice recognition. Written output in other modes was also collected and reviewed. The parents and teacher planned to communicate via email on progress reflected in the data collected. At the end of the trial period, the team planned a face-to-face meeting to review the data, discuss Chafic's progress, and plan the next steps.*

**KEY QUESTIONS**

- How will team members determine who is responsible for each aspect of evaluating the AT use?

- How does the team determine who will collect, analyze, and share data?

- How does the team decide how often the data will be collected, analyzed, and shared?

- What training or technical assistance may be needed to develop an evaluation of effectiveness plan or to carry it out?

2.  **Data are collected on specific student achievement that has been identified by the team and is *related to one or more goals*.**

    **Intent: In order to evaluate the success of AT use, data are collected on various aspects of student performance and achievement. Targets for data collection include the student's use of AT to progress toward mastery of relevant IEP and curricular goals and to enhance participation in extracurricular activities at school and in other environments.**

    The student's IEP documents the AT tools and the services that will be provided. The IEP will communicate whether the AT is being provided to help the student achieve one or more educational goals, to access the curriculum, or to support the student's participation in the general education environment. The implementation plan ensures that everyone on a student's team understands the reasons AT has been chosen, their personal role in supporting its use, and the expected change in student performance that has been identified. The reasons, roles, and expected changes are the basis for evaluating the effectiveness of the AT use. Evaluation of effectiveness is not a separate stand-alone event, but an ongoing process that is based on the IEP and the implementation plan.

    Reed, Bowser, and Korsten (2002) identified four primary methods to collect data about AT use. These are interview, review of a product created by the student, observation, and video or audio recording. The choice of how to collect data is based on the type of change expected and the evidence that can best reflect that change. In some cases data is recorded each time a student uses the AT device. In others, data is collected daily, weekly, or on some other reasonable pre-planned schedule. Using a form such as the *Plan for Evaluation of Effectiveness of AT Use* included in Appendix D facilitates planning. Table 6.1 includes the steps of planning for effective data collection. These questions lead the team through the process of planning for the evaluation of the impact of the AT.

---

**TABLE 6.1** Planning for evaluation of effectiveness of AT use

**Step 1:** What is the present level of performance on this goal?

**Step 2:** What changes are expected as a result of implementation?

**Step 3:** What aspects of performance will change (e.g., quality, quantity, frequency, independence)?

**Step 4:** What obstacles may inhibit success (e.g., physical access, opportunity, instruction, practice, student preference)?

**Step 5:** How will the occurrence of obstacles be reflected in the data?

**Step 6:** What format will be used to collect the data (e.g., interview, work samples, observation, audio or video recording)?

**Step 7:** What is the data collection plan (e.g., environments, activity, frequency, person responsible)?

---

The targeted performance identified in the IEP and implementation plan is the basis for data collection. The data collected provide information about the student's regular performance in relation to that task, such as initiating communication, producing legible written assignments, recording key facts during a lecture, and so on.

EXAMPLE

*Derek is an orally fluent third grader who struggles with written productivity. His most recent writing assessment indicates that he meets expectations in ideas, organization, voice, and word choice but struggles with sentence fluency, use of conventions, and presentation. His teacher reports that Derek's handwriting is very difficult to read and that he frequently shows frustration and fatigue when writing. His team determined that he may benefit from the use of a table computer with a word processing app. Team members agreed that the tool could be used in many settings where Derek needs to write, but had different expectations about how Derek's writing would change and how that change could be measured when he used the device. The teacher expected Derek to increase the number of sentences in a paragraph, the occupational therapist (OT) expected Derek to increase legibility and speed, and his parents expected Derek to complete written tasks more independently. The team realized that they needed to align their expectations, and after reviewing Derek's IEP goals, agreed that progress would be measured on the goal that read, "Derek will write a three to five sentence paragraph that meets expectations on the school's third grade writing rubric on four of five assignments." They were particularly interested in noting changes in fluency as well as use of writing conventions and presentation. They agreed to collect written samples weekly to place in his portfolio. They decided to meet in one month to review Derek's samples to determine if he was making progress. If progress was not satisfactory, the team would need to decide whether Derek needed more training, increased time, or some other change in his use of the tablet.*

**KEY QUESTIONS**

- How is student achievement expected to change as a result of the use of AT?
- What data is being collected?
- What does the analysis of the data show?
- What additional data is needed about student performance to clarify the effectiveness of the use of AT or identify barriers that may need to be addressed?

3. **Evaluation of effectiveness includes the *quantitative and qualitative measurement of changes* in the student's performance and achievement.**

   **Intent: Changes targeted for data collection are observable and measurable, so that data are as objective as possible. Changes identified by the IEP team for evaluation may include accomplishment of relevant tasks, method/manner of AT use, student preferences, productivity, participation, independence, quality of work, speed, accuracy of performance, and student satisfaction, among others.**

   Specific student behaviors are identified so that the data collected about them matches the intent of the goal. It is only when the correct data is collected that the resulting information can be used to make instructional decisions, and it is important that both quantitative and qualitative data are gathered and considered.

   Quantitative data refers to actions, behaviors, student responses, movements, and so on, that can be measured and counted. In the case of AT use, it might include factors like speed, accuracy, latency, quantity, task completion, or duration. Qualitative data, on the other hand, can be observed but not easily counted. It might include descriptions of what took place or the student's stated opinion, preference, or feeling. It may be gathered through interviews, observational and anecdotal reports, video recording, and use of rubrics.

   Comparing pre-intervention data, often referred to as baseline data, to the post-intervention data might also capture change. Such comparison can show whether the intervention (which includes AT paired with instruction) has been effective. It is critical to have both baseline data about the student's performance before using the AT and a clear understanding about how much change might be reasonably expected over a specific period of time.

   Many areas that were difficult to quantify in the past have been made easier by research. One example is the Developmental Writing Scale (Sturm, Nelson, Staskowski & Cali, 2010). Their research-based scale detects the smallest developmental progressions as students move from drawing and scribbling to paragraph writing. Another example is the Communication Matrix (Rowland, 2012) (*www.communicationmatrix.org*). The Communication Matrix identifies seven levels of development in the earliest stages of communication. Using tools like the Developmental Writing Scale or the Communication Matrix can make it much easier to identify progress in an area otherwise difficult to quantify.

**EXAMPLE**

*Shane uses an augmentative and alternative communication (AAC) device to support his expressive communication. His team felt that changes in the number of Shane's spontaneous communications as well as the length of his utterances were important skills related to his device use and they collected data on these skills to determine if there was quantitative improvement. In addition, they collected data on the elements (words) he put in sequence to communicate his message. They identified that Shane used many single word noun labels to identify objects, but these words were rarely combined with verbs, even though appropriate verbs were included in his vocabulary choices on the AAC device. Shane received intensive specialized instruction in expressive language intended to increase both initiation of interactions and use of noun-verb combinations when talking about topics of interest to him. The team then collected data on these skills during three identified times. After reviewing two weeks of data, it was clear that Shane was making steady progress toward meeting these goals in structured activities while less growth was documented in unstructured activities.*

---

**KEY QUESTIONS**

- What behaviors can be observed and measured to demonstrate progress toward goals?

- How will the expected change in performance be captured in the data?

- How will progress be monitored over time?

- What other information is needed?

4. **Effectiveness is evaluated *across environments* during naturally occurring and structured activities.**

   **Intent: Relevant tasks within each environment where the AT is to be used are identified. Data needed and procedures for collecting those data in each environment are determined.**

   It is essential that success be demonstrated on more than one occasion and in more than one environment. In developing the implementation plan and the method for evaluating the effectiveness of the AT use, the team identifies the environments in which the student participates at naturally occurring times. When collecting data in multiple environments and with multiple personnel, it is critical that team members identify a shared expectation and agreed upon criteria.

   Effective data are sufficiently specific and robust to provide information about what is occurring so that the team can analyze it and make needed changes. When data show the student is experiencing difficulty with a certain part of a task, it may be necessary to develop strategies to address the specific difficulty and then return to the task as a whole.

   In some cases, lack of student progress may be related to inconsistent opportunities to use the AT. This may be due to absences, schedule changes, or failure of team members to provide opportunities to use AT. It may be necessary to discuss the opportunities provided by team members and the consistency of implementation as well as student performance.

*The IEP team identified that Kathryn needs to use a switch-activated device for basic communication tasks such as asking for help and calling for attention. However, the specific motor ability with which Kathryn would activate a switch has not been determined. The OT met with Kathryn two times per week for five weeks and collected data on motor abilities and switch activations. When the team met, the OT shared the data and Kathryn's need for increased opportunities to use the switch each day. After discussion, the team created a chart listing natural and scripted ways that Kathryn could use a switch in multiple environments, so that they could determine preferred switch site and type, as well as intentionality of switch activations. Each team member identified a time and activity for which they would be responsible to support Kathryn's switch use and collect the necessary data. They met two weeks later and decided they had enough data to determine the switch site, switch type, and intentionality of switch use in multiple settings.*

**KEY QUESTIONS**

- How does the team ensure that data will be collected across environments?

- What are the targeted tasks in each environment?

- How many opportunities are needed to complete tasks using AT in each environment?

5. **Data are collected to provide teams with a means for *analyzing student achievement and identifying supports and barriers* that influence assistive technology use to determine what changes, if any, are needed.**

    **Intent: To guide decision-making, teams regularly analyze data on multiple factors that may influence success or lead to errors. Such factors include the student's understanding of expected tasks and ability to use AT, but also student preferences, intervention strategies, training, and opportunities to gain proficiency.**

    The criterion for success that was determined during device selection and goal setting is generally the basis for ongoing analysis of student progress. Data may reveal that there are unexpected barriers in one or more environments, that the original goal was not the most useful or feasible, or that team expectations were greater than the actual progress. Data provide not only information about the student's level of performance but can also help identify essential supports for continued student achievement. In the absence of adequate progress, data can identify causative factors to suggest program adjustments. Student and staff expectations, attendance, lack of practice opportunities, relevant research, and performance of same age peers may all contribute valuable information when reflecting on the appropriateness of goals.

The use of interventions based on research is another requirement in IDEA. It states that the IEP should include, "A statement of the special education and related services and supplementary aids and services, *based on peer-reviewed research to the extent practicable,* to be provided to the child...." 300.320 (a) (4) (emphasis added) Educators need to know the research about AT use and need to assess how its use is advancing the student toward attaining his or her annual goals and supporting student progress in the general education curriculum.

Research can provide a better understanding of what should be expected, as well as help when choosing specific AT tools and evaluating progress. For example, there are several software programs and apps that pair pictures or symbols with words. They were developed specifically for use in teaching reading to students with disabilities. However, Erickson, Hanser, Hatch, and Sanders (2009) studied the practice of pairing picture symbols with words and found that it slows down the rate at which students learn to read the word. If the goal is only to provide access to limited, specific content, then the use of paired picture symbols might increase comprehension of content that otherwise would not be accessible. However, if the goal is to further the development of literacy skills, pairing pictures with text is likely to slow down the rate at which a student develops those skills. In either case, making decisions about the use of these AT tools requires consideration of relevant research.

Research also provides valuable information about the length of time data should be collected. For example research on improving reading comprehension through use of text-to-speech (TTS) indicates that a four- or five- week trial will not be enough to show the potential impact. Several research studies demonstrated that long intervention periods and extended training are linked to improved outcomes when using TTS (Strangman & Dalton, 2005; Olson, Wise, & Ring, 1997; Olson & Wise, 1992; and Elbro, Rasmussen, & Spelling, 1996). Gersten and Edyburn (2007) recommended a minimum of nine weeks of training with extended training being desirable. Similarly, Dimmitt, Hodapp, Judas, Munn, and Rachow (2006) found at least 11 weeks was needed to show increases in passage comprehension. Hodapp and Rachow (2010) found that in a second year of training, as long as limitations in teacher's ability to support the use of TTS did not interfere, students accessed twice as much text with TTS as they did with paper texts. In addition, students maintained their level of comprehension when using TTS even when the difficulty of comprehension questions increased significantly.

*Jenna was expected to participate in history class by answering a minimum of three questions posed to her by her teacher. The team analyzed her performance data after the first two weeks of school and found that Jenna had only answered one question each week. They realized the vocabulary words specific to the history chapter were not programmed into her AAC device for those weeks. Jenna was supported by a paraprofessional who was new to the role and did not have experience with AAC devices. Due to busy schedules, the teacher and paraprofessional had been unable to collaborate to enter the vocabulary. The team arranged professional development and scheduled additional time for team members to collaborate and program the device. The school administration provided classroom coverage during training. Jenna's post-training performance was reviewed two weeks after the training. She was now answering all three of the questions posed each day, but was only 50% accurate in her answers. The team decided to have the speech language pathologist (SLP) observe in the class. The SLP noted that Jenna was sometimes slow in finding the answer she wanted and in those cases often answered incorrectly. They decided to have the paraprofessional go over the new vocabulary on Monday morning and collect data for two more weeks to see if Jenna would become more proficient in finding the vocabulary words she needed. The new data showed that Jenna was making excellent progress and no more changes were needed at that time.*

**KEY QUESTIONS**

- What performance criteria have been identified and agreed upon?
- How will the data identify barriers that should be removed?
- How will the data identify supports that need to be included?

6. *Changes are made* in the student's assistive technology services and educational program when evaluation data indicate that such changes are needed to improve student achievement.

   **Intent: During the process of reviewing evaluation data, the team decides whether changes or modifications need to be made in the AT, expected tasks, or factors within the environment. The team acts on those decisions and supports their implementation.**

   Flexibility in the provision of AT services is needed in order to support student progress. Evaluation of effectiveness data are collected in an ongoing manner and reviewed periodically in order to be responsive to changes in student need, achievement, environment and/or tasks. In the absence of sufficient progress, the team analyzes the data to decide what changes are needed such as additional scaffolding or adjustments to AT services or AT tools. Changes may also include specific intensive instruction to overcome an identified barrier. Some changes in student performance may result in a need for the IEP team to be reconvened to adjust the IEP goals. Analyzing data helps to pinpoint specific training or supports the student needs in order to support adequate progress in relationship to the predetermined criteria.

A consistent process of data collection, review, and sharing supports the team in determining the effectiveness of AT tools, services, and strategies. When the team analyzes the student performance, team members can make necessary adjustments and avoid errors such as assuming the student has skills that are not present, assuming the student does not have skills that are actually mastered, or prematurely abandoning the AT device.

*Mary Ellen showed minimal, unsatisfactory gains in comprehension as a result of using reading software that included text-to-speech. The team had expected a significant increase in comprehension as demonstrated on classroom quizzes. In reviewing the data, the team realized that her performance could be related to insufficient opportunities to use the program across settings since she was only using it in language arts. The team extended the trial period and identified additional environments (social studies and health classes) and natural opportunities in each of those classes (reading assignments at least three out of five days each week) in which the AT for reading could be used. The team agreed to meet again in one month to review the data gathered during the extended time frame and determine if the increased opportunities had been sufficient to increase Mary Ellen's comprehension.*

**KEY QUESTIONS**

- How is the performance data shared with all team members?
- When do periodic progress reviews take place?
- How are changes in the student's program determined in response to data?

7. **Evaluation of effectiveness is a dynamic, responsive, *ongoing process* that is reviewed periodically.**

   **Intent: Scheduled data collection occurs over time and changes are made in response to both expected and unexpected results. Data collection reflects measurement strategies appropriate to the individual student's needs. Team members evaluate and interpret data during periodic progress reviews.**

   In some instances the original data collection strategies planned by the team may not provide sufficient information to show what is happening. When creating and/or modifying the plan for evaluation of effectiveness, the team addresses the desired student outcomes as well as current skills in observation and data review. In developing the original evaluation plan, the team also determines the circumstances that will trigger the need to reexamine or initiate new data collection activities.

EXAMPLE

*During the IEP meeting, Stuart's team agreed to meet monthly to review data and make necessary changes in his AT use in response to the data. Stuart's goal was to complete math assignments with 90% accuracy using a talking calculator. At the first meeting, the data revealed that Stuart's accuracy on assignments had gone from 45% to 75%, but that his test performance had not changed. A plan was developed to observe Stewart during testing to provide additional data about his use of the calculator. The observational data showed that Stuart did not understand fractions and spent more than half of the test time struggling with the problems related to fractions then hurried through the rest of the test making mistakes. The special education resource teacher worked directly with Stuart to teach fractions. The team met again in one month to review his progress. His understanding of fractions had increased and his test performance was on target. His use of the talking calculator was not changed.*

**KEY QUESTIONS**

- What processes will the team use to analyze and respond to data?

- What circumstances will generate a need to reevaluate the effectiveness of current tools and strategies?

Evaluating the effectiveness of the AT that has been provided is an essential part of AT services. Unfortunately errors can occur in several ways such as when the team does not identify specific performance or behavior as a target for change; AT is provided without a performance goal in mind, making it difficult to determine progress; an easy and environmentally appropriate means of data collection has not been identified; or a regular schedule for reviewing data is not planned. Effective teams identify observable, measurable behavior that can be recorded to show changes in performance. Educators face a demanding schedule and must meet the needs of many students. When planning for data collection, it will be more workable if the educators who will be recording it participate in all of the decisions.

If progress is not as expected, it's important to remember that it may not be the AT tool, but failure to teach needed skills or provide enough time to master skills, that results in poor performance. One of the most common errors is deciding that the student has the "wrong" AT without first collecting effective data, analyzing it, and making changes to that student's program based on that analysis.

# Exploring the Quality Indicators for Evaluation of Effectiveness of Assistive Technology with the Self-Evaluation Matrix

The Self-Evaluation Matrix for Evaluation of Effectiveness of AT focuses on identifying the core components of evaluation of an intervention. Through its variations from "unacceptable" to "best practice" the matrix

- highlights the core components of evaluation of effectiveness of AT use,

- guides the team in planning for quality evaluation of student progress,

- helps identify strengths and areas of need, and

- facilitates the identification of processes or practices that may need to be changed.

The first quality indicator highlights the need for the student's entire team to be involved in planning and conducting the evaluation components. Indicators two, three, and four address the need to focus on student achievement by assuring that the data being collected is about performance that relates to one or more of the student's IEP goals, is measurable, and is evaluated across environments.

Indicators five and six are about analyzing the student's performance and using the information to make any changes that are needed in the student's program. The last indicator reminds us that the entire process of evaluating the effectiveness of AT use must be an ongoing process that is reviewed periodically.

Following the matrices is a case study about Janet, a ninth grader who hopes to work in the field of health some day. Her team is able to pinpoint areas for improvement and take action after using the Self-Evaluation Matrix for Evaluation of Effectiveness of AT.

# Quality Indicators for Self-Evaluation Matrix for Evaluation of Effectiveness of Assistive Technology

| QUALITY INDICATOR | UNACCEPTABLE | | |
|---|---|---|---|
| 1. Team members share *clearly defined responsibilities* to ensure that data are collected, evaluated, and interpreted by capable and credible team members. | 1 Responsibilities for data collection, evaluation, or interpretation are not defined. | 2 Responsibilities for data collection, evaluation, or interpretation of data are assigned to one team member. | |
| 2. Data are collected on specific student achievement that has been identified by the team and is *related to one or more goals*. | 1 Team neither identifies specific changes in student behaviors expected from AT use nor collects data. | 2 Team identifies student behaviors and collects data, but the behaviors are either not specific or not related to IEP goals. | |
| 3. Evaluation of effectiveness includes the *quantitative and qualitative* measurement of changes in the student's performance and achievement. | 1 Effectiveness is not evaluated. | 2 Evaluation of effectiveness is not based on student performance, but rather on subjective opinion. | |
| 4. Effectiveness is evaluated *across environments* including during naturally occurring opportunities as well as structured activities. | 1 Effectiveness is not evaluated in any environment. | 2 Effectiveness is evaluated only during structured opportunities in controlled environments (e.g., massed trials data). | |
| 5. Data are collected to provide teams with a means for analyzing *student achievement and identifying supports and barriers* that influence AT use to determine what changes, if any, are needed. | 1 No data are collected or analyzed. | 2 Data are collected but are not analyzed. | |
| 6. *Changes are made* in the student's AT services and educational program when evaluation data indicate that such changes are needed to improve student achievement. | 1 Program changes are never made. | 2 Program changes are made in the absence of data. | |
| 7. Evaluation of effectiveness is a dynamic, responsive, *ongoing process* that is reviewed periodically. | 1 No process is used to evaluate effectiveness. | 2 Evaluation of effectiveness only takes place annually, but the team does not make program changes based on data. | |

| 3 | 4 | 5 |
|---|---|---|
| Responsibilities for collection, evaluation, and interpretation of data are shared by some team members. | Responsibilities for collection, evaluation, and interpretation of data are shared by most team members. | Responsibilities for collection, evaluation, and interpretation of data are consistently shared by team members. |
| 3<br>Team identifies specific student behaviors related to IEP goals, but inconsistently collects data. | 4<br>Team identifies specific student behaviors related to IEP goals, and generally collects data. | 5<br>Team identifies specific student behaviors related to IEP goals, and consistently collects data on changes in those behaviors. |
| 3<br>Evaluation of effectiveness is not consistent or is based on limited data about student performance. | 4<br>Evaluation of effectiveness is generally based on quantitative and qualitative data about student performance from a few sources. | 5<br>Effectiveness is consistently evaluated using both quantitative and qualitative data about student's performance obtained from a variety of sources. |
| 3<br>Effectiveness is evaluated during structured activities across environments and a few naturally occurring opportunities. | 4<br>Effectiveness is generally evaluated during naturally occurring opportunities and structured activities in multiple environments. | 5<br>Effectiveness is consistently evaluated during naturally occurring opportunities and structured activities in multiple environments. |
| 3<br>Data are superficially analyzed. | 4<br>Data are sufficiently analyzed most of the time. | 5<br>Data are sufficiently analyzed all of the time. |
| 3<br>Program changes are loosely linked to student performance data. | 4<br>Program changes are generally linked to student performance data. | 5<br>Program changes are consistently linked to student performance data. |
| 3<br>Evaluation of effectiveness only takes place annually and the team uses the data to make annual program changes | 4<br>Evaluation of effectiveness takes place on an on-going basis and the team generally uses the data to make program changes. | 5<br>Evaluation of effectiveness takes place on an on-going basis and the team consistently uses the data to make program changes. |

# Exploring the Quality Indicators for Evaluation of Effectiveness of Assistive Technology Through Janet's Case Study

Janet is in the ninth grade. Her future goals are to be involved in the sciences, possibly the health field. She has a learning disability and has had an IEP since fourth grade. Janet has average auditory comprehension and difficulty with reading and writing. Her specially designed instruction made a significant difference in her fourth through eighth grade experiences where she has been served in the general education setting with paraprofessional and special education support. Her parents are involved in educational planning, but their work sometimes makes it difficult for them to come to meetings. During middle school, Janet became a more active participant on her own team. She not only attended meetings but became a more comfortable and confident self-advocate.

Janet's IEP goals are to improve: (a) reading comprehension, (b) task completion, and (c) specific mechanics of writing. Audio books and audio notes have been effective in helping her get necessary information from texts and were included in her IEP under Supplementary Aids and Services.

In ninth grade Janet moved from the middle school to the high school. She began experiencing difficulty with academic tasks and her new team met at the beginning of the second term to look at how her goals were being addressed. Team members reported that she was doing well in science while math, English, social studies, and history were very difficult. Tools and strategies that had supported her well at her previous school were no longer adequate in the new environments.

A portable word processor had been provided to her in expectation that this might be helpful in completing written assignments but several team members felt that it didn't provide enough support because it did not have text-to-speech feedback. The special education teacher provided mostly anecdotal data regarding completion of work done in English class. The data on which the team members based their conclusion that the portable word processor did not work well and that text-to-speech was helpful to Janet were captured by reviewing whether or not she had completed an essay of sufficient length in her English class. The quality of the essay itself was not evaluated.

Janet has also had success with a trial version of a text-to-speech program in her English class where students are expected to read a major literary work and write an essay each month. In that class, the general education teacher and special education teacher have a collaborative relationship. Because the technology was only available to her in her English class, Janet had difficulty arranging additional time to complete written assignments that her classmates were able to complete at home. The special education teacher collected data in Janet's English class but had difficulty finding the opportunity to share that data with the English teacher or any other team member.

Janet was not provided digital text formats for math, social studies, or history, so she could not use text-to-speech. Her teachers for these classes were concerned about Janet's performance, but did not see why they needed to be involved in the planning.

The team members were not specific in their initial communication and analysis of reading and writing goals and monitored only the number of written assignments completed and scores on reading comprehension tests. Some members of the team have stated that Janet could also benefit from use of word prediction software in her writing.

The team reviewed Janet's data and determined that using the portable word processor alone had resulted in her completing more of the required written assignments but they did not review the quality of that work. Her grades in English had improved in response to increased completion of work as reported by her English teacher. As they discussed how to better meet Janet's needs in other settings they addressed her history and social studies grades, which had been poor for two grading periods.

Although limited in time, the trial data from English class indicated that using text-to-speech software had been successful. They thought that using it in math, social studies, and history classes might improve her reading comprehension. Grades on classroom assignments and district level multiple choice tests would also need to be monitored more closely to measure comprehension.

There are a number of general education team members involved with Janet. Communication among team members is difficult. Challenges with scheduling have resulted in infrequent meetings and the special education teacher had to contact each teacher and compile the information they had. This provides infrequent opportunity for the team to collaborate and identify how things might be done across the various settings. The principal has noted that Janet is struggling in many areas and has asked the team to use a structured process to improve the services she is receiving. They scheduled three meetings that include Janet and her family during the next six months and began by rating themselves on the QIAT Self-Evaluation Matrix for Evaluation of Effectiveness of Assistive Technology.

# Application of the QIAT Self-Evaluation Matrix for Evaluation of Effectiveness of Assistive Technology by Janet's Team

1.  **Team members share *clearly defined responsibilities* to ensure that data are collected, evaluated, and interpreted by capable and credible team members.**

    **Discussion:** The special education teacher collected data in the resource room and in English, but had not had time or opportunity to share the data with other team members. The team discussed whether they should give themselves a rating of 2 or 3 in this area. They agreed that several people were willing to take data but had not done so. Only the special education teacher had collected and interpreted data.

    The team discussed their systems for sharing responsibilities for Janet's AT services. All team members, including Janet, indicated that they were willing and able to support her AT use after they received training and scheduled some meeting opportunities. The administrative staff at the high school will schedule time each week, or as needed, for the team to meet. The team expects to move from a 2 in this area to a 4 fairly quickly.

| 1 | 2 | 3 | 4 | 5 |
|---|---|---|---|---|
| Responsibilities for collection, evaluation, or interpretation of data are not defined. | **Responsibilities for collection, evaluation, or interpretation of data are assigned to one team member.** | Responsibilities for collection, evaluation, and interpretation of data are shared by some team members. | Responsibilities for collection, evaluation, and interpretation of data are shared by most team members. | Responsibilities for collection, evaluation, and interpretation of data are consistently shared by team members. |

2.  **Data are collected on specific student achievement that has been identified by the team and is *related to one or more goals*.**

    **Discussion:** For this indicator, they rated themselves a 2 because while the behaviors were *related* to the goals, they did not address the goals specifically enough to guide the team in making good decisions about the degree and manner in which the AT supported Janet in achieving the goals. As they became aware of the possibilities the technology offered, they were able to better match the AT more specifically to her goals.

| 1 | 2 | 3 | 4 | 5 |
|---|---|---|---|---|
| Team neither identifies specific changes in student behaviors expected from AT use nor collects data. | **Team identifies student behaviors and collects data, but the behaviors are either not specific or not related to IEP goals.** | Team identifies specific student behaviors related to IEP goals, but inconsistently collects data. | Team identifies specific student behaviors related to IEP goals, and generally collects data. | Team identifies specific student behaviors related to IEP goals, and consistently collects data on changes in those behaviors. |

3. **Evaluation of effectiveness includes the *quantitative and qualitative measurement of changes* in the student's performance and achievement.**

   **Discussion:** The team rated themselves a 3 for this indicator because they had initially relied only on teacher reports of effectiveness and had not yet begun to collect sufficient data to evaluate Janet's progress. The team felt that the newly instituted team collaboration and the data they would be collecting they could move quickly to a 4 or 5.

| 1 | 2 | 3 | 4 | 5 |
|---|---|---|---|---|
| Effectiveness is not evaluated. | Evaluation of effectiveness is not based on student performance, but rather on subjective opinion. | **Evaluation of effectiveness is not consistent or is based on limited data about student performance.** | Evaluation of effectiveness is generally based on quantitative and qualitative data about student performance from a few sources. | Effectiveness is consistently evaluated using both quantitative and qualitative data about student performance obtained from a variety of sources. |

4. **Effectiveness is evaluated *across environments* including during naturally occurring opportunities as well as structured activities.**

   **Discussion:** Initially, data were only taken in one environment and were not reviewed by the team. As a result of reviewing the Quality Indicators for Evaluation of Effectiveness of Assistive Technology, the team identified a need to collect data in Janet's English, math, social studies, and history classes and to structure supports for her in all classes. The team rated their evaluation efforts as a 2 because they only evaluated Janet's performance with AT in the limited environment of the resource room and English class. They planned to begin taking the same data in all Janet's classes and to improve data analysis and interpretation by meeting more frequently.

| 1 | 2 | 3 | 4 | 5 |
|---|---|---|---|---|
| Effectiveness is not evaluated in any environment. | **Effectiveness is evaluated only during structured opportunities in controlled environments (e.g., massed trials data).** | Effectiveness is evaluated during structured activities across environments and a few naturally occurring opportunities. | Effectiveness is generally evaluated during naturally occurring opportunities and structured activities in multiple environments. | Effectiveness is consistently evaluated during naturally occurring opportunities and structured activities in multiple environments. |

5. **Data are collected to provide teams with a means for** *analyzing student achievement and identifying supports and barriers* **that influence assistive technology use to determine what changes, if any, are needed.**

   **Discussion:** Team members felt that while the data from English class had been analyzed, other staff members would need to be involved in the analysis of achievement and identification of needed supports in other classes. They rated themselves a 2 overall, but felt they would give themselves a 4 with respect to the data collected for English and agreed to use the same strategies for her other classes. Future planning efforts for Janet will involve her directly so that she can develop self-advocacy skills and help identify barriers and additional tools she may need. The team will work with her family to determine what changes are needed in her use of AT.

| 1 | 2 | 3 | 4 | 5 |
|---|---|---|---|---|
| No data are collected or analyzed. | **Data are collected but are not analyzed.** | Data are superficially analyzed. | Data are sufficiently analyzed most of the time. | Data are sufficiently analyzed all of the time. |

6. *Changes are made* **in the student's assistive technology services and educational program when evaluation data indicate that such changes are needed to improve student achievement.**

   **Discussion:** The team felt they could better structure their work to regularly link program changes to Janet's performance data, but currently probably were a 3. When they had recognized that the portable word processor had not provided Janet with the support they felt she needed and had not yielded the results they expected, they had offered text-to-speech. The team noted that having frequent and inclusive team reviews would allow the team to evaluate the data and make changes more quickly.

| 1 | 2 | 3 | 4 | 5 |
|---|---|---|---|---|
| Program changes are never made. | Program changes are made in the absence of data. | **Program changes are loosely linked to student performance data.** | Program changes are generally linked to student performance data. | Program changes are consistently linked to student performance data. |

7. **Evaluation of effectiveness is a dynamic, responsive, *ongoing process* that is reviewed periodically.**

   **Discussion:** The team scored their work in ongoing evaluation of effectiveness as a 4. They had set a schedule and process for on-going communication among team members. The team identified several strategies for data review that included regular check-in dates by email along with review of her achievement data at their regular quarterly meetings. The team also identified benchmarks in Janet's achievement that would trigger a data review to determine whether a change in her program was necessary. Review of data by all team members and collaborative problem solving were used to make their evaluation of effectiveness more responsive to Janet's performance.

| 1 | 2 | 3 | 4 | 5 |
|---|---|---|---|---|
| No process is used to evaluate effectiveness. | Evaluation of effectiveness only takes place annually, but the team does not make program changes based on data. | Evaluation of effectiveness only takes place annually and the team uses the data to make annual program changes. | **Evaluation of effectiveness takes place on an ongoing basis and the team generally uses the data to make program changes.** | Evaluation of effectiveness takes place on an ongoing basis and the team consistently uses the data to make program changes. |

## Summary

Throughout a student's educational experience there are many moves to new classes, schools, and programs. Successfully transferring AT to these new settings can be challenging. The next chapter highlights AT transition.

## Suggested Activities

1. Using Gordon's Case Study from Chapter 5, design a plan to collect data on Gordon's performance in first grade that would have helped the team realize his lack of progress and make changes earlier.

2. View the webinar evaluating the effectiveness of AT at Ablenet University Webinar Series *https://www.ablenetinc.com/resources/recorded_webinars/*. Sign in and search the list of recorded videos on AT.

   View *QIAT Session 6: Evaluation of Effectiveness* by Jane Korsten and Terry Foss. What three ideas were most significant to you? How will you implement them?

3. Use the form Plan for Evaluation of Effectiveness of AT Use from Appendix D to develop a plan to evaluate a student's AT usage. If you do not know a student personally, develop a plan for one of the students presented in a case study in another chapter.

4.  Search the Internet and find two ideas for collecting or analyzing data that you believe could be used to evaluate the effectiveness of an AT device for a student. Explain how and why you would use those two ideas.

5.  Review iPad apps and find one that you can use as part of a plan to evaluate the effectiveness of an AT device (or app) for a student. Explain how and why you believe your plan would work.

# CHAPTER 7

# Exploring the Quality Indicators for Assistive Technology in Transition

1. *Transition plans address assistive technology needs* of the student, including roles and training needs of team members, subsequent steps in assistive technology use, and follow-up after transition takes place.

2. Transition *planning empowers the student* using assistive technology *to participate* in the transition planning at a level appropriate to age and ability.

3. *Advocacy related to assistive technology use is recognized as critical* and planned for by the teams involved in transition.

4. *AT requirements in the receiving environment* are identified during the transition planning process.

5. Transition planning for students using assistive technology proceeds according to an *individualized timeline*.

6. Transition plans address specific *equipment, training, and funding issues* such as transfer or acquisition of assistive technology, manuals, and support documents.

Transitions in education agencies can be from early intervention to early childhood special education (Part C to Part B of IDEA services), early childhood special education to K–12 education, classroom to classroom within the same school, school to school, or school to post-secondary settings or work. There are themes and needs that are consistent across all transitions and planning for these transitions ensures that the student's use of assistive technology (AT) continues uninterrupted.

Transitions that include AT involve individuals from both sending and receiving settings working together. Transition plans for students who use AT address the ways in which the student's use of AT devices and services are transferred from one setting to another and how the student's needs will be met in the new environment. Self-determination and advocacy become increasingly important as the student approaches the transition to a post-secondary setting. In fact, the research about AT use by successful adults shows that in addition to being skilled at operating their AT, success may depend on being able to advocate for themselves and have skills that allow them to be, to the best of their ability, self-determined (Fried-Oken, Bersani, Anctil, & Bowser, 1998).

1. *Transition plans address the assistive technology needs* of the student, including roles and training needs of team members, subsequent steps in assistive technology use, and follow-up after transition takes place.

    **Intent: The transition plan assists the receiving agency/team to successfully provide needed supports for the AT user. This involves the assignment of responsibilities and the establishment of accountability.**

    As students prepare to transition to new settings within the same school or to a different location, it is important to plan for and address the continued need for AT. When the transition is to a post-secondary setting, a transition plan, which is part of the IEP, is developed and includes a specific focus on transition. The IEP team expands to include key stakeholders from the receiving environment, vocational rehabilitation, or other agency personnel as appropriate as the team determines who is important to include on the new team.

    The plan includes supports and services needed to ensure functional use of the individual's AT in the receiving environment. To facilitate accountability, the IEP team identifies training needs, assigns individual responsibilities, and establishes specific roles and tasks. Teams establish the expectation that AT will be used in the new environments and identify, in writing, the specifics of what, why, how, when, and where it will be used. Using a planning form such as the *Transition Planning Worksheet for AT Users* in Appendix D to guide planning can facilitate the process. A planning form will help the team address important issues such as those in Tables 7.1 and 7.2. It can also help to identify areas of instruction that the student may need in preparation for the new setting.

| GENERAL TRANSITION TASKS TO BE COMPLETED |
| --- |
| Staff members from current setting observe in future setting. |
| Student/family visit future setting. |
| Staff from both settings meet to plan. |
| Arrange enrollment in needed non-school services (e.g., Developmental Disabilities, Vocational Rehabilitation). |
| Other: |

**TABLE 7.1** General Transition tasks to be completed for transition.

| DEVICE-SPECIFIC TASKS TO BE COMPLETED |
| --- |
| Name/Type of AT Used: _____ |
| Arrange transfer of technology including manuals and service records. |
| Create artifacts to demonstrate current level of use and independence (e.g., video recording, work samples). |

**TABLE 7.2** Device specific tasks to be completed for transition.

| DEVICE-SPECIFIC TASKS TO BE COMPLETED |
|---|
| Identify any new AT that may be needed in future setting. |
| Identify sources of funding for new AT, if needed. |
| Identify persons to do troubleshooting in future setting. |
| Other: |

Once a plan is developed, teams designate individuals to take responsibility for all aspects of implementing it. An individual team member is assigned to monitor accomplishment of the overall plan and the student's progress toward meeting IEP goals. Perhaps the single most common error that occurs in transition is inadequate communication and coordination between the sending and receiving agencies. The individual student can be left without needed arrangements and supports when he or she arrives in the new setting. Sometimes there is a philosophical difference between sending and receiving agencies that can also lead to a failure to implement the use of AT that was beneficial to the student in the previous setting.

EXAMPLE

*Aaron was transitioning from Markham Elementary School to Parkview Middle School within the same district. At the elementary school he used a portable computer with word prediction software that assisted him in the writing process and digital text with supported reading software to access textbooks. The team from the elementary school met with the lead teacher and the AT case manager from the middle school.*

*During the meeting, they all worked together to identify concerns that needed to be addressed. Aaron would be transitioning from a single classroom to a setting where he would be moving between classrooms. Concerns included transport of equipment, battery life, charging responsibilities, printer access, assignment completion, and identification* of accommodations needed for instruction and testing. The challenges in the new setting included interactions with multiple teachers, security from possible theft, and teachers' experience with AT.

Based on the jointly created written transition plan for Aaron, the team at Parkview Middle School attended a summer workshop to learn the operational features and functional use of the portable computer that he would bring with him from his elementary school. The receiving case manager began the process of acquiring his new textbooks in a digital format. Each of the concerns was addressed with team members accepting specific roles and responsibilities. Aaron was assigned the responsibility to ensure that the portable computer was charged and to inform the case manager immediately if there were any additional issues, such as not being able to print.

The case manager for the middle school team wrote a description of Aaron's needs and the accommodations that would be a part of his program. She scheduled a meeting in one month to include his elementary school teacher, so that Parkview teachers could consult with her and ask clarifying questions about the use of his AT in middle school.

**KEY QUESTIONS**

- What are the guidelines for documenting AT transition needs in the IEP?

- How do sending and receiving teams participate in development of an IEP when preparing for transition?

- How are roles and responsibilities to support transition documented in the IEP?

- How is information about students' current AT use, skills, and needs conveyed to the receiving environment (e.g., written descriptions, video, observations)?

2. **Transition *planning empowers the student* using assistive technology to participate in the transition planning at a level appropriate to age and ability.**

   **Intent: Specific self-determination skills are taught that enable the student to gradually assume responsibility for participation and leadership in AT transition planning as capacity develops. AT tools are provided, as needed, to support the student's participation.**

   Self-determination is the ability to be a causal agent in one's own life and has been identified as a critical factor in the continued use of AT in new environments (Fried-Oken, Bersani, Anctil, & Bowser, 1998). Explicit instruction in skills needed for self-determination in relation to one's AT can begin as soon as a student starts to use AT devices, allowing many opportunities to practice.

Wehmeyer and Field (2007) list choice-making, decision-making, problem-solving, goal-setting and attainment, self-regulation/self-management, and self-advocacy and leadership as critical skill areas for self-determination. When specific instruction is provided in these areas, students develop more self-awareness, self-knowledge, and more positive perceptions of control, efficacy, and outcome expectations. Students can also develop self-determination skills, such as problem-solving and choice-making, as those skills relate to AT. Opportunities to use these skills help students increase independence, involvement in transition planning, and success in the new setting.

Students who have been appropriately involved in IEP development throughout their school experience have greater access and independence during transitions and are better prepared to participate in transition planning. Participation can include tools and strategies that help the student plan the agenda, organize ideas, present thoughts, or use an AT device as a planning tool (e.g., use an AAC device during transition planning meetings). As members of their own IEP team, they are empowered to participate in expressing their needs and preferences regarding use of AT and other aspects of their program. Over time, students who use AT have the opportunity to learn self-determination skills at a level commensurate with their age, ability, and comfort level.

**EXAMPLE**

*Emily was a junior at Lincoln High School. During her IEP meeting, she advocated for herself using her AAC device to narrate a computer slide presentation she developed explaining the kinds of work she was hoping to be able to do after high school. Emily used her AAC device to ask questions about the kind of assistance she could expect if she entered college or a vocational-technical program and her personal goals were included in her plan. Another meeting was planned after Emily visited two post-secondary settings and learned what strategies she would need for successful transitions.*

**KEY QUESTIONS**

▪ How does the agency ensure that students are active participants in transition planning?

▪ What instruction do students receive to learn and demonstrate self-determination skills at an appropriate level?

▪ How do students use AT to support and increase participation in transition planning?

3. ***Advocacy related to assistive technology use is recognized as critical*** **and planned for by the teams involved in transition.**

   **Intent: Everyone involved in transition advocates for the student's progress, including the student's use of AT. Specific advocacy tasks related to AT use are addressed and may be carried out by the student, the family, staff members, or a representative.**

   As students transition to new environments, advocacy may be needed to support the continued use of AT, provide technical assistance when the AT is not working, and help determine when new AT devices are needed. Some students can self-advocate, while parents, caregivers and others in the new environment may need to provide additional encouragement and support for continued AT use. Advocacy activities, with roles and assigned tasks, ensure the students' continued progress. To the greatest extent possible, students learn and use self-advocacy skills and apply them before, during, and after transitions to participate in AT decision-making as well as other aspects of the transitions.

   For some students, the complexity of the disability makes it difficult to self-advocate. In these situations, it is important that a family member, supportive adult, friend, or professional who understands the student's AT use and preferences for future use of AT, can advocate during and after the transition. Without someone to advocate for continued AT use, the chances that AT will be a part of a successful transition are significantly reduced. For students who have limited advocacy skills there are processes that can help ensure that their interests are well represented. One of these processes, Person Centered Planning (Amado & McBride, 2001), can be used very effectively in transition planning that includes the use of AT. Using a process such as Person Centered Planning assists students, educators, family members, and other advocates chosen by the student to identify dreams, goals, and concerns for the future. It also helps to create a vision of how the student can begin to take leadership and advocate for quality of life issues. When AT is included in person centered planning discussions, everyone on the team can better understand the purpose of AT use in new environments.

EXAMPLE

*When Sven entered kindergarten, his IEP included the services of a teacher of the Deaf and Hard of Hearing (DHH). One of her responsibilities was to check his hearing aid batteries on a regular basis to make sure that they were functioning properly. By the third grade, the DHH teacher had taught Sven to check his own hearing aid batteries on the same schedule. He had also learned to replace batteries himself and he used a chart to keep track of the times when he had to replace the batteries.*

*After Sven had become independent with the management of his own hearing aides, his teachers began to help him develop some new self-advocacy skills. In fourth grade, Sven attended meetings with his DHH teacher and general education teachers. The DHH teacher explained the accommodations that Sven needed because of his hearing loss and helped teachers identify the things they needed to do in order to provide the accommodations that were listed on his IEP. By the time Sven moved to middle school, he had learned to lead the conversations about accommodations with his new teachers and the DHH teacher attended the meetings as an observer and extra support. In high school, Sven began to talk with his teachers independently. If his IEP accommodations were not being provided, he knew how to contact the DHH teacher and ask for help. By the time he moved from the K–12 educational system to a community college program, he knew what accommodations were important for him and how to request them from the college.*

**KEY QUESTIONS**

- How do team members actively advocate for students?

- How do students demonstrate self-advocacy skills during planning?

- If a student needs assistance to advocate for AT in the new environment, what is the process for identifying an advocate?

4. **Assistive technology requirements in the receiving environment are identified during the transition planning process.**

   **Intent: Environmental requirements, skill demands, and needed AT support are determined in order to plan appropriately. This determination is made collaboratively and with active participation by representatives from both sending and receiving environments.**

   The transition process includes opportunities for communication between settings; visits by the students, parents, and teachers; and planning meetings that include all needed team members. Team members from both sending and receiving environments work collaboratively during transition planning. In order to plan appropriately, team members identify environmental requirements, new tasks, equipment needs, and training needs, as well as services, service providers, and supports that will be needed in the new setting. Examples of tasks related to AT that may be necessary in the new environment include the need to move the technology from class to class, to access a remote printer for written assignments, or to use a new computer platform. In some instances, the new setting will have increased demands to communicate with multiple teachers, school staff, and peers. Team members in the sending environment help prepare the student by providing experiences and practice in using new skills that will be needed before the time for transition arrives.

*Shayna used text-to-speech and word prediction software for all writing tasks of more than three sentences. As Shayna's team began to plan for her move to middle school, the middle school team members pointed out that the new school has Windows platform computers rather than the Mac OS computers used at the elementary school. The team made plans to help Shayna with her transition by acquiring a Windows platform computer and the Windows-based version of the software she used for reading and writing. The team developed a plan to provide training for her in the operational use of the Windows computer and software during the spring before she moved to her new school.*

KEY QUESTIONS

- What does a review of the new environment reveal about the range of required tasks?

- What changes in the AT, if any, will be needed for the student to participate and achieve in the new environment?

- What opportunities to practice needed skills will the student have before the transition?

5. **Transition planning for students using assistive technology proceeds according to an *individualized timeline*.**

   **Intent: Transition planning timelines are adjusted based on specific needs of the student and differences in environments. Timelines address well-mapped action steps with specific target dates and ongoing opportunities for reassessment.**

   Timelines are developed and adjusted based on specific student needs or changes in the environment, required tasks, and changes in student abilities. Timelines include action steps, when they will be taken, persons responsible for those actions, and target dates for completion. Skills and use of AT are reviewed periodically and the review includes plans for ongoing re-assessment before, during, and after the transition. New timelines and new use of tools may be necessary based on data gathered.

   For transitions to post-secondary services, federal law requires that an individualized timeline is developed and documented for the transition no later than age 16. In some states, the age required to begin transition planning is earlier than age 16. It is important to know the specific rules for your state when beginning transition planning. In the timeline, AT needs and activities that require use of AT are addressed. The timeline may include tasks such as acquisition of a new device or software, AT practice in the new environment, direct instruction in communication with new people, guidance in independent AT use, visitations to potential settings, and meetings with service providers.

EXAMPLE

*Kristoff began using an AAC device during his early elementary years. His device was upgraded as upgrades became available and moved with him from setting to setting, including from elementary to middle school. Before each transition, meetings were scheduled with staff in the new setting to share information regarding use of his AAC device, introduction of new skills, development of new vocabulary, and inclusion strategies for instruction and assessment.*

*Because of Kristoff's complex communication needs and the number of teachers involved, planning for his transition to high school started in February. The team from the high school attended training on his AAC device in May, so that they knew the basics of operating and managing his AAC device and had a plan to address potential issues. They also visited the middle school to observe classroom strategies that were effective for him in that setting. A contact person was identified from both the middle school and the high school to quickly address any issues that might arise. They also met with the high school vice principal, so that she would be aware and informed about Kristoff's needs and their plan to address them should specific support be needed.*

**KEY QUESTIONS**

- How and when are timelines for preparing for transition developed?
- When are timelines reviewed and adjusted?
- Where and how are timelines and responsibilities documented in the IEP?

6. **Transition plans address specific *equipment, training, and funding* issues, such as transfer or acquisition of assistive technology, manuals, and support documents.**

   **Intent: A plan is developed to ensure that the AT equipment, hardware, and/ or software arrive in working condition accompanied by any needed manuals. Provisions for ongoing maintenance and technical support are included in the plan.**

   Equipment, training, and funding needs are identified and addressed when students transition to new environments. A review of the tasks that the student will need to accomplish in the receiving environment includes an evaluation to determine if the student's current AT is appropriate in the new environment or if different equipment is needed. If new equipment is needed, local funding options are explored as appropriate and a plan to obtain equipment, training, and supports for the student in the receiving environment becomes part of the transition planning process. Next steps are identified, roles are assigned, and appropriate agencies are notified. If necessary service providers have not been identified, the plan includes developing strategies to include the needed providers.

During any transition, whether the student remains in school or moves on to a new program or setting, just providing equipment is not enough. People who have never seen the student in action will need help in understanding how AT helps with functional capabilities and what is needed to support that AT use. For example, when Lance moved from middle school to high school, he stopped turning in the written assignments created on his portable computer. When his new teachers asked him why, he reported that he needed a printer cable that was accessible from the front of the computer attached to printers in each of his classes. Once cables were provided, Lance began to turn in his written assignments with the same frequency that he had in middle school. When a student stops using AT in the new environment, it may be because day-to-day management of equipment is not supported, making AT use difficult.

EXAMPLE

*Ahmed and his transition planning team, which included representatives of the school district, developmental disabilities services, the supported work site, and the group home to which Ahmed was moving, identified the specific equipment he had been using at school. This included a direct select augmentative and alternative communication (AAC) device with 32 options, a single talking switch used to ask for assistance, and a jig for an electric stapler that allowed proper alignment and insertion of papers. The school also provided a portfolio of information about how Ahmed used the AAC devices.*

*The supported work site had the equipment needed for the stapling task but was not able to provide either of the communication devices. The team determined that additional funding would be required to purchase these and also realized that services available to Ahmed did not include a speech language pathologist (SLP). A community-based SLP was identified and the team acquired funding through Medicaid for equipment purchase and periodic review and updating of vocabulary on Ahmed's AAC device.*

When the school owns the current AT, what arrangements are made to provide needed AT in the new environment?

If needed, when and how are funding options for new AT identified and accessed?

In post-secondary transitions, what is the process for identifying AT services and potential providers that will be needed in the new setting?

In post-secondary transitions, what are the referral processes for the agencies that should be contacted?

## Exploring the Quality Indicators for Assistive Technology in Transition with the QIAT Self-Evaluation Matrix

The Self-Evaluation Matrix for Assistive Technology in Transition focuses on a key part of effective transition, the planning that takes place in preparation for the transition. The matrix describes situations ranging from the unacceptable to promising practices for each of the Quality Indicators for Assistive Technology in Transition. Although the descriptors may not match exactly the situation in a given education agency, the user will evaluate each statement to determine which most closely describes practice in that agency. The choice of five alternatives

- helps users evaluate the status of their performance on each aspect of transition,

- provides a means to recognize areas of strength and areas in need of improvement,

- identifies characteristics of promising practices in each core component, and

- serves as a means to monitor improvements in transition planning.

Planning is a theme that runs throughout the six Quality Indicators for Assistive Technology in Transition. The first indicator addresses the importance of AT needs being included in transition planning. The second indicator is about empowering student participation in the planning process. The third indicator is about advocacy related to the use of the AT, whether it is done by the student or by a representative. Indicator five focuses on having an appropriate and effective timeline, while indicators four and six are about ensuring that AT needs are well-addressed in the receiving environments.

Following the matrix, the case study about Emma illustrates the importance of all the components of AT transition.

# Quality Indicators for Assistive Technology in *Transition*

| QUALITY INDICATOR | UNACCEPTABLE | | |
|---|---|---|---|
| **1.** *Transition plans address the AT needs* of the student, including roles and training needs of team members, subsequent steps in AT use, and follow-up after transition takes place. | 1<br>Transition plans do not address AT needs. | 2<br>Transition plans rarely address AT needs, critical roles, steps, or follow-up. | |
| **2.** Transition *planning empowers the student* using AT to participate in the transition planning at a level appropriate to age and ability. | 1<br>Student is not present. | 2<br>Student may be present but does not participate or input is ignored. | |
| **3.** *Advocacy related to AT use is recognized as critical* and planned for by the teams involved in transition. | 1<br>No one advocates for AT use or the development of student's self-determination skills. | 2<br>Advocacy rarely occurs for AT use or the development of student self-determination skills. | |
| **4.** *AT requirements in the receiving environment* are identified during the transition planning process. | 1<br>AT requirements in the receiving environment are not identified. | 2<br>AT requirements in the receiving environment are rarely identified. | |
| **5.** Transition planning for students using AT proceeds according to an *individualized timeline.* | 1<br>Individualized timelines are not developed to support transition planning for students using AT. | 2<br>Individualized timelines are developed, but do not support transition planning for students using AT. | |
| **6.** Transition plans address specific *equipment, training, and funding* issues, such as transfer or acquisition of AT, manuals, and support documents. | 1<br>The plans do not address AT equipment, training, and funding issues. | 2<br>The plans rarely address AT equipment, training, and/or funding issues. | |

| | | |
|---|---|---|
| 3<br><br>Transition plans sometimes address AT needs but may not include critical roles, steps, or follow-up. | 4<br><br>Transition plans always address AT needs and usually include critical roles, steps, or follow-up. | 5<br><br>Transition plans consistently address AT needs and all team members are involved and knowledgeable about critical roles, steps, and follow-up. |
| 3<br><br>Student sometimes participates and some student input is considered. | 4<br><br>Student participates and student input is generally reflected in the transition plan. | 5<br><br>Student is a full participant and student input is consistently reflected in the transition plan. |
| 3<br><br>Advocacy sometimes occurs for AT use and the development of student self-determination skills. | 4<br><br>Advocacy usually occurs for AT use and the development of student self-determination skills. | 5<br><br>Advocacy consistently occurs for AT use and the development of student self-determination skills. |
| 3<br><br>AT requirements in the receiving environment are identified, some participants are involved, and some requirements are addressed. | 4<br><br>AT requirements in the receiving environment are identified, most participants are involved, and most requirements are addressed. | 5<br><br>AT requirements in the receiving environment are consistently identified by all participants. |
| 3<br><br>Individualized timelines are sometimes developed and support transition planning for students using AT. | 4<br><br>Individualized timelines are generally developed and support transition planning for students using AT. | 5<br><br>Individualized timelines are consistently developed and support transition planning for students using AT. |
| 3<br><br>The plans sometimes address AT equipment, training, or funding issues. | 4<br><br>The plans usually address AT equipment, training, and funding issues. | 5<br><br>The plans consistently address AT equipment, training, and funding issues. |

# Exploring the Quality Indicators for Assistive Technology in Transition Through Emma's Case Study

Emma is a senior in high school and has been identified as a student on the Autism Spectrum with a learning disability in the area of written communication. She plans to walk through graduation with her senior class, although she has not completed all of the requirements for a full diploma. She will continue her school district enrollment in the fall but attend classes at the local community college. During her junior and senior year in high school, Emma explored several post-secondary education options and visited a local community college that offers a computer-maintenance and repair program. During her spring IEP meeting, a plan was developed that would allow Emma to be dually enrolled in the high school and in the community college, completing requirements for her high school diploma at the same time that she began taking the initial computer-maintenance and repair  classes.

During the summer, Emma and her parents attended an open house at the college. It was sponsored by the Office of Disability Services. The counselor who spoke at the orientation reminded everyone that, if students with disabilities were using AT as a part of their educational program, they should bring in documentation of that AT use as soon as possible. He also gave everyone a list of the AT options that the office supported. Emma and her parents agreed to look over the list and bring it to a summer IEP meeting that had been planned by the school district to help with her transition to community college.

Emma had used a computer program for writing for many years. The program has a text-to-speech feature, a talking dictionary and thesaurus, and word prediction that also could be read aloud when needed. She was partially independent in using it and was working with a paraprofessional to learn new features of the software.

A problem arose when everyone on Emma's IEP team realized that the college list of supported software did not include the software that she was accustomed to using. Some of the team members were under the impression that the college had to provide any software that Emma needed, but other team members were pretty sure that there were only a few options for AT software programs at the community college. The IEP team decided to invite one of the counselors from the Office of Disability Services to another IEP meeting to help explain how the program supported AT use.

At the second IEP meeting of the summer, the main topic of conversation was Emma's need for AT. Her college counselor attended and shared with the team that the college did not provide all the possible AT programs that students might use, but had a selection of AT available that could meet the needs of most students with disabilities. The college did provide similar software to what Emma needed in several computer labs but it was not the same program. The counselor also explained that the college would not install specialized software on Emma's computer. Their responsibility was to make sure that students have access, but not to provide all possible AT solutions.

The team, including Emma and her parents, discussed which option she should use. They questioned whether she should use software provided by the college or continue using the software she already knew. After much discussion, a poll showed that the majority of team members thought Emma should learn the program provided at the community college so that there would always be someone who could help her with it.

Even though most of the team members were in agreement, Emma was not convinced. She said in the meeting that she didn't like change and learning a new software program, even though it was very similar, would be very hard for her. Emma thought that a new school and new classes would be really hard and she did not want to do another hard thing. Because she would be dually enrolled, the team agreed that the school district would install the familiar software on Emma's laptop computer and arrange to transfer the license so that she could use it at the college. The vocational rehabilitation counselor committed to arranging for purchase of the needed software after graduation from high school.

Emma's mom and dad were proud of her participation in the meeting. It was the first time they had seen her actively advocate for her own educational goals. They volunteered to monitor her progress in college classes and supported her decision to stick with the familiar software. Because she was over 18, Emma needed to give the college permission to share information with her parents. She signed a release of information form so that they could see her grades and talk to her college counselor about her progress.

As they completed the transition planning activities for AT, Emma's team realized they had waited too long to address them. The team decided to use the Quality Indicators for Assistive Technology in Transition to review what they had done and to identify steps they might have addressed in a different way.

# Application of the QIAT Self-Evaluation Matrix for Assistive Technology in Transition by Emma's Team

1. *Transition plans address assistive technology needs* of the student, including roles and training needs of team members, subsequent steps in assistive technology use, and follow-up after transition takes place.

   **Discussion:** Emma's team realized they had not addressed her AT use when developing her transition plan. They had not collected information about technology in the new educational setting and were surprised when they found that her technology use might need to change. If it had not been for the reminder about AT from the college, they would not have addressed it at all. They rated their performance on this indicator a 1.

| 1 | 2 | 3 | 4 | 5 |
|---|---|---|---|---|
| **Transition plans do not address AT needs.** | Transition plans rarely address AT needs, critical roles, steps, or follow-up. | Transition plans sometimes address AT needs but may not include critical roles, steps, or follow-up. | Transition plans always address AT needs and usually include critical roles, steps, or follow-up. | Transition plans consistently address AT needs and all team members are involved and knowledgeable about critical roles, steps, and follow-up. |

2. Transition *planning empowers the student* using assistive technology *to participate* in the transition planning at a level appropriate to age and ability.

   **Discussion:** Emma had attended all of her own IEP meetings. She was an active participant and knew how to present her own ideas. With support from other team members and her parents, she was able to present her ideas about her future AT use. Because the team focused on Emma's self-determination, she was able to advocate for her position about the technology she would use at college. As they reviewed this indicator, they felt they had done a good job of including and addressing Emma's concerns and rated their performance a 5.

| 1 | 2 | 3 | 4 | 5 |
|---|---|---|---|---|
| Student is not present. | Student may be present but does not participate or input is ignored. | Student sometimes participates and some student input is considered. | Student participates and student input is generally reflected in the transition plan. | **Student is a full participant and student input is consistently reflected in the transition plan.** |

3. *Advocacy related to assistive technology use is recognized as critical* and **planned for by the teams involved in transition.**

   **Discussion:** As Emma moved from a public school program to college participation, her parents agreed to take a more active role in advocating for and monitoring her AT use. However, as the district reviewed their own involvement in AT planning, they realized that district staff members were not taking an active role in advocating for Emma's AT use. Their rating for this indicator was a 3.

| 1 | 2 | 3 | 4 | 5 |
|---|---|---|---|---|
| No one advocates for AT use or the development of student's self-determination skills. | Advocacy rarely occurs for AT use or the development of student self-determination skills. | **Advocacy sometimes occurs for AT use and the development of student self-determination skills.** | Advocacy usually occurs for AT use and the development of student self-determination skills. | Advocacy consistently occurs for AT use and the development of student self-determination skills. |

4. *Assistive technology requirements in the receiving environment* are identified **during the transition planning process.**

   **Discussion:** Once it had been called to their attention, the team worked hard to include Emma's AT use in her transition plan. But by that time, it was almost too late to make all the arrangements. The team rated their performance a 2.

| 1 | 2 | 3 | 4 | 5 |
|---|---|---|---|---|
| AT requirements in the receiving environment are not identified. | **AT requirements in the receiving environment are rarely identified.** | AT requirements in the receiving environment are identified, some participants are involved and some requirements are addressed. | AT requirements in the receiving environment are identified, most participants are involved and most requirements are addressed. | AT requirements in the receiving environment are consistently identified by all participants. |

5. **Transition planning for students using assistive technology proceeds according to an** *individualized timeline.*

   **Discussion:** The team felt the timeline for Emma's transition had been reasonable. But realized that if they had addressed her AT needs in relation to her dislike of change, they would have started sooner to address the differing technology at the post-secondary setting. Their self-rating was a 2.

| 1 | 2 | 3 | 4 | 5 |
|---|---|---|---|---|
| Individualized timelines are not developed to support transition planning for students using AT. | **Individualized timelines are developed, but do not support transition planning for students using AT.** | Individualized timelines are sometimes developed and support transition planning for students using AT. | Individualized timelines are generally developed and support transition planning for students using AT. | Individualized timelines are consistently developed and support transition planning for students using AT. |

6. **Transition plans address specific *equipment, training, and funding issues* such as transfer or acquisition of assistive technology, manuals, and support documents.**

   **Discussion:** Once they became aware of Emma's transition needs around AT, the team felt that they did good planning for her equipment use and ensured that all of the AT software she needed was available to her. Because they realized there would be future changes in Emma's AT needs as she left the public school system, their self-rating was a 4.

| 1 | 2 | 3 | 4 | 5 |
|---|---|---|---|---|
| The plans do not address AT equipment, training, and funding issues. | The plans rarely address AT equipment, training, and funding issues. | The plans sometimes address AT equipment, training, and funding issues. | **The plans usually address AT equipment, training, and funding issues.** | The plans consistently address AT equipment, training, and funding issues. |

## Summary

The next chapter is the first of two chapters that address agency-wide aspects of AT services rather than child-specific actions. It explores the importance of administrative support of AT service delivery and highlights core components.

## Suggested Activities

1. Research the issue of self-determination. What are the components of self-determination? How is it developed? How does it relate to successful AT use?

2. View the webinar on AT in transition at Ablenet University at *https://www .ablenetinc.com/resources/recorded_webinars/*. Sign in and search the recorded videos on AT. View *QIAT Session 7: AT Transition* by Gayl Bowser and Diana Carl. What three points are most significant to you? What do you feel is often overlooked in transition planning? How can you implement their suggestions?

3. Search the Internet for AT Transition checklists or packets. Choose two and compare and contrast them. How do they differ? How do you see either of them being useful in preparing for a smooth transition?

4. Using the *Transition Planning Document for AT Users* in Appendix D, develop a plan for a student that you know or a student described in one of the case studies from any chapter. What timeline do you think is needed? What areas are of most concern? What steps will the sending and receiving teams need to take?

5. Read the *Family Information Guide to Assistive Technology and Transition Planning* from *www.fctd.info/show/fig_summary*. How would you use this resource with families? What are the most useful aspects of the guide?

# CHAPTER 8

# Exploring the Quality Indicators for Administrative Support of Assistive Technology Services

1.  The education agency has *written procedural guidelines* that ensure equitable access to assistive technology devices and services for students with disabilities, if required, for a free, appropriate, public education (FAPE).

2.  The education agency *broadly disseminates* clearly defined procedures for accessing and providing assistive technology services, and supports the implementation of those guidelines.

3.  The education agency includes appropriate assistive technology responsibilities in *written descriptions of job requirements* for each position in which activities impact assistive technology services.

4.  The education agency employs *personnel with the competencies* needed to support quality assistive technology services within their primary areas of responsibility at all levels of the organization.

5.  The education agency includes *assistive technology in the technology planning and budgeting process.*

6.  The education agency provides access to *ongoing learning opportunities about assistive technology* for staff, family, and students.

7.  The education agency uses a *systematic process to evaluate* all components of the agency-wide assistive technology program.

$S$upport from administration is absolutely essential for quality AT services to be developed and sustained. This chapter addresses the core components of administrative support for AT services, providing examples and resources.

Sometimes administrators do not recognize the important role they play in establishing and supporting fair, efficient, and cost-effective AT services. They may assume that the AT team members "take care of all of that," but without knowledgeable and supportive administrators, AT services may fail. The most common error in the area of administrative support occurs when there is no formal support provided. There may be personal support where one or more administrators express their personal appreciation of an individual or a team, but do not take action to provide guidance, allocate resources, or understand procedures. Personal support without programmatic support leads to statements such as, "Oh, assistive technology? I leave all of that to our AT specialist, John. He does a terrific job." When this happens, it's typical that AT leadership personnel try to or are expected to be the sole source all of the effort required to provide AT devices and services.

As evidenced by the previous chapters, especially consideration, implementation, and evaluation of effectiveness, all educators who come into contact with a student using AT have a role to play in supporting that student. This will occur only when an informed administrator holds every educator accountable to make it happen. Administrators have influence over multiple aspects of the agency including funding, allocation of resources, meeting time, staff accountability, staff recognition, and other incentives. The individuals involved in the direct provision of AT services have little or no control over these areas.

Administrators can be leaders of change, cheerleaders, supporters, motivators, and providers of resources. The administrator sets the climate in the building or agency he or she leads, and one who is knowledgeable about the core components of effective AT services is more likely to recognize the importance of AT for students with disabilities and to value the provision of those services.

This chapter includes specific suggestions for addressing each indicator for administrative support of AT services.

1. **The education agency has *written procedural guidelines* that ensure equitable access to assistive technology devices and services for students with disabilities, if required for a free, appropriate, public education (FAPE).**

   **Intent: Clearly written procedural guidelines help ensure that students with disabilities have the AT devices and services they require for educational participation and benefit. Access to AT is ensured regardless of severity of disability, educational placement, geographic location, or economic status.**

   While AT decisions are made on a case-by-case basis, guidelines outline the steps to be followed for the provision and support of AT. Written guidelines are a core component of AT services and support consistent delivery of services that are legal, ethical, and equitably available to all students. Guidelines include clarification of processes and procedures for referral, consideration, assessment, documenting in the IEP, device acquisition, and implementation. In addition to general procedural guidelines, education agencies may find it helpful to develop guidelines for actions such as determining when AT needs to be taken home, addressing damages to AT devices, providing services to private schools, and resolving conflicts related to AT. Such guidelines enable educators and families to understand and follow agency practices. The Assistive Technology Model Operating Guidelines for Oregon, available from *www.otap-oregon.org*, provide an example of the type of wording that might be used in guidelines for AT services. Of course, all processes and procedures are reviewed regularly and updated as necessary.

**EXAMPLE**

*Mr. Mattson had a third-grade student with an IEP who was struggling in several areas of the curriculum, particularly with understanding print materials. He conferred with the student's parents and it was decided that the student's possible need for AT to support comprehension of print material should be explored. Mr. Mattson looked up the district's procedures for making an AT referral. He used the recommended form, followed the steps, and made the referral according to the procedure outlined in the guidelines.*

**KEY QUESTIONS**

- What written procedures are in place to support equitable access to AT?

- What is the process for keeping the procedures current and adequate?

- How are current and emerging trends incorporated into the written procedures document?

2. **The education agency *broadly disseminates* clearly defined procedures for accessing and providing assistive technology services, and supports the implementation of those procedures.**

   **Intent: Procedures are readily available in multiple formats to families and school personnel in special and general education. All are aware of how to locate the procedures and are expected to follow procedures whenever appropriate.**

   Procedural guidelines are made available in multiple formats, such as in print, on a website, and in the languages used by families in the agency's service area. These guidelines are disseminated to staff members at regular intervals and they confirm they have been received. All team members, including families, have access to the procedures and are provided opportunities to learn more about them. All staff members learn about AT procedures through mandatory in-service presentations and are held accountable by their supervisors to follow the guidelines.

*At the beginning of the year staff members in the Springfield School District received written AT guidelines and verified their receipt. They were also given the web address for the guidelines. The school principal gave magnets with the web address to all staff members in his building. When Mr. Brown joined the faculty in January, one of his colleagues shared the web address with him. Prior to a conference to discuss Johnny's possible AT needs, Mr. Brown provided the web address to Johnny's parents so that they could prepare for a discussion about AT.*

**KEY QUESTIONS**

- When and how are families and staff informed about the procedures and how to access them?

- How does the agency ensure that staff members know the guidelines?

- How is staff implementation of procedural guidelines supported?

3. **The education agency includes appropriate assistive technology responsibilities in *written descriptions of job requirements* for each position in which activities impact assistive technology services.**

   **Intent: Appropriate responsibilities and the knowledge, skills, and actions required to fulfill them are specified for positions from the classroom through the central office. These descriptions will vary depending upon the position and may be reflected in a position description, assignment of duty statement, or some other written description.**

   AT is part of the collective responsibility of all educators who provide services to students who use AT devices (e.g., general and special education teachers, administrators, related service providers, curriculum directors, paraprofessionals). Job descriptions across the agency include the AT-related responsibilities of each position, such as ensuring that AT required in the IEP is available and in working order on a daily basis, and that the student is supported in using it to carry out classroom tasks. A teacher's job description, for example, could include having knowledge of AT for academic tasks and the ability to include it in instruction for students with disabilities. Similarly, speech and language pathologists (SLPs), generally knowledgeable about communication and language development, may not be skilled in the area of augmentative and alternative communication (AAC). Including knowledge about AAC in position announcements and job descriptions for all SLP's can increase the availability of skilled service providers.

Job descriptions that include statements of basic AAC and other relevant AT skills can guide administrators to seek and hire staff members who can enhance the district's ability to meet the needs of children who use AT. Written descriptions provide clarity about expectations for current knowledge and the ability to implement the identified AT responsibilities. Administration and staff are mutually accountable for acknowledging and addressing the AT-related job responsibilities within their primary role.

EXAMPLE

*Ms. Williams, the principal, interviewed Mr. Chiba for a teaching position at Lake Middle School. They reviewed the AT portion of the job description. Job responsibilities included the ability to manage and support AT use for students in that classroom and collaborate with colleagues on the selection, acquisition, and use of AT. Mr. Chiba explained that he had worked in a classroom previously where students used text-to-speech, AAC, and aids for daily living. He talked about lesson plans that he developed that allowed students using AT to participate fully in classroom activities.*

*After the interview, Ms. Williams felt comfortable that Mr. Chiba had the skills required for the job and proceeded to check his references.*

**KEY QUESTIONS**

- Where are the AT responsibilities of each position described?

- How are the AT responsibilities reflected in hiring practices?

- How are job descriptions reviewed and updated to ensure that AT is included?

4. **The education agency employs *personnel with the competencies* needed to support quality assistive technology services within their primary areas of responsibility at all levels of the organization.**

   **Intent: Although different knowledge, skills, and levels of understanding are required for various jobs, all understand and are able to fulfill their parts in developing and maintaining a collaborative system of effective AT services to students.**

   While competencies vary across positions, there are critical roles that are inherent in direct service, support, and administrative positions that are necessary to ensure an effective and efficient system for acquiring and implementing AT. For example, administrators must have a vision of the importance of AT and actively support its use by doing the following: seeking, hiring, and retaining knowledgeable personnel; having expectations for effective AT implementation; acknowledging instances of high quality AT use; and encouraging ongoing learning and growth. Effective implementation of this indicator requires that all educators recognize, value, and support the use of AT for students who need it to demonstrate what they know or to participate actively in instructional activities. The administrator holds teachers accountable so that students have access to their education and learning opportunities in all educational settings where they receive instruction. Figure 8.1 lists some the components of effective AT use by students. It is part of the form, *Administrators' Planner for Effective Technology Supervision and Leadership*, found in Appendix D.

**TABLE 8.1** Components of effective technology use by students.

- Students regularly use technology, including AT, as required, to participate in learning activities, complete assignments and interact with peers.

- Students who experience difficulty with reading use technology to access information, acquire knowledge, and demonstrate skills.

- Students who experience difficulty with writing use technology to demonstrate knowledge and skills.

- Students who experience difficulty with physical or sensory access to classroom materials use technology to access the curriculum and demonstrate knowledge and skills.

- Students who experience difficulty with math use technology to access information, acquire knowledge, and demonstrate skills.

- Students who experience difficulty with oral communication use technology to support communication efforts.

In addition to AT-related competencies, personnel have skills, knowledge, and attitudes needed to collaborate and communicate with other professionals, departments, agencies, and families. AT services require the ability to work in teams, solve problems, and listen to and work with other people.

Initial job interviews and performance evaluations provide opportunities for personnel to demonstrate AT knowledge and skills. Experience and practice may be demonstrated by answering specific questions, sharing sample portfolios and case studies, and demonstrating AT skills. Performance evaluations are conducted regularly and include assessment of the employee's performance related to all competencies of their position, including the AT components. Good performance evaluations provide data and information necessary to develop and implement an effective professional development plan for each individual.

*During Ms. Edgar's interview for a position in the business department, the administrator asked questions that allowed her to talk about the importance of collaboration across departments. Ms. Edgar gave an example of working with a purchasing agent who knew which AT device vendors were sole sources for purchases, so time was not spent on an unnecessary bidding process. Ms. Edgar offered to work with the appropriate personnel, such as teachers, SLPs, OTs, and AT resource personnel to create a database of items available from sole source vendors.*

- How does the agency determine if employees across departments and positions have the knowledge and skills to support quality AT services?

- How do employee performance evaluations assess the AT expectations included in job descriptions?

- What opportunities are provided to staff to improve or increase skills/competencies in response to performance evaluations?

5. **The education agency includes *assistive technology in the technology planning and budgeting process.***

   **Intent: A comprehensive, collaboratively developed technology plan provides for the technology needs of all students in general education and special education.**

   Education agencies' technology plans address the need for access for *all* students. Students in special education are recognized as part of the total school district population who need access to instructional technology as well as specialized services that may include AT. Recognition of the AT needs of students with disabilities is part of agency-wide technology planning, (e.g., allowing access to specialized software and hardware on the school network, and avoiding purchase of academic courseware and assessments which have a closed environment that does not allow AT use). The district can acquire universally designed technology that is usable by students with the broadest possible range of abilities and needs, including those with identified disabilities. The acquisition and provision of AT are included in the agency's periodic assessment of overall technology competence.

   Technology planning committees include personnel with AT skills and competencies to articulate the unique technology needs of students with disabilities. Information is gathered from multiple stakeholders regarding current and anticipated needs for AT. Planning includes a recognition of the need for access for all students, as well as recognition of school technology concerns for security, capacity, and infrastructure (e.g., communication about the system requirements for specialized software and devices and how it will match the district's protocols).

Funding sources (e.g., general funds, IDEA funds, E-rate funds, discretionary grants) are identified when purchases are needed to provide curriculum access for students with disabilities. The members of IEP teams know how to request funding for needed AT purchases.

EXAMPLE

*Mrs. Dubbels, a resource room teacher, is an active member of the school technology planning and budgeting committee. Her participation increases her understanding of district-wide technology needs and ability to help others understand how universally designed technology is both inclusive and cost-effective. When the technology committee acquired interactive boards for every classroom in the building, the special education classrooms were included. The special education director and the technology director collaborated on funding the purchases. Interactive boards were purchased with general technology funds. Special education funds were used to purchase AT needed for specific students to access and use the interactive boards.*

**KEY QUESTIONS**

- How does the agency regularly seek and use input from general and special education staff so that budgets include both accessible technology and AT?

- How do administrators ensure there is special education participation on technology committees?

- How do technology-funded initiatives involve special education programs?

6. **The education agency provides access to *ongoing learning opportunities about assistive technology* for staff, family, and students.**

   **Intent: Learning opportunities are based on the needs of the student, the family, and the staff, and are readily available to all. Training and technical assistance include any topic pertinent to the selection, acquisition, or use of AT or any other aspect of AT service delivery.**

   Professional development and training needs of staff members and families are systematically identified based on program evaluation findings, needs assessments, and specific student needs. A comprehensive plan is developed that provides ongoing opportunities for learning about various aspects of AT devices and services that address identified needs.

The education agency ensures that a range of professional development activities is available to all staff, students, and families, and effective administrators support the participation of educators and others in relevant training. Administrators set expectations that people will take advantage of professional development related to their professional goals, provide time for learning activities, and hold staff responsible for meeting learning goals. Individuals who provide AT support are recognized and used as a valuable resource for training others and offering technical assistance within the agency. Errors in meeting the AT needs of students occur when it is not clearly understood that the primary purpose of AT in school settings is to support the implementation of the IEP for the provision of FAPE.

The agency ensures access to text-based resources, technical assistance, support for technology problem-solving, and a variety of training alternatives (e.g., face-to-face training, virtual learning, coaching, and mentoring). Agencies will need to develop targeted professional development to meet their own unique local needs. There are many training resources available from national, state, and local AT programs, universities, and vendors. Proactive leadership provides information about training opportunities and supports staff participation.

EXAMPLE

*Bayview School District conducted a needs assessment to identify the knowledge and skills needed by staff and families to improve systemic and student-specific AT services. The needs assessment identified three priority areas: accessible instructional materials, AT decision-making, and appropriate documentation. Mrs. Kriss, the director of special education, worked with others to identify a variety of internal and external resources that could be used to provide needed information and build identified skills. A comprehensive plan was then developed that used local, regional, and national entities. Workshops, study groups, and individualized support were made available online and in person to staff and family members at a variety of convenient times. Mrs. Kriss also provided resources and time for staff to attend the state AT conference as a means to network and build internal resources.*

**KEY QUESTIONS**

- What evidence is used to identify the need for ongoing learning opportunities?

- How does the administrator facilitate and monitor staff learning about AT?

- How is staff participation in learning opportunities supported (e.g., release time or other incentives)?

- How is family participation in AT training supported and encouraged?

- What agency resources (time, personnel, and money) are allocated for ongoing learning opportunities?

7. **The education agency uses a *systematic process to evaluate all* components of the agency-wide assistive technology program.**

   **Intent: The components of the evaluation process include, but are not limited to, planning, budgeting, decision-making, delivering AT services to students, and evaluating the impact of AT services on student achievement. There are clear, systematic evaluation procedures that all administrators know about and use on a regular basis at central office and building levels.**

   Program evaluation is the systematic assessment of the processes and outcomes of a program. Whenever possible, the same framework that is used throughout the agency to evaluate similar programs is used to evaluate the AT program. The Quality Indicators can be used to identify aspects of the program that should be evaluated and the QIAT Self-Evaluation Matrices highlight strengths and weaknesses within AT services. This information is used to further develop and improve the agency's AT services to support student achievement.

   Failure to evaluate the provision of AT services is a common error. All programs, including AT programs, need to be evaluated on a regular basis in order to improve and to better meet student needs. Three critical views of AT services that might be assessed as a part of the evaluation are the effect of AT devices and services on student achievement, the AT skills and competencies of staff members, and the satisfaction of service providers and parents with AT service received.

   Data collected about these aspects will help to show program strengths and challenges. For example, an agency may find that AT services are ethical, effective, and efficient in some settings but not in others. Data may indicate that a particular group of key people does not have the skills and competencies needed in order to support AT use. Student data may show that particular groups of students are underrepresented in their use of AT.

   Program evaluation findings lead the agency to determine priorities for program improvement and also suggest actions that might be taken to facilitate necessary changes. As a result of program evaluation activities, the agency can make both short and long term plans for improvements in design of AT services, allocation of resources, and provision of administrative supports in order to facilitate improved outcomes.

**EXAMPLE**

*As a part of regular program evaluation activities, the Big Valley School District conducted a comprehensive evaluation of the district's instructional technology services every three years. Most recently, the agency made the decision to include its AT services in the evaluation cycle. The data gained from the evaluation demonstrated that when students transitioned from elementary to middle school, achievement decreased disproportionately in comparison to past performance. The QIAT Self-Evaluation Matrices were used to analyze whether AT services could be related to the decreased achievement.*

*The analysis suggested that the staff in the middle school settings did not have the knowledge and skills needed to support implementation of AT. They needed staff development in both transition planning and implementation of AT. In the past there were insufficient opportunities for them to learn about AT and the new professional development plan focused improvement efforts on these identified areas for the next three years.*

**KEY QUESTIONS**

- How are the AT services evaluated?

- How is AT included in the agency-wide program evaluation process?

- How and to whom are results of program evaluations communicated?

- What actions are taken in response to the results of program evaluation?

- When and how are improvement actions and results monitored?

## Exploring the Quality Indicators for Administrative Support of Assistive Technology with the QIAT Self-Evaluation Matrix

The Self-Evaluation Matrix for Administrative Support of Assistive Technology focuses on the specific activities that administrators can do to enhance the likelihood that AT devices and services will be provided in an equitable, efficient, and cost effective manner. Through its variations from "unacceptable" to "best practice" the matrix

- provides a way to address the core components of administrative support in relation to AT service delivery,

- facilitates the understanding of the broad scope of impact that administrative support can have, and

- helps identify actions that may need to be undertaken to improve the delivery of AT services throughout the agency.

The first two indicators address the development and dissemination of procedures for AT service delivery. The third, fourth, and sixth indicators focus on highlighting important AT responsibilities in recruitment, supervision, and training of agency personnel. The fifth indicator addressed the inclusion of AT in technology planning and budgeting. The seventh indicator highlights the necessity of evaluating the AT program.

Following the Self-Evaluation Matrix is a case study about Frankie. It illustrates the importance of administrative support in AT service delivery.

# Quality Indicators for *Administrative Support* of Assistive Technology

| QUALITY INDICATOR | UNACCEPTABLE | | |
|---|---|---|---|
| **1. The education agency has *written procedural guidelines* that ensure equitable access to AT devices and services for students with disabilities, if required, for a free, appropriate, public education (FAPE).** | 1<br>No written procedural guidelines are in place. | 2<br>Written procedural guidelines for few components of AT service delivery are in place. | |
| **2. The education agency *broadly disseminates* clearly defined procedures for accessing and providing AT services, and supports the implementation of those guidelines.** | 1<br>No procedures disseminated and no plan to disseminate. | 2<br>A plan for dissemination exists, but has not been implemented. | |
| **3. The education agency includes appropriate AT responsibilities in *written descriptions of job requirements* for each position in which activities impact AT services.** | 1<br>No job requirements relating to AT are written. | 2<br>Job requirements related to AT are written only for a few specific personnel who provide AT services. | |
| **4. The education agency employs *personnel with the competencies* needed to support quality AT services within their primary areas of responsibility at all levels of the organization.** | 1<br>AT competencies are not considered in hiring, assigning, or evaluating personnel. | 2<br>AT competencies are recognized as an added value in an employee but are not sought. | |
| **5. The education agency includes *AT in the technology planning and budgeting process.*** | 1<br>There is no planning and budgeting process for AT. | 2<br>AT planning and budgeting is a special education function that is not included in the agency-wide technology planning and budgeting process. | |
| **6. The education agency provides access to *ongoing learning opportunities about AT* for staff, family, and students.** | 1<br>No learning opportunities related to AT are provided. | 2<br>Learning opportunities related to AT are provided on a crisis-basis only. Learning opportunities may not be available to all who need them. | |
| **7. The education agency uses a *systematic process to evaluate* all components of the agency-wide AT program.** | 1<br>The agency-wide AT program is not evaluated. | 2<br>Varying procedures are used to evaluate some components of the agency-wide AT program. | |

| | | |
|---|---|---|
| 3<br>Written procedural guidelines that address several components of AT service delivery are in place. | 4<br>Written procedural guidelines that address most components of AT service delivery are in place. | 5<br>Comprehensive written procedural guidelines that address all components of AT service delivery are in place. |
| 3<br>Procedures are disseminated to a few staff who work directly with AT. | 4<br>Procedures are disseminated to most agency personnel and generally used. | 5<br>Procedures are disseminated to all agency personnel and consistently used. |
| 3<br>Job requirements related to AT are written for most personnel who provide AT services but are not clearly aligned to job responsibilities. | 4<br>Job requirements related to AT are written for most personnel who provide AT services and are generally aligned to job responsibilities. | 5<br>Job requirements related to AT are written for all personnel who provide AT services and are clearly aligned to job responsibilities. |
| 3<br>AT competencies are recognized and sought for specific personnel. | 4<br>AT competencies are generally valued and used in hiring, assigning, and evaluating personnel. | 5<br>AT competencies are consistently valued and used in hiring, assigning, and evaluating personnel. |
| 3<br>AT is sometimes included in the agency-wide technology planning and budgeting process, but is inadequate to meet AT needs throughout the agency. | 4<br>AT is generally included in agency-wide technology planning and budgeting process in a way that meets most AT needs throughout the agency. | 5<br>AT is included in the agency-wide technology planning and budgeting process in a way that meets AT needs throughout the agency. |
| 3<br>Learning opportunities related to AT are provided to some individuals on a pre-defined schedule. | 4<br>Learning opportunities related to AT are provided on a pre-defined schedule to most individuals with some follow-up opportunities. | 5<br>Learning opportunities related to AT are provided on an ongoing basis to address the changing needs of students with disabilities, their families, and the staff who serve them. |
| 3<br>A systematic procedure is inconsistently used to evaluate a few components of the agency-wide AT program. | 4<br>A systematic procedure is generally used to evaluate most components of the agency-wide AT program. | 5<br>A systematic procedure is consistently used throughout the agency to evaluate all components of the agency-wide AT program. |

## Exploring the Quality Indicators for Administrative Support of Assistive Technology Services Through Frankie's Story

When Susan took on her new position as director of special education for Amherst School District, she was pleased to learn about all the interesting initiatives and programs that the district had in place. The district had a budget for special education services that was adequate for most student and staff needs. Highly qualified staff was employed in all aspects of special education services. Student placements for special education ranged from full inclusion to self-contained and special school environments with over 80% of the students with disabilities in the district attending their home school. There were well-established programs of Positive Behavioral and Instructional Supports (PBIS), high quality services for students with low incidence disabilities such as visual impairments and hearing loss, and an AT program that had been provided for over 10 years. Information regarding these programs was posted on the district website. She looked forward to working with the parent advisory council to identify areas where the excellent array of services could be enhanced.

At the end of the second month of school, Susan was surprised to receive a message from the state's department of education (DOE) telling her that a parent was filing an official complaint about AT. The parent stated in her official letter to the DOE that Western School District did not have an adequate process for addressing her son's AT needs and that, as a result, he was being denied FAPE. The following specific concerns were listed:

- The parent had asked that the IEP team consider her child's need for a personal amplification system as AT and the request had not been addressed.

- Subsequently the parent had asked, in writing, for an AT assessment of her son's need for a personal amplification system and had been told that, since he did not have a hearing impairment, the system was not needed. No assessment had been completed.

- The parent stated that the district had failed to provide FAPE for her son because the district had not fully evaluated his needs for requested special education services, accommodations, and modifications.

- Finally, the parent requested that the district immediately complete an assessment of her son's need for AT and specifically evaluate his need for a personal amplification system.

Susan immediately contacted the educational team and scheduled a meeting to talk about the complaint. During the meeting, the team explained more of the story. Frankie, a student with an intellectual disability, was placed in a general education third grade classroom and received pull-out instruction for reading and motor skills. In addition to his special education teacher, his team included an occupational therapist (OT), a speech and language pathologist (SLP), and a paraprofessional who was assigned to work with him and three other students with disabilities in the general education setting.

Frankie's special education teacher acknowledged that Frankie's mother had in fact asked about his use of a personal amplification system. His mom had stated that Frankie had a lot of trouble listening in the general education environment. His third-grade class also included a student with a hearing impairment who used a personal amplification system, and Frankie's mom wondered if having the sound directly in his ear would help him understand what the teacher was saying and also minimize auditory distractions.

The special education teacher told Frankie's mom that she would ask the SLP about the potential benefit of a personal amplification system for Frankie. The teacher and the SLP discussed the idea and agreed that they didn't think a personal amplification system would help him. The teacher sent a note home in Frankie's notebook stating that they did not think the system would help him.

About a week later, Frankie's mom wrote a letter requesting a formal AT evaluation for him and listed the need for a personal amplification system as one of the concerns to be addressed. The letter was forwarded to the district's AT specialist who responded that she only served students with low incidence disabilities like physical disabilities, hearing impairments, and vision impairments. The teacher wondered what she should do next, but didn't know who to ask about this problem so the request for assessment sat on her desk until she could figure out what to do.

Susan could see that there were some important issues to address in this case. She realized that a request from any IEP team member should trigger formal consideration of a student's need for AT. She was also very concerned that a formal, written request for an evaluation of the need for a special education service had not been addressed and immediately asked the AT specialist to complete the requested evaluation. She also called Frankie's mom to make sure that she had all the facts in the case.

Susan knew that, without some changes in the district's system of AT services, more parent dissatisfaction was likely. She and the AT specialist sat down to talk about this case and try to identify the reasons that things had gone so badly. After they had reviewed all the written district guidelines and procedures, they agreed that there were some flaws in Amherst District's procedures and continuum of services. Because they needed a format for identifying the issues, the AT specialist suggested that they use the Quality Indicators for Administrative Support of Assistive Technology Services as a basis for their conversation.

## Application of the QIAT Self-Evaluation Matrix for Administrative Support of Assistive Technology Services by Frankie's Team

1. **The education agency has *written procedural guidelines* that ensure equitable access to assistive technology devices and services for students with disabilities, if required for a free and appropriate public education (FAPE).**

   **Discussion:** Amherst District had a complete manual of operating guidelines for AT. Upon review, however, Susan realized that the guidelines did not address the consideration of the need for AT for students with high incidence disabilities, such as intellectual disabilities and learning disabilities. The district's focus had been on high-tech AT solutions such as augmentative communication devices, alternative computer access, and braille. Resource room teachers whose primary caseloads included these students had never received training about the guidelines nor been told that they applied to them. They were not aware of any procedures to follow when a formal request for AT evaluation was received. Susan and the AT specialist agreed on a rating of 4 on this indicator and made a plan to modify the guidelines to ensure that the needs of all students were addressed.

| 1 | 2 | 3 | 4 | 5 |
|---|---|---|---|---|
| No written procedural guidelines are in place. | Written procedural guidelines for few components of AT service delivery are in place. (e.g., assessment or consideration). | Written procedural guidelines that address several components of AT service delivery are in place. | **Written procedural guidelines that address most components of AT service delivery are in place.** | Comprehensive written procedural guidelines that address all components of AT service delivery are in place. |

2. **The education agency *broadly disseminates* clearly defined procedures for accessing and providing assistive technology services and supports the implementation of those guidelines.**

   **Discussion:** The Operating Guidelines were posted on the agency's website and were available to both parents and staff under the Special Education tab. Susan and the AT specialist realized, however, that after the guidelines had been posted, they had not been mentioned again. They suspected this was part of the trouble in Frankie's case. Because people didn't know about the guidelines, they weren't being used. Only staff members working directly with AT knew about them. They rated their district process at a 3 for this indicator.

| 1 | 2 | 3 | 4 | 5 |
|---|---|---|---|---|
| No procedures disseminated and no plan to disseminate. | A plan for dissemination exists, but has not been implemented. | **Procedures are disseminated to a few staff who work directly with AT.** | Procedures are disseminated to most agency personnel and generally used. | Procedures are disseminated to all agency personnel and consistently used. |

3. **The education agency includes appropriate assistive technology responsibilities in *written descriptions of job requirements* for each position in which activities impact assistive technology services.**

**Discussion:** Susan checked on the AT specialist position description and felt that it was fairly complete. It listed all of the AT services that were included in IDEA. However, there was no mention of services for students with high incidence disabilities. Additionally, there was no mention of AT in other teaching roles. Susan and the AT specialist rated their district's performance a 2 in this area and agreed to create a task force to better define how services such as assessment and evaluation of effectiveness would be provided for students with high incidence disabilities.

| 1 | 2 | 3 | 4 | 5 |
|---|---|---|---|---|
| No job requirements relating to AT are written. | **Job requirements related to AT are written only for a few specific personnel who provide AT services.** | Job requirements related to AT are written for most personnel who provide AT services but are not clearly aligned to job responsibilities. | Job requirements related to AT are written for most personnel who provide AT services and are generally aligned to job responsibilities. | Job requirements related to AT are written for all personnel who provide AT services and are clearly aligned to job responsibilities. |

4. **The education agency employs *personnel with the competencies needed* to support quality assistive technology services within their primary areas of responsibility at all levels of the organization.**

**Discussion:** Because she was new to her role, Susan took a look at job interview questions that had been used in previous hiring procedures. She was pleased to note that for the AT specialist position as well as for all related service providers, there were questions about the applicant's knowledge of AT devices and services. The AT specialist also noted that OTs, PTs, and SLPs who worked in self-contained classroom settings were expected to contribute to the consideration and assessments of AT needs for the students in those settings. While they were pleased with the results of this indicator assessment, they realized that there was a persistent pattern of failure to address the needs of students with learning disabilities. They rated the district performance on this indicator as a 4 and agreed to place it on the agenda of the newly formed AT task force.

| 1 | 2 | 3 | 4 | 5 |
|---|---|---|---|---|
| AT competencies are not considered in hiring, assigning, or evaluating personnel. | AT competencies are recognized as an added value in an employee but are not sought. | AT competencies are recognized and sought for specific personnel. | **AT competencies are generally valued and used in hiring, assigning, and evaluating personnel.** | AT competencies are consistently valued and used in hiring, assigning, and evaluating personnel. |

5. The education agency includes *assistive technology in the technology planning and budgeting process.*

   **Discussion:** Amherst District's budget included funds for purchase of AT devices and for hiring personnel for AT services. Susan and the AT specialist agreed that this budget was adequate to meet the demand and were able to rate the district's AT services a 5 for this indicator.

| 1 | 2 | 3 | 4 | 5 |
|---|---|---|---|---|
| There is no planning and budgeting process for AT. | AT planning and budgeting is a special education function that is not included in the agency-wide technology planning and budgeting process. | AT is sometimes included in the agency-wide technology planning and budgeting process, but is inadequate to meet AT needs throughout the agency. | AT is generally included in agency-wide technology planning and budgeting process in a way that meets most AT needs throughout the agency. | **AT is included in the agency-wide technology planning and budgeting process in a way that meets AT needs throughout the agency.** |

6. The education agency provides access to *ongoing learning opportunities about assistive technology* for staff, family, and students.

   **Discussion:** The pattern of focus on students with low incidence disabilities was also apparent here. The AT specialist reviewed a list of all the training sessions and support meetings that he had offered in the past year and realized that most had been offered only to those who worked with students in self-contained settings. In addition, most of these training opportunities had been related to highly specialized equipment that was not usually available in general education settings. A rating of 3 resulted in the addition of expanded training opportunities to the agenda for the AT task force.

| 1 | 2 | 3 | 4 | 5 |
|---|---|---|---|---|
| No learning opportunities related to AT are provided. | Learning opportunities related to AT are provided on a crisis-basis only. Learning opportunities may not be available to all who need them. | **Learning opportunities related to AT are provided to some individuals on a pre-defined schedule.** | Learning opportunities related to AT are provided on a pre-defined schedule to most individuals with some follow-up opportunities. | Learning opportunities related to AT are provided on an ongoing basis to address the changing needs of students with disabilities, their families, and the staff who serve them. |

7. **The education agency uses a *systematic process to evaluate* all components of the agency-wide assistive technology program.**

   **Discussion:** Susan asked what had been done in previous years to evaluate the AT program. Neither she nor the AT specialist could find any indication that the overall program had ever been evaluated. While the AT specialist did send a satisfaction survey to parents and educators, it did not provide enough information to identify results for students or increased skills and learning for teachers. Because it was a satisfaction survey, it had not been sent to parents or to educators of students with disabilities who were not currently receiving AT services. They rated the district efforts on this indicator a 2 and planned that program evaluation would be the first activity when the newly formed task force met.

| 1 | 2 | 3 | 4 | 5 |
|---|---|---|---|---|
| The agency-wide AT program is not evaluated. | **Varying procedures are used to evaluate some components of the agency-wide AT program.** | A systematic procedure is inconsistently used to evaluate a few components of the agency-wide AT program. | A systematic procedure is generally used to evaluate most components of the agency-wide AT program. | A systematic procedure is consistently used throughout the agency to evaluate all components of the agency-wide AT program. |

## Summary

The next chapter addresses the importance of ongoing professional development and training for AT and explores the core components of effective, high quality programs.

## Suggested Activities

1. Review the Assistive Technology Policy Checklist at: *http://natri.uky.edu/resources/reports/cheklst.html* and compare it to the Model Operating Guidelines from *www.otap-oregon.org*. What similarities do you see? What do you see as missing from either of them? Which do you find most useful?

2. Watch the webinar on administrators and AT at AbleNet University *https://www.ablenetinc.com/resources/recorded_webinars/*. Sign in and search the recorded videos for *What Administrators Need to Know about Assistive Technology* by Kirk Behnke. Watch the webinar and write a short paper about what you think are the three most important things that administrators need to know about AT. Justify your choices.

3. Complete the QIAT Self-Evaluation Matrix for Administrative Support of Assistive Technology Services using a school district with which you are familiar.

4. Using your ratings, determine the two greatest needs in that school district.

5. Review the Connecticut Assistive Technology Guidelines at *www.sde.ct.gov/sde/cwp/view.asp?a=2663&q=334976*. How do they reflect the Quality Indicators for Assistive Technology? What areas, if any, are included in the Connecticut Guidelines that are not addressed in the Quality Indicators? Write one or more Quality Indicators related to an area not already included in the Quality Indicators.

# CHAPTER 9

# Exploring the Quality Indicators for Professional Development and Training in Assistive Technology

1. Comprehensive assistive technology professional development and training *support the understanding that assistive technology devices and services enable students to accomplish IEP goals and objectives and make progress in the general curriculum.*

2. The education agency has an AT professional development and training *plan that identifies the audiences, purposes, activities, expected results, evaluation measures, and funding* for assistive technology professional development and training.

3. The content of comprehensive AT professional development and training *addresses all aspects of the selection, acquisition, and use* of assistive technology.

4. AT professional development and training addresses and is *aligned with other local, state, and national professional development initiatives.*

5. Assistive technology professional development and *training includes ongoing learning opportunities that utilize local, regional, and/or national resources.*

6. Professional development and training in assistive technology follows *research-based models for adult learning* that include multiple formats and are delivered at multiple skill levels.

7. The effectiveness of assistive technology professional development and training is *evaluated by measuring changes* in practice that result in improved student performance.

It is essential that educational agency staff members are knowledgeable about assistive technology (AT), so each student's need for AT is appropriately considered and all staff are aware of and in compliance with federal and state laws about AT. There are no current figures about the percentage of educators who are knowledgeable about AT, but evidence suggests that most educators do not learn about AT in their pre-service programs. Edyburn (2004) reported that general education teacher certification standards in most states require only one course in instructional technology that may or may not include anything about assistive technology. Even for special education teachers, if there is a course on AT, it is an elective rather than a requirement, in the majority of pre-service training programs (Edyburn, 2004).

Studies indicate that educators who were asked to consider the need for AT in the IEP, did not feel confident in their knowledge of AT nor in their ability to make an informed decision about its use (Ashton & Wahl, 2004; Ashton, Lee, & Vega, 2005; Marsters, 2011; Wilcox, Dugan, Campbell, & Guimond, 2006; Wilcox, Guimond, Campbell, & Weintrab Moore, 2006). This may result in students not having their AT needs met (Marsters, 2001). Ashton and Wahl (2004) also found that educators without knowledge of AT placed less importance on access to it.

The goal of AT professional development and training is to increase educators' and families' knowledge and skills in a variety of areas related to AT including, but not limited to: legal issues; collaborative processes; tools, strategies, and services continuum; resources; action planning; and data collection and analysis. Audiences for professional development and training include: special education teachers, related services personnel, general education teachers, paraprofessionals, administrators, AT specialists, students, parents or caregivers, and others involved with students with disabilities. When professional development and training is provided for special educators but not for administrators, general educators, and other staff a significant problem occurs. This targeted training leads other educators to believe that they have no role in the provision or support of AT.

The most effective AT professional development and training efforts arise out of an ongoing, well-defined, comprehensive plan. That plan is designed to develop and maintain the abilities to participate in the creation and provision of quality AT services for individuals at all levels of the agency.

1.  **Comprehensive assistive technology professional development and training** *supports the understanding that assistive technology devices and services enable students to accomplish IEP goals and objectives and make progress in the general curriculum.*

    **Intent: The Individuals with Disabilities Education Act (IDEA) requires the provision of a free, appropriate, public education (FAPE) for all children with disabilities. The Individualized Education Program (IEP) defines FAPE for each student. The use of AT enables students to participate in and benefit from FAPE. The focus of all AT professional development and training activities is to increase the student's ability to make progress in the general curriculum and accomplish IEP goals and objectives.**

Quality AT professional development and training is based on the philosophy that AT is used when needed to eliminate or reduce barriers to student participation and progress in the curriculum. Target audiences include general and special education teachers, administrators, AT providers, related service providers, students, and families. It reaches all staff members that provide services to students with disabilities including general educators and administrators. Effective professional development and training activities include information on the federal mandate to provide AT in order to ensure FAPE for any student who needs it. Learning opportunities include a wide spectrum of training from awareness of the need for AT to specific training on the application and use of identified AT devices.

Throughout the district, AT professional development and training includes a focus on eliminating misconceptions about AT (e.g., AT is only computers, is always expensive, doesn't apply to my students, is not my responsibility, gives an unfair advantage). Professional development and training promotes understanding that AT devices are tools that provide students an alternate means of access to complete assigned tasks and achieve IEP goals. Understanding that AT exists for a broad range of activities increases awareness of the need to consider AT as a strategy to support student achievement. Educators who have had 40 or more hours of training about AT are more comfortable with AT and are more likely to believe access to AT is critical for students with disabilities (Ashton, Lee, & Vega, 2005).

The list of AT services in IDEA includes the provision of AT training for the student, family, and staff. When AT professional development and training is part of the overall district professional development plan, it becomes integrated into training opportunities (e.g., time for training is designated on professional development and training days, substitute teachers are available , importance of knowledge about AT is recognized).

EXAMPLE

*Mrs. Reynolds saw a television program about a tool she thought might help her son, Mike, process information better, and told his teacher she would like Mike to have the opportunity to try it. Mike is identified as being on the autism spectrum. The school district had provided professional development and training on AT decision-making. Mike's teacher reviewed her notes and then followed district procedures to request assistance in determining whether this AT tool was needed in order for Mike to accomplish his IEP goals and make progress in the general education curriculum. The team met to plan the specific steps and necessary timelines for determining his need for AT and to identify the tools with the features he needs.*

How does the district ensure that AT professional development and training reaches all educators who serve students with disabilities including general education teachers and administrators?

How are AT learning opportunities integrated into the overall district professional development and training plan?

How is AT aligned with and outlined in the continuous improvement plan for special education?

2. **The education agency has an assistive technology professional development and training** *plan that identifies the audiences, purposes, activities, expected results, evaluation measures, and funding* **for assistive technology professional development and training.**

**Intent: The opportunity to learn the appropriate techniques and strategies is provided for each person involved in the delivery of AT services. Professional development and training is offered at a variety of levels of expertise and are pertinent to individual roles.**

An effective plan for AT professional development and training is aligned to district-wide goals and initiatives as well as the individual needs of students with AT. When developing an AT professional development and training plan, consideration is given to the responsibilities and needs of all adults who support or are involved in the provision of AT services (e.g., administrators, teachers, related services staff, paraprofessionals, and parents).

It is common for educators to believe that their greatest need is to learn primarily about AT devices. However, learning about the devices alone is not sufficient. Knowledge about the processes of consideration, assessment, implementation, and evaluation of effectiveness is equally important.

AT professional development and training activities are based on the roles and responsibilities of individuals involved. Planning the activities that meet the differing roles and responsibilities include clearly identifying the purpose, expected results, and evaluation measures that will be used to determine the extent to which results have been achieved. *The Assistive Technology Professional Development and Training Planner* (Appendix D) may be a useful tool when developing or expanding a program of training. There are many ways to provide training and to foster professional development. The use of social media and online, web-based training is growing exponentially. These formats offer greater flexibility than the "traditional" model of face-to-face workshops. Table 9.1 shows the formats included in the Planner.

TABLE 9.1 Format considerations for training and follow-up

| Formats for Training: | |
|---|---|
| Face to face | Online learning module |
| Ongoing class | Blog or Wiki |
| Online workshop | Podcast |
| Online credit course | Video training |
| Webinar | Community of practice |

| Formats for follow-up: | |
|---|---|
| Coaching | Social media |
| Mentoring | Professional Learning Community |
| Email/phone support | |

Comprehensive professional development and training incorporates adult learning principles and considers skill level of the participants (e.g., awareness, knowledge, application, and mastery). Conducting needs-based assessments to inform planning improves the quality and utility of the AT learning opportunities.

**EXAMPLE**

*Mary was excited when her special education director asked her to provide a workshop on AT for the special education staff during the school's beginning of the year professional development and training days. Mary asked about how the training would fit into the district's technology plan and about the expected results for this session. The director told her it was a two hour time block and offered a great opportunity to get staff up to speed with AT tools. Mary was not given, nor did she seek, input from the rest of the staff to inform her planning. Mary thought about the AT devices she used most often with her students with significant physical disabilities as she planned the introductory training for the entire special education staff.*

*On the training day, Mary delivered a well-prepared session on her chosen AT devices. Some participants found relevance and left excited to try the tools with their students; others were disappointed in the training because they already knew those tools and needed more advanced knowledge or examples. Others did not understand how the products would apply to their students and felt their time had been wasted. Mary was surprised by some of the feedback she received on the evaluation forms and determined that in the future she would ask her audience about their interests, knowledge, and needs prior to providing training.*

*When Mary and the special education director debriefed, they recognized that they should have gotten involvement from staff members. They developed a plan to get input from district educators representing a cross-section of students with disabilities.*

In what ways are responsibilities and needs of all adults involved in support or provision of AT services reflected in the plan?

How does the professional development and training plan encompass the variability of participants' knowledge (e.g., basic awareness to mastery)?

What formats do trainers consider for presentations (e. g., workshops, webinars, podcasts, video stream, other web-based resources, just-in-time, coaching, mentoring)?

How do evaluation results drive changes in practice?

3. **The content of comprehensive assistive technology professional development and training** *addresses all aspects of the selection, acquisition, and use* **of assistive technology.**

   **Intent: AT professional development and training addresses the development of a wide range of assessment, collaboration, and implementation skills that enable educators to provide effective AT interventions for students. The AT professional development and training plan includes, but is not limited, to collaborative processes; the continuum of tools, strategies, and services; resources; legal issues; action planning; and data collection.**

   When a comprehensive professional development and training plan is being developed, all aspects of the provision of AT devices and services are addressed, as appropriate, for agency personnel and their roles. AT devices and processes (e.g., consideration, assessment, inclusion in the IEP, implementation, and evaluation of effectiveness) necessary for the selection, acquisition, and use of AT are certainly the focus. Additional content might include collaborative processes, legal issues, specific implementation strategies, and other topics identified by target audiences. The overall concern is that the planned professional development and training teaches about and supports performance of critical roles in each indicator area. This includes identification of student needs in the customary environment, identification of features needed in AT devices, matching identified features to AT devices, providing trials and long-term use in customary environments, and evaluating effectiveness of AT devices and services in meeting identified needs.

**EXAMPLE**

*Staff at Washington Elementary decided they wanted to expand the use of technology in an attempt to increase student learning in language arts. They established a committee to investigate the research about the impact of technology use on student learning. After studying the research, they decided to increase the use of technology in specific settings.*

*They added white boards and projection systems to all upper elementary classrooms and began collecting data on changes in participation and learning. Regular education staff worked with the special education staff to develop a list of software teachers could provide to students as needed. This included text-to-speech, word prediction, and phonics programs that support a range of student needs. They realized it's important to remember that for a student with disabilities, if such technology is required to increase, maintain, or improve functional capabilities, it would be considered AT for that student, and be included in the IEP.*

**KEY QUESTIONS**

- How does the overall program of AT professional development and training address all aspects of selection, acquisition, and use?

- How is the need to integrate AT use within the general education curriculum addressed in the plan?

- How does the professional development and training support acquisition of critical knowledge and skills for team members and additional stakeholders?

4. **Assistive technology professional development and training addresses and is *aligned with other local, state, and national professional development initiatives.***

   **Intent: For many students with disabilities, AT is required for active participation in local, state, and national educational initiatives. Content of the professional development and training includes information about how the use of AT supports the participation of students with disabilities in these initiatives.**

   Districts have undertaken a variety of federal, state, and local initiatives (e.g., multi-tiered systems of support, Universal Design for Learning (UDL), core curriculum, literacy, math) to improve educational outcomes of all students. For some children and youth with disabilities, AT is often required to participate in and benefit from these initiatives. Teacher effectiveness is increased when educators understand how AT tools and strategies can be used to support inclusion of students with disabilities in initiatives that are being implemented.

   Professional development on selected initiatives provides an excellent opportunity to imbed AT training in those sessions. UDL and Accessible Educational Materials (AEM) have an obvious connection to AT, but it is also critical to help all educators understand how it can be an important part of any academic or behavioral initiative. AT tools and strategies can be used to model ways to include students with disabilities in goals and activities of broader training.

*Mr. Michaels was contacted by Deep River School District and asked to present a half-day training on AT supports for students with complex communication needs in the general education classroom. As an experienced AT trainer, Mr. Michaels was aware that the training would have a much greater impact if it framed the AT supports within typical activities in which AT would be used. Mr. Michaels inquired about the major initiatives in the Deep River SD, looked up the most salient aspects of each of those initiatives and included two of those initiatives in his training. At the opening of the session, Mr. Michaels and participants discussed activities and barriers that participants had encountered in attempting to engage students with complex communication needs in the initiative activities. He modeled AT tools and strategies that could be used to broaden participation of students with disabilities in targeted initiatives.*

**KEY QUESTIONS**

- How are AT professional development and training activities aligned with and infused in the district's professional development initiatives?

- How does content of AT professional development and training reflect the ways in which AT supports participation of students with disabilities in these initiatives?

- Have the purpose and expected results of each activity been clearly defined?

5. **Assistive technology professional development and training include** *ongoing learning opportunities that utilize local, regional, and/or national resources.*

   **Intent: Professional development and training opportunities enable individuals to meet present needs and increase their knowledge of AT for use in the future. Training in AT occurs frequently enough to address new and emerging technologies and practices and is available on a repetitive and continuous schedule. A variety of AT professional development and training resources are used.**

   Effective AT learning opportunities are provided on an ongoing basis to meet the continual need related to rapid advances in technology and changing needs of staff, students, and families. In addition, training is needed on an ongoing basis due to staff turnover and the needs of educators and related service personnel supporting students using new or unfamiliar AT.

   Local educational agencies often provide training opportunities, if they have staff with the expertise, and there are numerous regional, state, and national resources that can be used as part of a comprehensive plan. Professional development that is valuable and useful includes all levels and types of resources to keep staff members current. Learning opportunities are available in many formats; some are face-to-face and/or hands-on and some are offered via the

Internet. Local, state, and regional conferences and workshops are often a source of information and expertise. Many states now offer AT conferences. In addition, there are several national conferences where the primary focus is AT. Currently, these include the Closing the Gap Conference in the fall in Minneapolis, the Assistive Technology Industry Association Conference in the winter in Orlando, the Annual International Technology and Persons with Disabilities Conference in the spring in San Diego and the Rehabilitation Engineering and Assistive Technology Society of North America (RESNA) Conference in different locations in the summer. Attending any of these can become part of an individual's professional development plan.

Other opportunities are available via online courses, self-study modules, webinars, virtual communities of practice, and social networking tools. The Accessible Technology Coalition, *atcoalition.org*, provides at no cost a comprehensive collection of free webinars from all over the United States. There are many websites, electronic mailing lists, webcasts, podcasts, blogs, and wikis that can be part of a teacher's available tools for training and for technical assistance. The QIAT website, *www.qiat.org*, contains resources from multiple state agencies and other AT projects and programs and is a good place to begin. The QIAT Resource Bank contains materials developed by QIAT Community members, and there is a link to the archives of the QIAT list. These searchable archives include many discussions on important topics. From the QIAT website, you can sign-up for the QIAT list, an electronic mailing list with several thousand participants in a community of practice.

**EXAMPLE**

*When students using technology moved into the South Washington County district, the teachers identified a gap in their ability to implement the AT components of IEPs. Although there had been a few awareness level training sessions in recent years, the bulk of the staff members were not comfortable with their level of knowledge. Teachers asked the director for support in expanding learning opportunities. A staff survey identified specific needs as well as individuals with expertise in specific aspects of AT, including a speech language pathologist with extensive experience in augmentative communication and a teacher who was using a wide variety of AT to support student reading and writing. The director formed a task force to develop a plan to train peers and identify additional sources for ongoing professional development and training using this expertise. They learned that the technology department was willing to include an AT strand in their summer "Tech Camp" and began to identify how to maximize that opportunity and support skilled AT implementation across all settings. The task force also joined the QIAT electronic list where they asked practitioners for additional suggestions and they requested specific days be set aside throughout the next three years to further develop and implement a comprehensive plan.*

How do staff members, including all of those who serve on IEP teams, learn about professional development opportunities, including those on AT?

How are ongoing learning opportunities in AT supported and funded?

How is information obtained in professional development and training about AT shared and disseminated?

6. **Professional development and training in assistive technology follow** *research-based models for adult learning* **that include multiple formats and are delivered at multiple skill levels.**

   **Intent: The design of professional development and training for AT recognizes adults as diverse learners who bring various levels of prior knowledge and experience to the training and can benefit from differentiated instruction using a variety of formats and diverse timeframes (e.g., workshops, distance learning, follow-up assistance, ongoing technical support).**

   Effective adult professional development incorporates information from adult education and learning style research. To meet the needs of adult learners, professional development and training plans involve ways for adults to find meaning in what they are learning, create professional learning communities, implement learning immediately, and establish attainable goals for their learning. Training strategies may include time for reflection and discussion, small group interaction, hands-on opportunities with AT products, and video vignettes for further study. Training is more successful if it relates to the individual's current role and is immediately applicable.

   Unfortunately, among those who receive training alone, only about 5% actually make a change in their practices (Joyce & Showers, 2002). The only support strategy that dramatically increases the implementation of new knowledge and skills is coaching. Coaching has been shown to increase the implementation of information and strategies learned in training to over 90% (Joyce & Showers, 2002). Coaching is a support strategy designed to expand an individual's capacity to create a desired outcome. Rather than telling someone what to do, the coach gives his or her full attention, asking thought provoking questions, and listening carefully (Hargrove, 2000). Coaching is most effective when the person being coached wants to become more resourceful, informed, and skillful in applying the skills learned in training (Reed & Bowser, 2012).

   Coaching is not a quick fix. It is a strategy that allows time and support for the coach and the individual receiving the coaching to reflect, discuss, explore, and practice a new way of thinking about and carrying out instructional activities. It includes the coach using positive presuppositions (e.g., assuming teachers are doing their best), asking insightful questions, listening carefully, and giving reflective feedback (Cheliotes & Reilly, 2010). The coach's role is not be a "buddy" but to be a change agent who guides without giving direction, asking questions that cause reflection about how AT could be used to help a struggling student, and when and how AT use could best fit in the student's schedule to support accomplishment of difficult tasks.

Changes occur when coaches ask thought-provoking questions, uncover assumptions, have challenging or difficult conversations, and engage teachers in dialogue about their beliefs and goals related to AT rather than their knowledge and skills. "The purpose of interaction at the belief and goal level rather than the knowledge and skills level is to facilitate teachers' exploration of who they are as teachers as much or more than what they do as teachers. It is at this level where deep reform can occur." (Killion, 2009, Pg. 24)

**EXAMPLE**

*Wild Prairie School System purchased comprehensive scan and read software for all of their secondary schools. To ensure that it would be used, they conducted a survey to assess teachers' knowledge and skills related to the technology. Based on the information received, the agency offered awareness training to all staff and introductory operational training from the sales representative to those expected to use it. Regular follow-up sessions from the agency's AT team were scheduled throughout the year. A professional learning community including coaching relationships with experienced users was formed for ongoing support. Additionally, a web-based refresher tutorial with answers to frequently asked questions was made available for on-demand training. At the end of the year a post survey was conducted to see what needed to be changed or improved for the coming year.*

**KEY QUESTIONS**

- How do trainers incorporate adult learning principles and strategies when providing professional development and training?

- How is information presented in multiple formats and at multiple levels of engagement?

- How is training designed to consider the differing needs of digital natives and digital immigrants?

7. **The effectiveness of assistive technology professional development and training is *evaluated by measuring changes* in practice that result in improved student performance.**

   **Intent: Evidence is collected about the results of AT professional development and training. The professional development and training plan is modified based on these data to ensure changes in educational practice that result in improved student performance.**

The goal of all AT learning opportunities is to provide staff and families with the knowledge and skills needed to increase student access to the curriculum and make progress toward achievement of IEP goals. In order to determine effectiveness of the professional development and training, evidence is collected about student outcomes. Data that is collected may include individual and aggregate student data about access, engagement, and participation, implementation of new skills by the people involved in the training, and attitudinal factors.

Serious problems can arise when effectiveness is not measured in terms of changes in professional practice and improvement in student performance. These are the overall goals of AT professional development and training. Changes in practice are measured through use of data collection systems, including the QIAT Self-Assessment Matrices, other innovation configuration matrices, rubrics, self-ratings, aggregate student and agency data, surveys, interviews, observations, and so on. The data collected help to determine what will be needed in future learning opportunities to address agency goals for student performance.

**EXAMPLE**

*Typically, the Salem school district offered AT professional development and training to all staff and advertised it on the district calendar. When the district evaluated outcomes of AT professional development and training, results indicated that implementation was inconsistent. Analysis indicated that the major factor influencing implementation breakdown was the expectation that staff learn and use many similar software applications. Often teams were required to learn more than one multimedia software program to support students on their caseload. This appeared to be the reason that implementation was inconsistent. Movement of staff between buildings and time constraints were additional factors. The district realized that teachers had to learn so many skills that they never acquired proficiency in any one software application. To investigate this problem further the district administered a survey, which asked classroom teachers to respond to questions such as, "Are you still using the software?," "For what tasks do you use it?," "How did you get training?," "What software features do you use to support student learning?," and "How do these software features address student need?"*

*Examination of the survey data showed that one of the software solutions provided more global access than the others. The district made plans to focus professional development and training primarily on the most universally designed software application while acknowledging that some students might need to use one of the other software applications. Those needs would be addressed on an individual basis. The district would continue to evaluate the effectiveness of professional development and training to build capacity, enable teachers to work with software independently, and improve student outcomes.*

- What measures are used to determine the effectiveness of AT professional development and training?

- How is the effectiveness data used to plan for future professional development and training?

- What data is available to show the relationship between professional development and training efforts and student outcomes?

## Exploring the Quality Indicators for Professional Development and Training in Assistive Technology with the Self-Evaluation Matrix

The Quality Indicators for Professional Development and Training in Assistive Technology focus on the many inter-related components necessary to improve the knowledge and skills of the personnel who work with students with disabilities in all capacities. The Self-Evaluation Matrix is a tool to

- Assess current performance in a building or education agency,

- Identify areas of strength and areas needing improvement,

- Increase awareness of what constitutes high quality professional development and training, and

- Provide a framework of components that constitute a successful program of professional development and training about AT.

The first indicator addresses the importance of building in an underlying focus on the role of assistive technology in supporting and empowering students with disabilities. Indicators two and three talk about the critical components of the plan. Indicator four addresses the need to be aware of and aligned with other professional development initiatives.

The fifth and sixth indicators speak to the need for an ongoing plan that incorporates the research on adult learning. The final indicator reminds us that the goal of professional development is to improve learner outcomes and that a program of professional development and training is evaluated by changes in practice resulting in improved student performance.

A case study of the Madison School District follows the matrix and helps to illustrate its use. Even though Madison School District had many components in place, they still benefitted from the use of the Quality Indicators.

# Quality Indicators for *Professional Development and Training* in Assistive Technology

| QUALITY INDICATOR | UNACCEPTABLE | | |
|---|---|---|---|
| **1. Comprehensive AT professional development and training *support the understanding that AT devices and services enable students to accomplish IEP goals and objectives and make progress in the general curriculum.*** | 1<br>There is no professional development and training in the use of AT. | 2<br>Professional development and training address only technical aspects of AT tools and/or are not related to use for academic achievement. | |
| **2. The education agency has an AT professional development and training plan that *identifies the audiences, purposes, activities, expected results, evaluation measures, and funding* for AT professional development and training.** | 1<br>There is no plan for AT professional development and training. | 2<br>The plan includes unrelated activities done on a sporadic basis for a limited audience. | |
| **3. The content of comprehensive AT professional development and training *addresses all aspects of the selection, acquisition, and use* of AT.** | 1<br>There is no professional development and training related to selection, acquisition, and use of AT. | 2<br>Professional development and training address few aspects of selection, acquisition, and use of AT. | |
| **4. AT professional development and training address and are *aligned with other local, state, and national professional development initiatives.*** | 1<br>Professional development and training do not consider other initiatives. | 2<br>Professional development and training rarely align with other initiatives. | |
| **5. AT professional development and training *include ongoing learning opportunities that utilize local, regional, and/or national resources.*** | 1<br>There are no professional development and training opportunities. | 2<br>Professional development and training occur infrequently. | |
| **6. Professional development and training in AT follow *research-based models for adult learning* that include multiple formats and are delivered at multiple skill levels.** | 1<br>Professional development and training never consider adult learning. | 2<br>Professional development and training rarely consider models for adult learning strategies. | |
| **7. The effectiveness of AT professional development and training is *evaluated by measuring changes* in practice that result in improved student performance.** | 1<br>Changes in practice are not measured. | 2<br>Changes in practice are rarely measured. | |

| 3 | 4 | 5 |
|---|---|---|
| Some professional development and training include strategies for use of AT devices and services to facilitate academic achievement. | Most professional development and training include strategies for use of AT devices and services to facilitate academic achievement. | All professional development and training include strategies for use of AT devices and services to facilitate academic achievement. |
| The plan includes some elements (e.g., variety of activities, purpose, levels) for some audiences. | The plan includes most elements of a comprehensive plan for most audiences. | The comprehensive AT professional development plan encompasses all elements, audiences, and levels. |
| Professional development and training address some aspects of selection, acquisition, and use of AT. | Professional development and training address most aspects of selection, acquisition, and use of AT. | Professional development and training address all aspects of selection, acquisition, and use of AT. |
| Professional development and training sometimes align with other initiatives. | Professional development and training generally align with other initiatives. | Professional development and training consistently align with other initiatives as appropriate. |
| Professional development and training are sometimes provided. | Professional development and training are generally provided. | Professional development and training opportunities are provided on a comprehensive, repetitive, and continuous schedule, utilizing appropriate local, regional, and national resources. |
| Professional development and training sometimes consider research-based adult learning strategies. | Professional development and training generally consider research-based adult learning strategies. | Professional development and training consistently consider research-based adult learning strategies. |
| Changes in practice are measured using a variety of measures but may not be related to student performance. | Changes in practice are usually measured using a variety of reliable measures linked to improved student performance. | Changes in practice are consistently measured using a variety of reliable measures linked to improved student performance. |

# Exploring the Quality Indicators for Assistive Technology Professional Development and Training in Assistive Technology Through Madison School District's Case Study

Madison School District, a district of approximately 80,000 students, created an AT professional development plan to support a school-based AT service model. Prior to this change, the district used an expert model of AT service delivery that began with two staff members designated to assess individual students. As the district grew, and as AT became more available, these two professionals could not keep up with the demand to provide timely AT supports to students across campuses. The school district planned to move assessment from this expert model to a model where one or two people who were knowledgeable about basic AT consideration, assessment, and implementation could take an AT leadership role in their school. As part of the restructuring, the AT planning task force developed a rubric of expected skills and identified levels of knowledge for current and potential staff who could support AT within each school.

The AT planning task force also decided to use professional development services at their local education support agency (ESA). The ESA maintains an AT professional development program with content experts in augmentative communication, low vision and blindness, occupational therapy, and systems for hearing and listening. Madison School District sent a team, including an administrator, to this comprehensive training, focusing on promising practices and tool-specific training. At the initial ESA AT Teams meeting, the training plan was explained. It used Novice, Apprentice, Practitioner, and Veteran to designate levels of knowledge.

| Background | Novice | Apprentice | Practitioner | Veteran |
|---|---|---|---|---|
| AT Knowledge | Interested in formal AT team training | Completed basic-AT team training | Completed intermediate level AT team training | Completed advanced level AT team training |
| Years of Experience | 0-1 year experience | 1+ years' experience | 3+ years' experience | 10+ years' experience |
| AT Device training | Basic computer skills and knowledge of IT | Some AT/IT tools knowledge | Substantial knowledge of AT/IT tools | Knowledge of all or most AT/IT tools across categories |
| AT Service Training | Laws and core components of AT services (e.g., consideration, assessment, implementation, and evaluation of effectiveness) | In depth focus on consideration and assessment/evaluation | In depth focus on implementation and evaluation of effectiveness | Focus on training others, coaching, and program evaluation |

| Background | Novice | Apprentice | Practitioner | Veteran |
|---|---|---|---|---|
| Coaching and Mentoring Activities | Observes AT evaluation process with Practitioner or Veteran. May follow implementation plan created by Practitioners and Veterans. | Participates in AT evaluations with Practitioners and Veterans. Follows implementation plans created by Practitioners and Veterans. May create implementation plans with coaching and collaboration from Practitioners or Veterans. | Can lead student centered teams in AT evaluations and creation of implementation plans. | Mentor and coach Novices and Apprentices in performing AT evaluations and developing implementation plans. |

Later, the expected knowledge of AT tools for different staff groups was further defined. The team began to create professional development plans for each staff grouping. If staff members were rated as novices, the AT team specified the training the group would need in the next year and identified opportunities for them to receive coaching and mentoring in AT evaluation and implementation strategies.

As the AT team developed training for staff at the four levels, they conferred with colleagues from the school district's professional development team and AT staff from the ESA regarding training content. They wanted to be sure the training they were putting together was in tune with strategies and methods that were research based and used within the state. They also wanted to take advantage of opportunities to connect to literacy initiatives that were taking place within their district. The AT team began the project with school buildings where they felt the most success could be realized in the shortest amount of time.

The AT Planning task force's last step was to outline a three year plan to include all campuses in the AT professional development efforts. As a result, there was an increase in the number of school-based teams with the ability to identify gaps in AT services as well as increased independence and participation from IEP team members when AT was considered.

At the end of the second year of this three-year project, the task force used the QIAT matrix to evaluate their professional development efforts and make adjustments to their activities. One area they rated low in their self-evaluation was indicator #7: evaluation of changes in practice. While they had much anecdotal evidence that school-based professional development activities were having an impact, they felt they needed quantitative data to show the kinds of differences the program was making. Future plans for the task force included increased program data collection about the model so the impact of AT staff training on student performance could be monitored.

# Application of the QIAT Self-Evaluation Matrix for Professional Development and Training in Assistive Technology by Madison School District

1. **Comprehensive AT professional development and training** *support the understanding that AT devices and services enable students to accomplish IEP goals and objectives and make progress in the general curriculum.*

   **Discussion:** Prior to the redesign of the professional development model, AT training for students and staff was solely focused on tools. The new model incorporated information on how AT was to be included into the IEP and the role of multiple staff members in AT assessment and implementation activities. When rating this area, however, the team did recognize that they were at 3 because training was only occurring for some schools and was not yet offered to all staff at all schools in the district.

| 1 | 2 | 3 | 4 | 5 |
|---|---|---|---|---|
| There is no professional development and training in the use of AT. | Professional development and training only address technical aspects of AT tools and/or are not related to use for academic achievement. | **Some professional development and training include strategies for use of AT devices and services to facilitate academic achievement.** | Most professional development and training include strategies for use of AT devices and services to facilitate academic achievement. | All professional development and training include strategies for use of AT devices and services to facilitate academic achievement. |

2. **The education agency has an AT professional development and training plan** that *identifies the audiences, purposes, activities, expected results, evaluation measures, and funding* **for AT professional development and training.**

   **Discussion:** The team not only identified the audiences, purposes, and activities of the AT professional development plan, but was able to rate individual staff members' skills using their new system. After developing and defining the levels of Novice, Apprentice, Practitioner, and Veteran, the team rated their performance on this indicator at a 5.

| 1 | 2 | 3 | 4 | 5 |
|---|---|---|---|---|
| There is no plan for AT professional development and training. | The plan includes unrelated activities done on a sporadic basis for a limited audience. | The plan includes some elements (e.g., variety of activities, purpose, levels) for some audiences. | The plan includes most elements of a comprehensive plan for most audiences. | **The comprehensive AT professional development plan encompasses all elements, audiences, and levels.** |

3. **The content of comprehensive AT professional development and training** *addresses all aspects of the selection, acquisition, and use* **of AT.**

   **Discussion:** Prior to the redesign of the district's AT service model, only the "expert" AT team was involved in seeking professional development in the areas of selection and acquisition of AT. Afterward, professional development within the district was offered to all staff and was coordinated with the needs of staff members at the four levels of AT knowledge. Initial training within the district was focused on the AT needs of students in high incidence disabilities. The team rated their performance in this area at a 4 and made plans to increase the staff training about AT needed by those student with low incidence disabilities in the future.

| 1 | 2 | 3 | 4 | 5 |
|---|---|---|---|---|
| There is no professional development and training related to selection, acquisition, and use of AT. | Professional development and training addresses few aspects of selection, acquisition, and use of AT. | Professional development and training addresses some aspects of selection, acquisition, and use of AT. | **Professional development and training addresses most aspects of selection, acquisition, and use of AT.** | Professional development and training addresses all aspects of selection, acquisition, and use of AT. |

4. **AT professional development and training address and are** *aligned with other local, state, and national professional development initiatives.*

   **Discussion:** The AT task force members rated this area a 5 for two reasons. First, they conferred with colleagues as they developed training for staff at the four levels to make sure the training was in tune with strategies that were being promoted within the state and at national levels. Second, they infused AT into other professional development opportunities, such as literacy initiatives within their district.

| 1 | 2 | 3 | 4 | 5 |
|---|---|---|---|---|
| Professional development and training do not consider other initiatives. | Professional development and training rarely align with other initiatives. | Professional development and training sometimes align with other initiatives. | Professional development and training generally align with other initiatives. | **Professional development and training consistently align with other initiatives as appropriate.** |

5. **AT professional development and** *training include ongoing learning opportunities that utilize local, regional, and/or national resources.*

   **Discussion:** The team was distributing information about ongoing trainings offered by the ESC and the district, however, national trainings were still not an option to many staff to attend, so they rated this area at 4.

| 1 | 2 | 3 | 4 | 5 |
|---|---|---|---|---|
| There are no professional development and training opportunities. | Professional development and training occur infrequently. | Professional development and training are sometimes provided. | **Professional development and training is generally provided.** | Professional development and training opportunities are provided on a comprehensive, repetitive, and continuous schedule, utilizing appropriate local, regional, and national resources. |

6. **Professional development and training in AT follow** *research-based models for adult learning* **that include multiple formats and are delivered at multiple skill levels.**

   **Discussion:** As the team reviewed this indicator area, they were able to reflect positively on the plan that they had developed for the four levels of staff AT knowledge. Also in conferring with the district's professional development team, they ensured the training they had developed within the district was following researched-based models. That training was being delivered in multiple formats from onsite, in district labs, as well as through downloadable videos and Power-Points. Although the trainings were being rated at the four levels, staff members were able to self-select the information that was most pertinent to their needs. Since other districts were starting to copy their model, the team rated this area at a 5.

| 1 | 2 | 3 | 4 | 5 |
|---|---|---|---|---|
| Professional development and training never consider adult learning. | Professional development and training rarely consider models for adult learning strategies. | Professional development and training sometimes consider research-based adult learning strategies. | Professional development and training generally consider research-based adult learning strategies. | **Professional development and training consistently consider research-based adult learning strategies.** |

7. **The effectiveness of AT professional development and training is *evaluated by measuring changes* in practice that result in improved student performance.**

   **Discussion:** When reviewing this indicator, the AT team rated this area at a 2. They realized that staff members were evaluating their satisfaction with the professional development opportunities, and they had put into place measures for rating staff levels of knowledge. Their data could not measure specific increases in student performance as a result of staff members having made changes in AT practice. They made a plan to focus on evaluation of changes in practice and student outcomes during the third year of the project.

| 1 | 2 | 3 | 4 | 5 |
|---|---|---|---|---|
| Changes in practice are not measured. | **Changes in practice are rarely measured.** | Changes in practice are measured using a variety of measures but may not be related to student performance. | Changes in practice are usually measured using a variety of reliable measures linked to improved student performance. | Changes in practice are consistently measured using a variety of reliable measures linked to improved student performance. |

## Suggested Activities

1. Watch the webinar on professional development at Ablenet University. *https://www.ablenetinc.com/resources/recorded_webinars/*. Sign in and search the recorded videos on AT for *QIAT Session 8: Professional Development and Training in AT* by Scott Marfilius and Kathy Lalk. What were the three most important things you learned from the webinar? Write a short paper telling how you would use that information.

2. Read the *Assistive Technology Trainer's Handbook* from *www.natenetwork.org/manuals-forms*. Write a short paper on three techniques that you would like to employ when doing professional development.

3. Using what you learned from the *AT Trainer's Handbook*, critique an experience you have had as a learner (either during in-service training or university class). What would you do to improve it?

4. Your school has just purchased a school license for a voice recognition software program to improve writing for struggling writers in high school. A survey shows only 10% of the teachers are familiar with it. Using the *Assistive Technology Professional Development and Training Planner* from Appendix D, develop a plan to increase the knowledge of critical staff.

5. Review the professional development about AT that has been provided in a school district with which you are familiar. Based on the Quality Indicators for Professional Development and Training in Assistive Technology, what would you add to that training and why?

# CHAPTER 10

# Using the Quality Indicators to Improve Assistive Technology Services

The goal of every educational agency is to establish effective, sustainable practices across the agency and across service areas. High quality educational practices are planned and supported so that changes in personnel or leadership do not change a course of action in the service programs, including AT services. The many demands on individual AT service providers' time and the many components to provision of high quality AT devices and services make it challenging to look at the big picture of AT service.

The previous chapters in *Quality Indicators for Assistive Technology (QIAT): A Comprehensive Guide to Assistive Technology Services* have highlighted the core components of quality AT services and provided examples of ways that teams use QIAT to help improve their practices and develop effective, efficient AT services. This chapter will discuss the implementation of new practices to build and sustain system change. The focus of this chapter is application of research-based steps identified in the science of implementation (Fixsen, Naoom, Blase, Friedman, & Wallace, 2005; Wallace, Blase, Fixsen, & Naoom, 2008) to the improvement of AT services. The science of implementation is based on research about successfully adopting a systemic change throughout an agency. Education agencies can use the processes identified in implementation science research to plan, implement, and evaluate their efforts to address AT services and, when needed, adjust them to meet their desired goals. This research shows that in order to make positive, lasting change, it is wise to begin with the end in mind, develop a system-wide plan to make progress toward that end, take strategic action, evaluate progress, modify the plan if progress is not made, and identify potential barriers.

As defined by Wallace et al. (2008), there are five stages of implementation. They are

- exploration,

- installation,

- initial implementation,

- full implementation, and

- sustainable implementation.

In this chapter, each of these stages will be described as they relate to the provision of high quality AT services.

## Exploration of Quality Assistive Technology Services

**Exploration** is the initial stage of implementation of any system change. During the exploration stage a group of people within an agency determines goals, identifies the current status in relation to those goals, begins to develop a plan, and takes initial action steps toward sustainable implementation. System change cannot be planned and carried out by one or two people. Michael Fullan (2003) who has researched educational change across many countries has found that sustainable change requires a core group of people struggling though the challenges of identifying problems and working toward shared solutions. When addressing AT services in the exploration phase, critical actions may include

- forming an implementation planning group that includes key stakeholders,

- assessing individual or agency needs using the Quality Indicators Self-Evaluation Matrices,

- analyzing the results of the self-evaluation to identify areas of need and possible solutions (programs and interventions) to address those needs, and

- determining how and when program change will be measured.

The implementation planning group plays a key role in determining and orchestrating the specific activities that are part of the system change. Collectively, the members of this group must have the knowledge, skills, abilities, and time to dedicate to all phases of implementation of the plan for change. The planning group includes members from one or more AT teams within the agency, but must not be limited to them. Some planning group members must have administrative authority to make agency-wide decisions and must represent other critical programs, such as instructional technology, curriculum, and staff development. The involvement of one or more active and knowledgeable parents of students with disabilities on the planning group is also critical as they provide a unique perspective. Other stakeholders to be included on the implementation planning group will be identified based on the specific needs of the agency. Overall the planning group actively provides the structure, oversight, and supports to make the desired change happen. An important responsibility of the planning group is communication with others who are directly involved in or who will be impacted by the changes.

The implementation planning group collectively needs

- knowledge of the multiple components of an AT program,

- awareness of the use of AT with students with disabilities,

- connections to all key stakeholders,

- awareness of other agency change and improvement initiatives,

- knowledge of research about implementation science, and

- experience in applying data analysis to measure program improvement.

In the exploration stage, the planning group identifies needed core components of quality AT services for the agency. Core components are the critical aspects of an intervention that are essential for success. The QIAT indicators and intent statements offer an ideal resource for this stage of change by providing descriptions of quality AT services that members of the planning group may not have experienced or considered. For example, in some education agencies all AT assessments are completed by an AT team while in other agencies there are non-centralized models for AT assessments. The Quality Indicator for Assistive Technology Assessment #1, "*Procedures* for all aspects of assistive technology assessment are clearly defined and consistently applied," supports a consistent process for completing an AT assessment no matter what the model.

Use of the QIAT Self-Evaluation Matrices can facilitate assessment of both quality of individual teams' practices and the collective practice across the agency. By clearly identifying core components of consideration, assessment, implementation, and so on, the Quality Indicators and matrices provide the planning group and agency administrators with a way to think about and discuss individual components that are in need of change. Knowing the core components that must be present for high quality services is important to successful implementation. Core components of a program or intervention are, by definition, essential to achieving good outcomes for students (Wallace, et al., 2008). They provide the basis for developing an implementation plan to improve practice by an individual team or throughout an agency. From their self-identified starting point, the planning group determines what achievable change will look like, and designs a plan to get to that point. Initially, the AT planning group identifies areas that are strong as well as areas that need improvement.

Administrators play a significant role in the implementation of new programs and the improvement of existing ones. Without the support of key administrators, change does not take place. Only administrators can commit resources, such as time for the planning group to meet and for staff to be trained, along with resources for needed actions. These actions, such as site visits or material purchase, and their associated costs are necessary first steps to begin any change in an education agency. Administrative leadership is critical to success of any system change. Only administrators can establish and maintain a culture that values learner-centered environments and communicates the importance of the role of AT in achieving that culture (TSSA Collaborative, 2001).

The implementation planning group needs knowledge of change-theory strategies and group interaction techniques to guide their decision-making and planning process. A facilitator skilled in leading group processes can greatly enhance the AT implementation planning group's potential for success. One process used to plan and implement change is Plan/Do/Study/Act (PDSA) (Langley, Nolan, Nolan, Norman, & Provost, 2009). The four steps of PDSA for AT exploration and planning might look something like the steps in Table 10.1. Note that every stage of implementation will have its own PDSA cycle, and it will vary based on the supports needed by the local system.

**TABLE 10.1** Plan/Do/Study/Act for exploration of AT service improvement

| **PLAN** |
| --- |
| Use the QIAT Self-Evaluation Matrices to analyze local practice, identify strengths and problem areas, and determine what change may be necessary for improved outcomes. |
| Set priority areas. |
| Identify barriers and challenges that need to be addressed for change to occur. |
| **DO** |
| Develop an AT improvement implementation plan that specifies the targets, timelines, and monitoring of outcomes in order to overcome the impact of barriers. |
| Provide for communication regarding the plan among impacted stakeholders, which includes the planning group, AT team members, and other key players. |
| **STUDY** |
| Gather feedback on reactions to the plan. |
| Analyze the feedback. |
| **ACT** |
| Make any necessary changes to the plan. |

**EXAMPLE**

*As a result of data from monitoring the local education agencies, the state education agency (SEA) in one state recognized the need to improve AT services in school districts throughout the state. They contracted with the state Assistive Technology Act (AT Act) project to take the lead in planning and implementing a system change project over five years. The state AT Act agency brought together an AT planning group that met several times over three months to plan an AT initiative. They chose to begin with the QIAT Indicators and the QIAT Self-Evaluation Matrices to guide the system change. Early in the fall of the following year teams from 45 school districts came together to begin analyzing AT services in their district using the QIAT tools. A facilitator provided instructions and guidance as each team member individually completed the matrices and then teams discussed their answers arriving at a consensus score for each indicator.*

*Each team then chose an indicator area on which to collectively develop their improvement plan. Nearly half (21) of the teams decided to focus on improving AT consideration*

*throughout their district. About a quarter (10) of the teams focused on developing or improving their AT assessment process. The remaining teams were fairly equally divided between working on administrative support (8) and AT transition services (6).*

*As they began to plan for the exploration stage in their districts, teams were reminded that implementation plans are fluid, and that strategies can be evaluated and adjusted over time. The teams were given print and online resources that they could use as they developed, documented, and implemented their plans. Throughout the year the project leaders from the state AT Act agency worked with the planning group and the individual teams to evaluate progress and adjust plans if indicated. They also brought in experts in the field of AT to provide training on topics identified by district teams. The training provided both motivation and information as the teams moved forward with their exploration.*

## Installation of Quality Assistive Technology Services

After determining the plan for improvement, the AT implementation planning group begins taking active steps on the agreed upon actions. During the installation stage, the planning group begins to build the supports and resources necessary to make effective change in their agency's AT practice. Many of the strategies critical to this stage are reflected in the Quality Indicators for Administrative Support for Assistive Technology (see Chapter 8), including

- written procedural guidelines for AT services that are broadly disseminated (Indicators 1 and 2),

- personnel with AT competencies and job descriptions that include AT (Indicators 3 and 4),

- AT included in the technology planning and budgeting process (Indicator 5),

- ongoing opportunities to learn more about AT (Indicator 6), and

- a process to evaluate components of the AT program (Indicator 7).

In the installation stage, the AT planning group addresses the question, "On which indicators should we focus our efforts in order to see the greatest improvement in student performance?" With this information they can determine which specific Quality Indicators to address in order to obtain the most improved outcomes in AT service for their unique situation. Since it would be overwhelming to address all areas of identified need at once, it is critical that planning group members understand that change takes time. Changes in skill levels of educators, organizational capacity, and agency culture require training, practice, and coaching, as well as time to mature (Fixsen, et al., 2005). While barriers may be encountered, planning group members should recognize that remaining true to their plan may be very difficult, but will result in positive change.

Teams will want to ensure that training and coaching opportunities are in place. The functions of training are well known. It is generally a quick and effective way to introduce new concepts and strategies, to discuss the rationale for the new systems, and to provide a "safe place" to try out new skills. In addition, training is essential in raising awareness about the importance of AT for students with disabilities. Ashton, Lee, and Vega (2005) found that educators who had 40 or more hours of training about AT felt it was essential to students' daily routine and were comfortable in identifying and using AT to ensure educational access. Educators without AT training felt it was not important to students' daily activities, and were not confident in identifying and using AT. Once key players have participated in AT training that is targeted to their needs and scope of practice, ongoing coaching helps ensure the targeted skills are integrated into the educational program.

Equally important is the development of a data management system to collect, analyze, and use data about the effectiveness of change efforts. The data management system may include regularly scheduled reviews using the QIAT Self-Evaluation Matrix for the targeted improvement area or other methods of data collection such as observations of staff members and students, review of IEPs to identify the presence of documentation, or other evidence of new performance.

The installation stage often begins with the development of written procedures and guidelines that provide educators with the directions they need to consistently implement the new strategies across settings. Guidelines that describe expectations for specific AT services help educators to understand and take ownership of their students' AT programs. Several of the QIAT areas begin with a focus on the need for written guidelines. For example:

- *Procedures* for all aspects of AT assessment are clearly defined and consistently applied. (Assessment area, Indicator 1)

- The education agency *has guidelines for documenting AT needs* in the IEP and requires their consistent application. (IEP area, Indicator 1)

- The education agency has *written procedural guidelines* that ensure equitable access to AT devices and services for students with disabilities if required for a free, appropriate, public education (FAPE). (Administrative Support area, Indicator 1)

- The education agency has an *AT professional development and training plan* that identifies the audiences, purposes, activities, expected results, evaluation measures, and funding for AT professional development and training. (Professional Development area, Indicator 1)

The need to develop and implement agency-wide procedures is one of the reasons that administrators are important members of the AT implementation planning group. They are also critical in the movement from paper implementation, where the policies and procedures are written but not yet acted upon (Wallace, et al., 2008), to performance implementation, where the core components are being used to benefit the consumers, in this case, students with disabilities (Paine, Bellamy & Wilcox, 1984).

*Clinton School District had not focused much on AT services until Ezra's family moved into the district. Clinton was a small district and relied on their education service agency (ESA) to send expert staff when they needed an AT evaluation or consultation. When Ezra, who has Angelman Syndrome, came to the district as a preschooler, the ESA team consulted with the district's preschool staff. Ezra needed support for augmentative and alternative communication (AAC) as well as some specific instructional programs. The ESA provided training to the preschool staff and things went fairly well for the rest of the year.*

*When Ezra transitioned to kindergarten, the district staff felt he should be placed in a self-contained special education classroom where it would be easier to meet his educational needs and provide AAC support. His parents requested that he be placed in a regular kindergarten class with the supports he needed in that setting. It was a difficult year that ended in a due process hearing. As a result of that hearing Clinton School District began to change their provision of special education services, related services, and AT services.*

*As a first step in improving the AT services, Norm Martin, the special education director, formed an AT planning group that represented a cross section of the school community, including teachers, administrators, instructional technology specialists, related services personnel, and parents. The group invited individuals to speak to them and made visits to other school districts to see how services were provided. When an AT representative from the ESA told them about QIAT they used the indicators to assess the district's provision of AT services and were shocked to learn how much they needed to change.*

*Change started with the development of written guidelines and provision of district-wide training, first on the law and the new procedures, and then on AT consideration. All potential IEP team members attended AT consideration trainings. All district administrators, including principals and vice-principals, attended a series of workshops regarding use of the Quality Indicators for Administrative Support. This workshop series focused on the importance of administrators' roles in the provision of AT services and described the other special education supports the team was addressing in their plan. Mr. Martin worked with the ESA staff and his superintendent to make sure that the training covered all of the important aspects of quality AT and other special education services.*

*Mr. Martin also used the knowledgeable AT team from the ESA to teach specific AT operating skills to his staff so that they would become comfortable supporting and training others in the future. During the second year of the project, the team focused on developing the district's capability to provide comprehensive AT assessments. As they proceeded with the installation process the team planned to emphasize implementation and evaluation of effectiveness during the next two years.*

# Initial Implementation of Quality Assistive Technology Services

Implementation is the stage at which the agency begins to put the desired change into place. It is common for AT planning groups to identify a need to train a broad cross section of staff members about AT devices and services. All individuals who will be involved in providing services in a new or revised model need to receive training and coaching on many topics, including the specific purpose and value of AT tools, the need for AT services to support those tools, the processes of consideration and assessment, the operation of specific tools, trouble shooting strategies, collection and use of meaningful data, and sources of technical assistance and support.

For many interventions, initial implementation may be a time of challenge and confusion as new ways to do things are introduced. This may be one of the most difficult times for everyone involved in improvement of AT services because people are asked to change their practice and integrate new technologies and teaching strategies into their daily routines. The proactive planning group will take steps to avoid derailing the new AT initiatives at this stage. Steps may include:

- AT team members who will train their colleagues about the new approaches to service delivery are provided with their own professional development on adult learning practices, as well as strategies and techniques to help individuals change systems of behaviors.

- Both AT team members and the individuals they train are coached to support implementation of new strategies and techniques. This coaching addresses ways to effectively support others in new endeavors, ways to deal with team processes that include AT, and ways to deal with conflict.

- The AT implementation planning group members are taught strategies to address obstacles as they emerge and develop systemic solutions that prevent problems from re-occurring.

Fixsen, et al. (2005) found that implementation requires a sustained effort in order to produce the desired outcome. During the initial stage of implementation, "the compelling forces of fear of change, inertia, and investment in the status quo combine with the inherently difficult and complex work of implementing something new" to make it very difficult to achieve the desired change" (Fixsen, et al., 2005, pg.16). Top management support and access to the needed resources during the initial implementation stage are directly related to achieving the desired outcomes (McCormick, Steckler, & McLeroy, 1995).

**EXAMPLE**

*Madison School District had a well established AT program that had been in place for many years. They had a large AT team that provided AT consultations, assessments, training, and follow-up to facilitate the implementation of the AT devices. In recent years, referrals for student with learning disabilities and mild cognitive disabilities had begun to overwhelm their system.*

*At the same time, Madison School District was involved with several initiatives, two of which focused on increasing the use of Universal Design for Learning (UDL) and Accessible Educational Materials (AEM). Both of these initiatives focused on many of the same students. Beth, one of the OTs on the AT team, had been serving on a special education implementation planning group and was the link that brought all three areas together. As the planning group worked to develop a plan for improving supports to students with mild disabilities through UDL, AEM, and AT, especially in the secondary schools in the district, she was able to share the results of the Quality Indicators Self-Evaluation that the AT team had recently completed. This self-evaluation had revealed the need to better integrate AT into the curriculum and have all persons supporting the student share responsibility for implementation of AT devices. Using the Plan/Do/Study/Act paradigm a comprehensive plan was developed.*

*Many different programs and service providers were asked to step up and help implement the plan. Within classrooms the AT team was charged with building capacity for using multimedia software for students with disabilities to provide better access to the curriculum. Multimedia software would read text that is beyond the learner's proficiency level, increase comprehension, organize complex thoughts, and help the students complete writing assignments and tests more independently. With features like text-to-speech, word prediction, talking dictionaries, and spell checking, multimedia software would address many of the reading and writing problems that were preventing these students from making the adequate progress.*

*As part of their planning, the team surveyed teachers to determine what current software was being used most frequently to support access to the curriculum for these students. The team used the results of the survey to identify one primary multimedia software program on which to focus. The planning group asked administration to increase the budget to provide sufficient copies of the software across the district. Software was purchased and installed on computers throughout the district's secondary schools.*

*During installation of this change in the system, the district provided information about the available training by communicating directly with all administrators. As a result, 80% of all registrants said they heard about the training from their administrators.*

*The team planned to track the use of the software over a three-year period. In addition to multiple face-to-face training sessions for small groups of teachers, there was access to online tutorials, tip sheets, individual training, and coaching. Staff members who participated in training were surveyed to determine if they were using the software to meet the needs of their students. At the end of the first semester survey results indicated that 61% of staff were able to successfully use the software with their students.*

# Full Implementation of Quality Assistive Technology Services

During full implementation AT providers are working steadily to provide enhanced services using promising practices. Classroom teachers, paraprofessionals and other support staff are well-trained and collaborating to carry out student and program-wide implementation plans in all settings. Administrators are informed and supportive, highlighting AT and its importance, and holding all educators accountable for their responsibilities. In general, AT devices and services are provided according to mutually developed plans.

Well-planned professional development and training is ongoing, both for experienced and new staff members. Coaching for AT promising practices continues to be a critical part of AT services as new practices continue to be used and expanded.

There are challenges unique to each agency, and supports developed during full implementation will help to ensure progress continues. The full implementation stage may be a time when stakeholders want more progress or competing priorities arise. It is worth repeating that at the full implementation stage, administrative support is crucial if the plan to improve AT services is to maintain a steady course toward the desired outcomes. Not all buildings, levels, or groups will progress at the same pace, and timeframes for full implementation will vary. A snapshot across the agency will show different classrooms and schools at all stages from exploration to full implementation at any given time.

The Quality Indicators for Assistive Technology are used during full implementation to provide one measure of progress, but also to pinpoint additional core components that need to be addressed. For example, if IEP teams had initially failed to consider the need for AT for all students, they may now be doing so at the full implementation stage, but then realize they need improved documentation of the AT in the IEP. Or, in planning for AT transitions, they may identify strategies they would like to use during implementation of AT with younger students.

Full implementation of a new intervention can only occur once the new learning becomes integrated into agency procedures and practices. It often takes two to four years to accomplish full implementation (Wallace et al., 2008).

**EXAMPLE**

*The following year, Madison School District had moved into full implementation in most aspects of their special education systems change. Second year results of the multimedia software project showed an increase in staff use of the software to 74%. It was going better in some buildings than in others. Turnover of staff in one site moved them back to the installation stage in that building with a need for rapid training to bring the new staff up to speed. In two buildings all staff reported success with each of the students who needed AT to access the curriculum. The team decided to focus on the approximately one quarter of the staff that still needed help.*

*They established a professional learning community that met both in person and digitally, and arranged intensive coaching by peer coaches who were successfully using the software. The professional learning community decided to create a wiki with ideas, templates, and directions for using the multimedia software. All teachers who were using the software had access to it.*

*Continued data collection was planned for the third year. The team evaluated the barriers identified in each year of training and adjusted the training opportunities as needed. One of the main barriers identified by teachers indicated that there was not enough time to customize the software to meet the needs of students with multiple disabilities. In response, the team increased their use of just-in-time training, through webinars and podcasts to address some of the frequently asked questions regarding the software and added this information to the wiki. This reduced the need for on-site coaching and increased opportunities for staff to learn new software skills at times when it was convenient for them.*

*At the end of the year, they felt that they were on track and were pleased with the student progress as a result of having this software readily available in all classes.*

## Sustainability of Quality Assistive Technology Services

During the sustainability stage, processes and procedures are in place, a broad range of individuals are successfully implementing the desired practices, and there is a plan to support them if there is a change in staff, budget modification, or other challenges. Sustainability includes written guidelines and procedures so that the ways AT services are provided are consistent and the processes sustainable. Ongoing professional development and training occurs to reach new staff and to provide new or more advanced information about the technologies. Regular support from administrators includes program review and evaluation as well as the development of budgets to ensure access to AT and training. The AT program receives agency recognition that helps to demonstrate the importance of the AT services.

Other aspects that may be seen when an AT program is effective and sustainable are

- an AT budget, which includes funding for staff, equipment, travel, appropriate professional development, and other supports, is established;

- administrative, instructional, and support staff have clearly identified responsibilities for AT;

- data shows that AT for student use is in place and a maintenance plan is established;

- the AT program has documented long-term goals and a plan for sustainability and the plan is reviewed and updated on a regular schedule;

- training, coaching, and measurement processes for making data driven decisions are ongoing;

- policies and procedures supporting and facilitating full implementation of the AT program are in place; and

- a plan is in place to deal with staff attrition, including attrition of administrative leadership.

The goal during the sustainability stage is the continued effectiveness and long-term survival of the core components of high quality AT services that have been achieved. This requires constant vigilance and continued attention to system supports in the context of a changing world.

EXAMPLE

*In 1995 the Jefferson School District developed an AT team that provided expert one-to-one assessments for about 10 years. Initially the team served only students with the most significant disabilities. In 2006, the team was introduced to the Quality Indicators for Assistive Technology and used the QIAT Self-Evaluation Matrices to review their service design. As a result of this self-evaluation, team members identified two specific agency-wide needs: 1) to provide AT devices and services to a broader range of students with disabilities, including those with academic challenges in reading and writing; and 2) to involve all special educators and related services staff members in the assessment, acquisition, and use of AT. The team planned many activities to address these goals. Operating guidelines and policies were written and disseminated. An increased AT budget was developed. Targeted training was provided to various groups. All educators in the district participated in basic training about AT while case managers and special education resource room teachers received training that allowed them to be the initial point of contact for their students who needed or might need AT. All special education staff participated in training about how the district implemented consideration of AT during IEP meetings and for two years, professional observations and evaluations by supervisors included specific AT questions.*

*In 2012, Jefferson District's AT team again identified some areas in the district's AT service design where improvements were needed. While the team had made significant progress in attaining the district's initial AT goals, new challenges had arisen. Team members used the QIAT Self-Evaluation Matrices to reassess the status of their AT services. They were pleased to note that the initial AT goals they had set had been addressed and, although there was still work to be done in those areas, their overall ratings had moved from ones and twos to fours in most areas. The team identified actions they needed to take to ensure continued progress in these two goal areas.*

*There were also new challenges. The increased use of mobile technology and the fact that some schools were purchasing tablet computers for each student in the school was having an enormous impact on the types of AT that students needed and the way in which services were provided. The team decided they needed to explore possible approaches to meet this challenge. They met with their special education director to talk about their concerns and to request establishment of a planning group to investigate possible solutions. As they moved into this first stage of system change, they felt confident that using their self-evaluation data and the Plan/Do/Study/Act model they would soon be moving forward.*

## Summary

When undertaking system change for AT, agencies anticipate that the stages of exploration, installation, initial implementation, full implementation, and sustainability often overlap. In addition, there are activities that may be needed during more than one stage. However, each stage is critical and must be recognized, planned for, and supported at multiple levels of the education agency in order to improve AT services. The amount of time and effort will vary, and progress will depend on many factors. Smaller education agencies with fewer teachers and fewer levels of administration may more quickly and easily decide to adopt a change in practice at the conclusion of the exploration stage. However, during the initial implementation stage, larger education agencies with more resources and greater flexibility are more likely to implement more of the planned changes. A positive organizational climate (e.g., job satisfaction, perceived risk-taking, conflict management, involvement in decision-making) is associated with both the adoption decision and with the extent of implementation (McCormick, et al., 1995).

Agency climate and teacher involvement in decision-making are key factors. Bowser and Reed (2011) point out red flags related to the provision of quality AT services in Table 10.2. These can be a sign of problems with climate and teacher involvement in AT.

| RED FLAGS RELATED TO ASSISTIVE TECHNOLOGY PROGRAM |
| --- |
| AT Consideration in the IEP meeting is typically cursory with little or no discussion and few recommendations. |
| Teachers do not seem to know that AT is included in a student's IEP or how it's being implemented. |
| Negative conversations about AT devices or AT service providers take place frequently. |
| The AT specialist seems to be working in isolation with little or no involvement of teachers. |
| AT is rarely mentioned when brainstorming about how student progress can be increased. |

**TABLE 10.2** Red Flags in AT services.

During each stage, a PDSA cycle can be used to make sure that as change progresses, the implementation planning group knows what that change will look like, and keeps that vision in mind. Through each phase and with the actions taken, results are reviewed, determination of their effectiveness is made, and changes are made to ensure movement is in the desired direction. It is critical that planning groups develop strategies for innovations that are teachable, learnable, doable, and can be assessed in classrooms and schools with documentation that shows there are positive outcomes for students

Winter and Szulanski (2001) found that the speed and effectiveness of implementation of any new program depends on knowing exactly what has to be in place to achieve the desired results for consumers and stakeholders—no more and no less. At all stages of implementation, the Quality Indicators, Intent Statements, and the Self-Evaluation Matrices are the tools needed to identify the core components that need to be in place for quality AT services.

## Suggested Activities

1. Identify three to five individuals from a single school district and have them complete the entire set of Quality Indicator Self-Evaluation Matrices.

2. Review their answers and identify the two top areas of concern for that district.

3. Go to the Active implementation hub (*http://implementation.fpg.unc.edu*). Using the *Stages of Implementation Analysis-Where Are We?*, determine the status of your team in making systemic changes in practice. What resources and tools are helpful in identifying barriers to sustainable change?

4. Download the *Guide to using data in school improvement efforts* from Learning Point Associates (2004) *www.learningpt.org/expertise/schoolimprovement/guidebook.php*. How can this information be applied to improving AT services?

5. Several years ago, the Montgomery County (MD) Public Schools initiated a system change in their AT program, moving from a centralized, expert model to a decentralized model for their high incidence students. Go to the High Incidence Accessible Technology (HIAT) Montgomery County Public Schools—*www.montgomeryschoolsmd.org/departments/hiat*. How does this website illustrate the components of support necessary to implement a system change in AT? Identify the ways in which they are helping teachers and related service providers understand and use AT.

# Quality Indicators for Consideration of Assistive Technology Needs

Consideration of the need for AT devices and services is an integral part of the educational process contained in IDEA for referral, evaluation, and IEP development. Although AT is considered at all stages of the process, the Consideration Quality Indicators are specific to the consideration of AT in the development of the IEP as mandated by the Individuals with Disabilities Education Act (IDEA). In most instances, the Quality Indicators are also appropriate for the consideration of AT for students who qualify for services under other legislation (e.g., 504, ADA).

## Consideration Quality Indicators

1. **Assistive technology devices and services are *considered for all students with disabilities* regardless of type or severity of disability.**

   **Intent**: Consideration of assistive technology need is required by IDEA and is based on the unique educational needs of the student. Students are not excluded from consideration of AT for any reason (e.g., type of disability, age, administrative concerns).

2. **During the development of an individualized educational program, every IEP team consistently uses a *collaborative decision-making process* that supports systematic consideration of each student's possible need for assistive technology devices and services.**

   **Intent**: A collaborative process that ensures that all IEP teams effectively consider the assistive technology of students is defined, communicated, and consistently used throughout the agency. Processes may vary from agency to agency to most effectively address student needs under local conditions.

3. **IEP team members have the *collective knowledge and skills* needed to make informed assistive technology decisions and seek assistance when needed.**

   **Intent**: IEP team members combine their knowledge and skills to determine if assistive technology devices and services are needed to remove barriers to student performance. When the assistive technology needs are beyond the knowledge and scope of the IEP team, additional resources and support are sought.

4. **Decisions regarding the need for assistive technology devices and services are *based on the student's IEP goals and objectives, access to curricular and extracurricular activities, and progress in the general education curriculum.***

   **Intent**: As the IEP team determines the tasks the student needs to complete and develops the goals and objectives, the team considers whether assistive technology is required to accomplish those tasks.

5. **The IEP team *gathers and analyzes data* about the student, customary environments, educational goals, and tasks when considering a student's need for assistive technology devices and services.**

   **Intent**: The IEP team shares and discusses information about the student's present levels of achievement in relationship to the environments and tasks to determine if the student requires assistive technology devices and services to participate actively, work on expected tasks, and make progress toward mastery of educational goals.

6. **When assistive technology is needed, the IEP team *explores a range* of assistive technology devices, services, and other supports that address identified needs.**

   **Intent**: The IEP team considers various supports and services that address the educational needs of the student and may include no tech, low-tech, mid-tech, and/or high-tech solutions and devices. IEP team members do not limit their thinking to only those devices and services currently available within the district.

7. **The assistive technology consideration process and *results are documented in the IEP* and include a rationale for decisions and supporting evidence.**

   **Intent**: Even though IEP documentation may include a checkbox verifying that assistive technology has been considered, the reasons for the decisions and recommendations should be clearly stated. Supporting evidence may include the results of assistive technology assessments, data from device trials, differences in achievement with and without assistive technology, student preferences for competing devices, and teacher observations, among others.

## Common Errors

1. AT is considered for students with severe disabilities only.

2. No one on the IEP team is knowledgeable regarding AT.

3. The team does not use a consistent process based on data about the student, environment, and tasks to make decisions.

4. Consideration of AT is limited to those items that are familiar to team members or are available in the district.

5. Team members fail to consider access to the curriculum and IEP goals in determining if the student requires AT to receive FAPE.

6. If the student does not need AT, team fails to document the basis of its decisions.

## Quality Indicators for Assessment of Assistive Technology Needs

Applying the Quality Indicators for Assessment of Assistive Technology Needs is a process conducted by a team, used to identify tools and strategies to address a student's specific needs. The issues that lead to an AT assessment may be simple and quickly answered or more complex and challenging. Assessment takes place when these issues are beyond the scope of the problem solving that occurs as a part of normal service delivery.

1. *Procedures* for all aspects of assistive technology assessment are clearly defined and consistently applied.

   **Intent**: Throughout the educational agency, personnel are well informed and trained about assessment procedures and how to initiate them. There is consistency throughout the agency in the conducting of assistive technology assessments. Procedures may include—but are not limited to—initiating an assessment, planning and conducting an assessment, conducting trials, reporting results, and resolving conflicts.

2. Assistive technology assessments are conducted by a team with the *collective knowledge and skills needed* to determine possible assistive technology solutions that address the needs and abilities of the student, demands of the customary environments, educational goals, and related activities.

   **Intent**: Team membership is flexible and varies according to the knowledge and skills needed to address student needs. The student and family are active team members. Various team members bring different information and strengths to the assessment process.

3. All assistive technology assessments include a functional assessment in the student's *customary environments*, such as the classroom, lunchroom, playground, home, community setting, or work place.

   **Intent**: The assessment process includes activities that occur in the student's current or anticipated environments because characteristics and demands in each may vary. Team members work together to gather specific data and relevant information in identified environments to contribute to assessment decisions.

4. **Assistive technology assessments, including needed trials, are completed within *reasonable timelines.***

   **Intent**: Assessments are initiated in a timely fashion and proceed according to a timeline the IEP team determines to be reasonable based on the complexity of student needs and assessment questions. Timelines comply with applicable state and agency requirements.

5. **Recommendations from assistive technology assessments are *based on data* about the student, environments, and tasks.**

   **Intent**: The assessment includes information about the student's needs and abilities, demands of various environments, educational tasks, and objectives. Data may be gathered from sources, such as student performance records, results of experimental trials, direct observation, interviews with students or significant others, and anecdotal records.

6. **The assessment provides the IEP team with clearly *documented recommendations* that guide decisions about the selection, acquisition, and use of assistive technology devices and services.**

   **Intent**: A written rationale is provided for any recommendations that are made. Recommendations may include assessment activities and results, suggested devices and alternative ways of addressing needs, services required by the student and others, and suggested strategies for implementation and use.

7. **Assistive technology needs are *reassessed* any time changes in the student, the environments, and/or the tasks result in the student's needs not being met with current devices and services.**

   **Intent**: An assistive technology assessment is available any time it is needed due to changes that have affected the student. The assessment can be requested by the parent or any other member of the IEP team.

## Common Errors

1. Procedures for conducting AT assessment are not defined, or are not customized to meet the student's needs.

2. A team approach to assessment is not utilized.

3. Individuals participating in an assessment do not have the skills necessary to conduct the assessment, and do not seek additional help.

4. Team members don't have adequate time to conduct assessment processes, including necessary trials with AT.

5. Communication between team members is not clear.

6. The student is not involved in the assessment process.

7. When the assessment is conducted by any team other than the student's IEP team, the needs of the student or expectations for the assessment are not communicated.

## Quality Indicators for Including Assistive Technology in the IEP

The Individuals with Disabilities Education Improvement Act (IDEA) requires that the IEP team consider AT needs in the development of every Individualized Education Program (IEP). Once the IEP team has reviewed assessment results and determined that AT is needed for provision of a free, appropriate, public education (FAPE), it's important that the IEP document reflects the team's determination as clearly as possible. The Quality Indicators for AT in the IEP help the team describe the role of AT in the child's educational program.

1. **The education agency has *guidelines for documenting* assistive technology needs in the IEP and requires their consistent application.**

   **Intent**: The education agency provides guidance to IEP teams about how to effectively document assistive technology needs, devices, and services as a part of specially designed instruction, related services, or supplementary aids and services.

2. **All *services* that the IEP team determines are needed to support the selection, acquisition, and use of assistive technology devices are designated in the IEP.**

   **Intent**: The provision of assistive technology services is critical to the effective use of assistive technology devices. It is important that the IEP describes the assistive technology services needed for student success. Such services may include evaluation, customization or maintenance of devices, coordination of services, and training for the student, family, and professionals, among others.

3. **The IEP illustrates that assistive technology is a *tool to support achievement of goals* and progress in the general curriculum by establishing a clear relationship between student needs, assistive technology devices and services, and the student's goals and objectives.**

   **Intent**: Most goals are developed before decisions about assistive technology are made. However, this does not preclude the development of additional goals, especially those related specifically to the appropriate use of assistive technology.

4. **IEP content regarding assistive technology use is written in language that describes how assistive technology contributes to achievement of *measurable and observable outcomes*.**

**Intent**: Content that describes measurable and observable outcomes for assistive technology use enables the IEP team to review the student's progress and determine whether the assistive technology has had the expected impact on student participation and achievement.

5.  **Assistive technology is included in the IEP in a manner that provides a *clear and complete description* of the devices and services to be provided and used to address student needs and achieve expected results.**

    **Intent**: IEPs are written so that participants in the IEP meeting and others who use the information to implement the student's program understand what technology is to be available, how it is to be used, and under what circumstances. Jargon should be avoided.

### Common Errors

1.  IEP teams do not know how to include AT in IEPs.

2.  IEPs including AT use a formulaic approach to documentation. All IEPs are developed in a similar fashion and the unique needs of the child are not addressed.

3.  AT is included in the IEP, but the relationship to goals and objectives is unclear.

4.  AT devices are included in the IEP, but no AT services support the use.

5.  AT expected results are not measurable or observable.

## Quality Indicators for Assistive Technology Implementation

Assistive technology implementation pertains to the ways that assistive technology devices and services, as included in the IEP (including goals/objectives, related services, supplementary aids and services, and accommodations or modifications) are delivered and integrated into the student's educational program. Assistive technology implementation involves people working together to support the student using assistive technology to accomplish expected tasks necessary for active participation and progress in customary educational environments.

1.  **Assistive technology implementation proceeds according to a *collaboratively developed plan.***

    **Intent**: Following IEP development, all those involved in implementation work together to develop a written action plan that provides detailed information about how the AT will be used in specific educational settings, what will be done, and who will do it.

2.  **Assistive technology is *integrated* into the curriculum and daily activities of the student across environments.**

**Intent**: Assistive technology is used when and where it is needed to facilitate the student's access to, and mastery of, the curriculum. Assistive technology may facilitate active participation in educational activities, assessments, extracurricular activities, and typical routines.

3. **Persons supporting the student across all environments in which the assistive technology is expected to be used** *share responsibility* **for implementation of the plan.**

   **Intent**: All persons who work with the student know their roles and responsibilities, are able to support the student using assistive technology, and are expected to do so.

4. **Persons supporting the student provide opportunities for the student to use a** *variety of strategies—including assistive technology* **and to learn which strategies are most effective for particular circumstances and tasks.**

   **Intent**: When and where appropriate, students are encouraged to consider and use alternative strategies to remove barriers to participation or performance. Strategies may include the student's natural abilities, use of assistive technology, other supports, or modifications to the curriculum, task, or environment.

5. *Learning opportunities* **for the student, family, and staff are an integral part of implementation.**

   **Intent**: Learning opportunities needed by the student, staff, and family are based on how the assistive technology will be used in each unique environment. Training and technical assistance are planned and implemented as ongoing processes based on current and changing needs.

6. **Assistive technology implementation is initially based on assessment** *data* **and is adjusted based on performance data.**

   **Intent**: Formal and informal assessment data guide initial decision-making and planning for AT implementation. As the plan is carried out, student performance is monitored and implementation is adjusted in a timely manner to support student progress.

7. **Assistive technology implementation includes** *management and maintenance of equipment* **and materials.**

   **Intent**: For technology to be useful, it's important that equipment management responsibilities are clearly defined and assigned. Though specifics may differ based on the technology, some general areas may include organization of equipment and materials; responsibility for acquisition, set-up, repair, and replacement in a timely fashion; and assurance that equipment is operational.

### Common Errors

1. Implementation is expected to be smooth and effective without addressing specific components in a plan. Team members assume that everyone understands what needs to happen and knows what to do.

2. Plans for implementation are created and carried out by one IEP team member.

3. The team focuses on device acquisition and does not discuss implementation.

4. An implementation plan is developed that is incompatible with the instructional environments.

5. No one takes responsibility for the care and maintenance of AT devices and so they are not available or in working order when needed.

6. Contingency plans for dealing with broken or lost devices are not made in advance.

## Quality Indicators for Evaluation of the Effectiveness of Assistive Technology

This area addresses the evaluation of the effectiveness of the AT devices and services that are provided to individual students. It includes data collection, documentation, and analysis to monitor changes in student performance resulting from the implementation of assistive technology services. Student performance is reviewed in order to identify if, when, or where modifications and revisions to the implementation are needed.

1. **Team members share *clearly defined responsibilities* to ensure that data are collected, evaluated, and interpreted by capable and credible team members.**

   **Intent**: Each team member is accountable for ensuring that the data collection process determined by the team is implemented. Individual roles in the collection and review of the data are assigned by the team. Data collection, evaluation, and interpretation are led by persons with relevant training and knowledge. It can be appropriate for different individual team members to conduct these tasks.

2. **Data are collected on specific student achievement that has been identified by the team and is *related to one or more goals.***

   **Intent**: In order to evaluate the success of assistive technology use, data are collected on various aspects of student performance and achievement. Targets for data collection include the student's use of assistive technology to progress toward mastery of relevant IEP and curricular goals and to enhance participation in extracurricular activities at school and in other environments.

3. **Evaluation of effectiveness includes the** *quantitative and qualitative measurement of changes* **in the student's performance and achievement.**

    **Intent**: Changes targeted for data collection are observable and measurable so that data are as objective as possible. Changes identified by the IEP team for evaluation may include accomplishment of relevant tasks, how assistive technology is used, student preferences, productivity, participation, independence, quality of work, speed and accuracy of performance, and student satisfaction, among others.

4. **Effectiveness is evaluated** *across environments* **during naturally occurring and structured activities.**

    **Intent**: Relevant tasks within each environment where the assistive technology is to be used are identified. Data needed and procedures for collecting those data in each environment are determined.

5. **Data are collected to provide teams with a means for** *analyzing student achievement and identifying supports and barriers* **that influence assistive technology use to determine what changes, if any, are needed.**

    **Intent**: Teams regularly analyze data on multiple factors that may influence success or lead to errors in order to guide decision-making. Such factors include not only the student's understanding of expected tasks and ability to use assistive technology, but also student preferences, intervention strategies, training, and opportunities to gain proficiency.

6. *Changes are made* **in the student's assistive technology services and educational program when evaluation data indicate that such changes are needed to improve student achievement.**

    **Intent**: During the process of reviewing evaluation data, the team decides whether changes or modifications need to be made in the assistive technology, expected tasks, or factors within the environment. The team acts on those decisions and supports their implementation.

7. **Evaluation of effectiveness is a dynamic, responsive,** *ongoing process* **that is reviewed periodically.**

    **Intent**: Scheduled data collection occurs over time and changes in response to both expected and unexpected results. Data collection reflects measurement strategies appropriate to the individual student's needs. Team members evaluate and interpret data during periodic progress reviews.

## Common Errors

1. An observable, measurable student behavior is not specified as a target for change.

2. Team members do not share responsibility for evaluation of effectiveness.

3. An environmentally appropriate means of data collection and strategies has not been identified.

4. A schedule of program review for possible modification is not determined before implementation begins.

## Quality Indicators for Assistive Technology in Transition

Transition plans for students who use assistive technology address the ways the student's use of assistive technology devices and services are transferred from one setting to another. Assistive technology transition involves people from different classrooms, programs, buildings, or agencies working together to ensure continuity. Self-determination, advocacy, and implementation are critical issues for transition planning.

1. **_Transition plans address assistive technology needs_ of the student, including roles and training needs of team members, subsequent steps in assistive technology use, and follow-up after transition takes place.**

   **Intent**: The comprehensive transition plan required by IDEA assists the receiving agency/team to successfully provide needed supports for the AT user. This involves assigning responsibilities and establishing accountability.

2. **Transition _planning empowers the student_ using assistive technology _to participate_ in the transition planning at a level appropriate to age and ability.**

   **Intent**: Specific self-determination skills are taught that enable the student to gradually assume responsibility for participation and leadership in AT transition planning as capacity develops. AT tools are provided, as needed, to support the student's participation.

3. **_Advocacy related to assistive technology use is recognized as critical_ and planned for by the teams involved in transition.**

   **Intent**: Everyone involved in transition advocates for the student's progress, including the student's use of AT. Specific advocacy tasks related to AT use are addressed and may be carried out by the student, the family, staff members, or a representative.

4. **_AT requirements in the receiving environment_ are identified during the transition planning process.**

   **Intent**: Environmental requirements, skill demands, and needed AT support are determined in order to plan appropriately. This determination is made collaboratively and with active participation by representatives from sending and receiving environments.

5. **Transition planning for students using assistive technology proceeds according to an _individualized timeline_.**

**Intent**: Transition planning timelines are adjusted based on specific needs of the student and differences in environments. Timelines address well-mapped action steps with specific target dates and ongoing opportunities for reassessment.

6. **Transition plans address specific *equipment, training, and funding issues* such as transfer or acquisition of assistive technology, manuals, and support documents.**

   **Intent**: A plan is developed to ensure AT equipment, hardware, and software arrives in working condition accompanied by any needed manuals. Provisions for ongoing maintenance and technical support are included in the plan.

## Common Errors

1. Lack of self-determination, self-awareness, and self-advocacy on the part of the individual with a disability (or advocate).

2. Lack of adequate long-range planning on the part of sending and receiving agencies (timelines).

3. Inadequate communication and coordination.

4. Failure to address funding responsibility.

5. Inadequate evaluation process (e.g., lack of documentation, insufficient data, poor communication).

6. Philosophical differences between sending and receiving agencies.

7. Lack of understanding of the law and of their responsibilities.

# Quality Indicators for Administrative Support of Assistive Technology Services

This area defines the critical areas of administrative support and leadership for developing and delivering assistive technology services. It involves the development of policies, procedures, and other supports necessary to improve quality of services and sustain effective assistive technology programs.

1. **The education agency has *written procedural guidelines* that ensure equitable access to assistive technology devices and services for students with disabilities if required for a free, appropriate, public education (FAPE).**

   **Intent**: Clearly written procedural guidelines help ensure that students with disabilities have the assistive technology devices and services they require for educational participation and benefit. Access to assistive technology is ensured regardless of severity of disability, educational placement, geographic location, or economic status.

2. The education agency *broadly disseminates* clearly defined procedures for accessing and providing assistive technology services and supports the implementation of those guidelines.

   **Intent**: Procedures are readily available in multiple formats to families and school personnel in special and general education. All are aware of how to locate the procedures and are expected to follow procedures whenever appropriate.

3. The education agency includes appropriate assistive technology responsibilities in *written descriptions of job requirements* for each position in which activities impact assistive technology services.

   **Intent**: Appropriate responsibilities and the knowledge, skills, and actions required to fulfill them are specified for positions from the classroom through the central office. These descriptions will vary depending on the position and may be reflected in a position description, assignment of duty statement, or some other written description.

4. The education agency employs *personnel with the competencies* needed to support quality assistive technology services within their primary areas of responsibility at all levels of the organization.

   **Intent**: Although different knowledge, skills, and levels of understanding are required for various jobs, all understand and are able to fulfill their parts in developing and maintaining a collaborative system of effective assistive technology services to students.

5. The education agency includes *assistive technology in the technology planning and budgeting process.*

   **Intent**: A comprehensive, collaboratively developed technology plan provides for the technology needs of all students in general education and special education.

6. The education agency provides access to *ongoing learning opportunities about assistive technology* for staff, family, and students.

   **Intent**: Learning opportunities are based on the needs of the student, the family, and the staff and are readily available to all. Training and technical assistance include any topic pertinent to the selection, acquisition, or use of assistive technology or any other aspect of assistive technology service delivery.

7. The education agency uses a *systematic process to evaluate* all components of the agency-wide assistive technology program.

   **Intent**: The components of the evaluation process include, but are not limited to, planning, budgeting, decision-making, delivering AT services to students, and evaluating the impact of AT services on student achievement. There are clear, systematic evaluation procedures that all administrators know about and use on a regular basis at central office and building levels.

## Common Errors

1.  If policies and guidelines are developed, they are not known widely enough to assure equitable application by all IEP teams.

2.  It is not clearly understood that the primary purpose of AT in school settings is to support the implementation of the IEP for the provision of a free, appropriate, public education (FAPE).

3.  Personnel have been appointed to head AT efforts, but resources to support those efforts have not been allocated (time, a budget for devices, professional development, etc.).

4.  AT leadership personnel try or are expected to do all of the AT work and fail to meet expectations.

5.  AT services are established but their effectiveness is never evaluated.

# Quality Indicators for Professional Development and Training in Assistive Technology

This area defines the critical elements of quality professional development and training in assistive technology. Assistive technology professional development and training efforts should arise out of an ongoing, well-defined, sequential, and comprehensive plan. Such a plan can develop and maintain the abilities of individuals at all levels of the organization to participate in the creation and provision of quality AT services. The goal of assistive technology professional development and training is to increase educators' knowledge and skills in a variety of areas including, but not limited to these areas: collaborative processes; a continuum of tools, strategies, and services; resources; legal issues; action planning; and data collection and analysis. Audiences for professional development and training include students, parents or caregivers, special education teachers, educational assistants, support personnel, general education personnel, administrators, AT specialists, and others involved with students.

1.  **Comprehensive assistive technology professional development and training** *support the understanding that assistive technology devices and services enable students to accomplish IEP goals and objectives and make progress in the general curriculum.*

    **Intent**: The Individuals with Disabilities Education Act (IDEA) requires the provision of a free, appropriate, public education (FAPE) for all children with disabilities. The Individualized Education Program (IEP) defines FAPE for each student. The use of AT enables students to participate in and benefit from FAPE. The focus of all AT professional development and training activities is to increase the student's ability to make progress in the general curriculum and accomplish IEP goals and objectives.

2. **The education agency has an assistive technology professional development and training** *plan that identifies the audiences, the purposes, the activities, the expected results, evaluation measures, and funding* **for assistive technology professional development and training.**

   **Intent**: The opportunity to learn the appropriate techniques and strategies is provided for each person involved in the delivery of assistive technology services. Professional development and training are offered at a variety of levels of expertise and are pertinent to individual roles.

3. **The content of comprehensive assistive technology professional development and training** *addresses all aspects of the selection, acquisition, and use* **of assistive technology.**

   **Intent**: AT professional development and training address the development of a wide range of assessment, collaboration, and implementation skills that enable educators to provide effective AT interventions for students. The AT professional development and training plan includes, but is not limited to collaborative processes; the continuum of tools, strategies, and services; resources; legal issues; action planning; and data collection.

4. **Assistive technology professional development and training address and are** *aligned with other local, state, and national professional development initiatives.*

   **Intent**: For many students with disabilities, assistive technology is required for active participation in local, state, and national educational initiatives. Content of the professional development and training includes information about how the use of assistive technology supports the participation of students with disabilities in these initiatives.

5. **Assistive technology professional development and training include** *ongoing learning opportunities that utilize local, regional, and national resources.*

   **Intent**: Professional development and training opportunities enable individuals to meet present needs and increase their knowledge of AT for use in the future. Training in AT occurs frequently enough to address new and emerging technologies and practices, and is available on a repetitive and continuous schedule. A variety of AT professional development and training resources are used.

6. **Professional development and training in assistive technology follow** *research-based models for adult learning* **that include multiple formats and are delivered at multiple skill levels.**

   **Intent**: The design of professional development and training for AT recognizes adults as diverse learners who bring various levels of prior knowledge and experience to the training, and can benefit from differentiated instruction using a variety of formats and diverse timeframes (e.g., workshops, distance learning, follow-up assistance, ongoing technical support).

7.  **The effectiveness of assistive technology professional development and training is** *evaluated by measuring changes in practice that result in improved student performance.*

    **Intent**: Evidence is collected regarding the results of AT professional development and training. The professional development and training plan is modified based on these data in order to ensure changes to educational practice that result in improved student performance.

## Common Errors

1.  The educational agency does not have a comprehensive plan for ongoing AT professional development and training.

2.  The educational agency's plan for professional development and training is not based on AT needs assessment and goals.

3.  Outcomes for professional development are not clearly defined and effectiveness is not measured in terms of practice and student performance.

4.  A continuum of ongoing professional development and training is not available.

5.  Professional development and training focuses on the tools and not the process related to determining student needs and integrating technology into the curriculum.

6.  Professional development and training is provided for special educators but not for administrators, general educators, and instructional technology staff.

# Self-Evaluation Matrices for the Quality Indicators in Assistive Technology Services

# Introduction to the QIAT Self-Evaluation Matrices

The Quality Indicators in Assistive Technology (QIAT) Self-Evaluation Matrices were developed in response to formative evaluation data indicating a need for a model that could assist in the application of the Quality Indicators for Assistive Technology Services in Schools (Zabala, et al. 2000). The QIAT Matrices are based on the idea that change does not happen immediately, but rather, moves toward the ideal in a series of steps that take place over time. The QIAT Matrices use the Innovation Configuration Matrix (ICM) developed by Hall and Hord (1985) as a structural model. The ICM provides descriptive steps ranging from the unacceptable to the ideal that can be used as benchmarks to determine the current status of practice related to a specific goal or objective, and guide continuous improvement toward the ideal. It enables users to determine areas of strength that can be built upon as well as areas of challenge that need improvement.

When the QIAT Matrices are used to guide a collaborative self-assessment conducted by a diverse group of stakeholders within an agency, the information gained can be used to plan for changes that lead to improvement throughout the organization in manageable and attainable steps. The QIAT Matrices can also be used to evaluate the level to which expected or planned-for changes have taken place by periodically analyzing changes in service delivery over time.

When completed by an individual or team, the results of the self-assessment can be used to measure areas of strength and plan for needed professional development, training, or support for the individual or team. When an individual or team uses the QIAT Matrices, however, it is important to realize that the results can only reasonably reflect perceptions of the services in which that individual or team is involved and may not reflect the typical services within the organization. Since a primary goal of QIAT is to increase the quality and consistency of assistive technology (AT) services to *all* students throughout the organization, the perception that an individual or small group is working at the level of best practices does not necessarily mean that the need for quality and consistency of services has been met throughout the organization. The descriptive steps included in the QIAT Matrices are meant to provide illustrative examples and may not be specifically appropriate, as written, for all environments. People using the QIAT Matrices may wish to revise the descriptive steps to align them more closely for specific environments. However, when doing this, care must be taken that the revised steps do not compromise the intent of the quality indictor to which they apply.

The QIAT Matrices document is a companion document to the list of Quality Indicators and Intent Statements. The original six indicator areas were validated by research in 2004 and revisions were made in 2005, 2012, and 2015. For more information, please refer to the indicators and intent statements on the QIAT website at *http://www.qiat.org*. Before an item in the QIAT Matrices is discussed and rated, we recommend the groups read the entire item in the list of Quality Indicators and Intent Statements so that the intent of the item is clear.

# References

Hall, G. E. and Hord, S. M. (1987) *Change in Schools: Facilitating the Process.* Ithaca: State University of New York Press.

QIAT Community. (2015). Quality indicators for assistive technology services. Retrieved April 5, 2015 from http://qiat.org/indicators.html.

Zabala, J.S. (2007). *Development and evaluation of quality indicators for assistive technology services.* University of Kentucky Doctoral Dissertations. Paper 517. *http://uknowledge.uky.edu/gradschool_diss/517*

Zabala, J. S., Bowser, G., Blunt, M., Carl, D. F., Davis, S., Deterding, C., Foss, T., Korsten, J., Hamman, T., Hartsell, K., Marfilius, S. W., McCloskey-Dale, S., Nettleton, S. D., & Reed, P. (2000). Quality indicators for assistive technology services. *Journal of Special Education Technology, 15*(4), 25-36.

Zabala, J. S., & Carl, D. F. (2005). Quality indicators for assistive technology services in schools. In D.L. Edyburn, K. Higgins, & R. Boone (Eds.), *The handbook of special education technology research and practice* (pp. 179-207). Whitefish Bay, WI: Knowledge by Design, Inc.

# Quality Indicators for *Consideration* of Assistive Technology Needs

| QUALITY INDICATOR | UNACCEPTABLE | | |
|---|---|---|---|
| **1. Assistive technology (AT) devices and services are *considered for all students with disabilities* regardless of type or severity of disability.** | 1<br>AT is not considered for students with disabilities. | 2<br>AT is considered only for students with severe disabilities or students in specific disability categories. | |
| **2. During the development of the individualized educational program (IEP), every IEP team consistently uses a *collaborative decision-making process* that supports systematic consideration of each student's possible need for AT devices and services.** | 1<br>No process is established for IEP teams to use to make AT decisions. | 2<br>A process is established for IEP teams to use to make AT decisions but it is not collaborative. | |
| **3. IEP team members have the *collective knowledge and skills* needed to make informed AT decisions and seek assistance when needed.** | 1<br>The team does not have the knowledge or skills needed to make informed AT decisions. The team does not seek help when needed. | 2<br>Individual team members have some of the knowledge and skills needed to make informed AT decisions. The team does not seek help when needed. | |
| **4. Decisions regarding the need for AT devices and services *are based on the student's IEP goals and objectives, access to curricular and extracurricular activities, and progress in the general education curriculum*.** | 1<br>Decisions about a student's need for AT are not connected to IEP goals or the general curriculum. | 2<br>Decisions about a student's need for AT are based on either access to the curriculum/IEP goals or the general curriculum, not both. | |
| **5. The IEP team *gathers and analyzes data* about the student, customary environments, educational goals, and tasks when considering a student's need for AT devices and services.** | 1<br>The IEP team does not gather and analyze data to consider a student's need for AT devices and services. | 2<br>The IEP team gathers and analyzes data about the student, customary environments, educational goals, or tasks, but not all, when considering a student's need for AT devices and services. | |
| **6. When AT is needed, the IEP team *explores a range* of AT devices, services, and other supports that address identified needs.** | 1<br>The IEP team does not explore a range of AT devices, services, and other supports to address identified needs. | 2<br>The IEP team considers a limited set of AT devices, services, and other supports. | |
| **7. The AT consideration process and *results are documented in the IEP* and include a rationale for the decision and supporting evidence.** | 1<br>The consideration process and results are not documented in the IEP. | 2<br>The consideration process and results are documented in the IEP but do not include a rationale for the decision and supporting evidence. | |

| 3 | 4 | 5 |
|---|---|---|
| AT is considered for all students with disabilities but the consideration is inconsistently based on the unique educational needs of the student. | AT is considered for all students with disabilities and the consideration is generally based on the unique educational needs of the student. | AT is considered for all students with disabilities and the consideration is consistently based on the unique educational needs of the student. |
| 3 A collaborative process is established but not generally used by IEP teams to make AT decisions. | 4 A collaborative process is established and generally used by IEP teams to make AT decisions. | 5 A collaborative process is established and consistently used by IEP teams to make AT decisions. |
| 3 Team members sometimes combine knowledge and skills to make informed AT decisions. The team does not always seek help when needed. | 4 Team members generally combine their knowledge and skills to make informed AT decisions. The team seeks help when needed. | 5 The team consistently uses collective knowledge and skills to make informed AT decisions. The team seeks help when needed. |
| 3 Decisions about a student's need for AT sometimes are based on both the student's IEP goals and general education curricular tasks. | 4 Decisions about a student's need for AT generally are based on both the student's IEP goals and general education curricular tasks. | 5 Decisions about a student's need for AT consistently are based on both the student's IEP goals and general education curricular tasks. |
| 3 The IEP team sometimes gathers and analyzes data about the student, customary environments, educational goals, and tasks when considering a student's need for AT devices and services. | 4 The IEP team generally gathers and analyzes data about the student, customary environments, educational goals, and tasks when considering a student's need for AT devices and services. | 5 The IEP team consistently gathers and analyzes data about the student, customary environments, educational goals, and tasks when considering a student's need for AT devices and services. |
| 3 The IEP team sometimes explores a range of AT devices, services, and other supports. | 4 The IEP team generally explores a range of AT devices, services, and other supports. | 5 The IEP team always explores a range of AT devices, services, and other supports to address identified needs. |
| 3 The consideration process and results are documented in the IEP and sometimes include a rationale for the decision and supporting evidence. | 4 The consideration process and results are documented in the IEP and generally include a rationale for the decision and supporting evidence. | 5 The consideration process and results are documented in the IEP and consistently include a rationale for the decision and supporting evidence. |

# Quality Indicators for *Assessment* of Assistive Technology Needs

| QUALITY INDICATOR | UNACCEPTABLE | | |
|---|---|---|---|
| **1. *Procedures* for all aspects of AT assessment are clearly defined and consistently applied.** | 1<br>No procedures are defined. | 2<br>Some assessment procedures are defined, but not generally used. | |
| **2. AT assessments are conducted by a *team with the collective knowledge and skills needed* to determine possible AT solutions that address the needs and abilities of the student, demands of the customary environments, educational goals, and related activities.** | 1<br>A designated individual with no prior knowledge of the student's needs or technology conducts assessments. | 2<br>A designated person or group conducts assessments but lacks either knowledge of AT or of the student's needs, environments, or tasks. | |
| **3. All AT assessments include a functional assessment in the student's *customary environments*, such as the classroom, lunchroom, playground, home, community setting, or work place.** | 1<br>No component of the AT assessment is conducted in any of the student's customary environments. | 2<br>No component of the AT assessment is conducted in any of the customary environments, however, data about the customary environments are sought. | |
| **4. AT assessments, including needed trials, are completed within *reasonable timelines*.** | 1<br>AT assessments are not completed within agency timelines. | 2<br>AT assessments are frequently out of compliance with timelines. | |
| **5. Recommendations from AT assessments are *based on data* about the student, environments and tasks.** | 1<br>Recommendations are not data-based. | 2<br>Recommendations are based on incomplete data from limited sources. | |
| **6. The assessment provides the IEP team with clearly *documented recommendations* that guide decisions about the selection, acquisition, and use of AT devices and services.** | 1<br>Recommendations are not documented. | 2<br>Documented recommendations include only devices. Recommendations about services are not documented. | |
| **7. AT needs are *reassessed* any time changes in the student, the environments and/or the tasks result in the student's needs not being met with current devices or services.** | 1<br>AT needs are not reassessed. | 2<br>AT needs are only reassessed when requested. Reassessment is done formally and no ongoing AT assessment takes place. | |

| | | PROMISING PRACTICES |
|---|---|---|
| 3<br><br>Procedures are defined and used only by specialized personnel. | 4<br><br>Procedures are clearly defined and generally used in both special and general education. | 5<br><br>Everyone involved in the assessment process uses clearly defined procedures. |
| 3<br><br>A team conducts assessments with limited input from individuals who have knowledge of AT or of the student's needs, environments, and tasks. | 4<br><br>A collaborative team whose members have direct knowledge of the student's needs, environments, and tasks, and knowledge of AT generally conducts assessments. | 5<br><br>A collaborative, flexible team formed on the basis of knowledge of the individual student's needs, environments, and tasks, and expertise in AT consistently conducts assessments. |
| 3<br><br>Functional components of AT assessments are sometimes conducted in the student's customary environments. | 4<br><br>Functional components of AT assessments are generally conducted in the student's customary environments. | 5<br><br>Functional components of AT assessments are consistently conducted in the student's customary environments. |
| 3<br><br>AT assessments are completed within a reasonable timeline and may or may not include initial trials. | 4<br><br>AT assessments are completed within a reasonable timeline and include at least initial trials. | 5<br><br>AT assessments are conducted in a timely manner and include a plan for ongoing assessment and trials in customary environments. |
| 3<br><br>Recommendations are sometimes based on data about student performance on typical tasks in customary environments. | 4<br><br>Recommendations are generally based on data about student performance on typical tasks in customary environments. | 5<br><br>Recommendations are consistently based on data about student performance on typical tasks in customary environments. |
| 3<br><br>Documented recommendations may or may not include sufficient information about devices and services to guide decision-making and program development. | 4<br><br>Documented recommendations generally include sufficient information about devices and services to guide decision-making and program development. | 5<br><br>Documented recommendations consistently include sufficient information about devices and services to guide decision-making and program development. |
| 3<br><br>AT needs are reassessed on an annual basis or upon request. Reassessment may include some ongoing and formal assessment strategies. | 4<br><br>AT use is frequently monitored. AT needs are generally reassessed if current tools and strategies are ineffective. Reassessment generally includes ongoing assessment strategies and includes formal assessment, if indicated. | 5<br><br>AT use is frequently monitored. AT needs are generally reassessed if current tools and strategies are ineffective. Reassessment generally includes ongoing assessment strategies and includes formal assessment, if indicated. |

# Quality Indicators for Including Assistive Technology in the IEP

| QUALITY INDICATOR | UNACCEPTABLE | |
|---|---|---|
| 1. The education agency has *guidelines for documenting* AT needs in the IEP and requires their consistent application. | 1<br>The agency does not have guidelines for documenting AT in the IEP. | 2<br>The agency has guidelines for documenting AT in the IEP but team members are not aware of them. |
| 2. All *services* that the IEP team determines are needed to support the selection, acquisition, and use of AT devices are designated in the IEP. | 1<br>AT devices and services are not documented in the IEP. | 2<br>Some AT devices and services are minimally documented. Documentation does not include sufficient information to support effective implementation. |
| 3. The IEP illustrates that AT is a *tool to support achievement of goals* and progress in the general curriculum by establishing a clear relationship between the student's needs, AT devices and services, and the student's goals and objectives. | 1<br>AT use is not linked to IEP goals and objectives or participation and progress in the general curriculum. | 2<br>AT use is sometimes linked to IEP goals and objectives but not linked to the general curriculum. |
| 4. IEP content regarding AT use is written in language that describes how AT contributes to achievement of *measurable and observable outcomes*. | 1<br>The IEP does not describe outcomes to be achieved through AT use. | 2<br>The IEP describes outcomes to be achieved through AT use, but they are not measurable. |
| 5. AT is included in the IEP in a manner that provides a *clear and complete* description of the devices and services to be provided and is used to address student needs and achieve expected results. | 1<br>Devices and services needed to support AT use are not documented. | 2<br>Some devices and services are documented but they do not adequately support AT use. |

| 3 | 4 | 5 |
|---|---|---|
| The agency has guidelines for documenting AT in the IEP and members of some teams are aware of them. | The agency has guidelines for documenting AT in the IEP and members of most teams are aware of them. | The agency has guidelines for documenting AT in the IEP and members of all teams are aware of them. |
| 3 Required AT devices and services are documented. Documentation sometimes includes sufficient information to support effective implementation. | 4 Required AT devices and services are documented. Documentation generally includes sufficient information to support effective implementation. | 5 Required AT devices and services are documented. Documentation consistently includes sufficient information to support effective implementation. |
| 3 AT use is linked to IEP goals and objectives and sometimes linked to the general curriculum. | 4 AT is linked to IEP goals and objectives and is generally linked to the general curriculum. | 5 AT is linked to the IEP goals and objectives and is consistently linked to the general curriculum. |
| 3 The IEP describes outcomes to be achieved through AT use, but only some are measurable. | 4 The IEP generally describes observable, measurable outcomes to be achieved through AT use. | 5 The IEP consistently describes observable, measurable outcomes to be achieved through AT use. |
| 3 Devices and services are documented and are sometime adequate to support AT use. | 4 Devices and services are documented and are generally adequate to support AT use. | 5 Devices and services are documented and are consistently adequate to support AT use. |

# Quality Indicators for Assistive Technology *Implementation*

| QUALITY INDICATOR | UNACCEPTABLE | | |
|---|---|---|---|
| **1. AT implementation proceeds according to a** *collaboratively developed plan.* | 1<br>There is no implementation plan. | 2<br>Individual team members may develop AT implementation plans independently. | |
| **2. AT is** *integrated* **into the curriculum and daily activities of the student across environments.** | 1<br>AT included in the IEP is rarely used. | 2<br>AT is used in isolation with no links to the student's curriculum and/or daily activities. | |
| **3. Persons supporting the student across all environments in which the AT is expected to be used** *share responsibility* **for implementation of the plan.** | 1<br>Responsibility for implementation is not accepted by any team member. | 2<br>Responsibility for implementation is assigned to one team member. | |
| **4. Persons supporting the student provide opportunities for the student to use** *a variety of strategies—including AT*—**and to learn which strategies are most effective for particular circumstances and tasks.** | 1<br>No strategies are provided to support the accomplishment of tasks. | 2<br>Only one strategy is provided to support the accomplishment of tasks. | |
| **5.** *Learning opportunities* **for the student, family, and staff is an integral part of implementation.** | 1<br>AT needs for learning opportunities have not been determined. | 2<br>AT learning opportunity needs are initially identified for student, family, and staff, but no training has been provided. | |
| **6. AT implementation is initially based on assessment** *data* **and is adjusted based on performance data.** | 1<br>AT implementation is based on equipment availability and limited knowledge of team members, not on student data. | 2<br>AT implementation is loosely based on initial assessment data and rarely adjusted. | |
| **7. AT implementation includes management and** *maintenance of equipment* **and materials.** | 1<br>Equipment and materials are not managed or maintained. Students rarely have access to the equipment and materials they require. | 2<br>Equipment and materials are managed and maintained on a crisis basis. Students frequently do not have access to the equipment and materials they require. | |

| | | |
|---|---|---|
| 3<br>Some team members collaborate in the development of an AT implementation plan. | 4<br>Most team members collaborate in the development of AT implementation plan. | 5<br>All team members collaborate in the development of a comprehensive AT implementation plan. |
| 3<br>AT is sometimes integrated into the student's curriculum and daily activities. | 4<br>AT is generally integrated into the student's curriculum and daily activities. | 5<br>AT is fully integrated into the student's curriculum and daily activities. |
| 3<br>Responsibility for implementation is shared by some team members in some environments. | 4<br>Responsibility for implementation is generally shared by most team members in most environments. | 5<br>Responsibility for implementation is consistently shared among team members across all environments. |
| 3<br>Multiple strategies are provided. Students are sometimes encouraged to select and use the most appropriate strategy for each task. | 4<br>Multiple strategies are provided. Students are generally encouraged to select and use the most appropriate strategy for each task. | 5<br>Multiple strategies are provided. Students are consistently encouraged to select and use the most appropriate strategy for each task. |
| 3<br>Initial AT learning opportunities are sometimes provided to student, family, and staff. | 4<br>Initial and follow-up AT learning opportunities are generally provided to student, family, and staff | 5<br>Ongoing AT learning opportunities are provided to student, family, and staff as needed, based on changing needs. |
| 3<br>AT implementation is based on initial assessment data and is sometimes adjusted as needed based on student progress. | 4<br>AT implementation is based on initial assessment data and is generally adjusted as needed based on student progress. | 5<br>AT implementation is based on initial assessment data and is consistently adjusted as needed based on student progress. |
| 3<br>Equipment and materials are managed and maintained so that students sometimes have access to the equipment and materials they require. | 4<br>Equipment and materials are managed and maintained so that students generally have access to the equipment and materials they require. | 5<br>Equipment and materials are effectively managed and maintained so that students consistently have access to the equipment and materials they require. |

# Quality Indicators for *Evaluation of the Effectiveness* of Assistive Technology

| QUALITY INDICATOR | UNACCEPTABLE | | |
|---|---|---|---|
| 1. Team members share *clearly defined responsibilities* to ensure that data are collected, evaluated, and interpreted by capable and credible team members. | 1<br>Responsibilities for data collection, evaluation, or interpretation are not defined. | 2<br>Responsibilities for data collection, evaluation, or interpretation of data are assigned to one team member. | |
| 2. Data are collected on specific student achievement that has been identified by the team and is *related to one or more goals*. | 1<br>Team neither identifies specific changes in student behaviors expected from AT use nor collects data. | 2<br>Team identifies student behaviors and collects data, but the behaviors are either not specific or not related to IEP goals. | |
| 3. Evaluation of effectiveness includes the *quantitative and qualitative* measurement of changes in the student's performance and achievement. | 1<br>Effectiveness is not evaluated. | 2<br>Evaluation of effectiveness is not based on student performance, but rather on subjective opinion. | |
| 4. Effectiveness is evaluated *across environments* including during naturally occurring opportunities as well as structured activities. | 1<br>Effectiveness is not evaluated in any environment. | 2<br>Effectiveness is evaluated only during structured opportunities in controlled environments (e.g., massed trials data). | |
| 5. Data are collected so teams can analyze *student achievement and identify supports and barriers* that influence AT use and determine what changes, if any, are needed. | 1<br>No data are collected or analyzed. | 2<br>Data are collected but are not analyzed. | |
| 6. *Changes are made* in the student's AT services and educational program when evaluation data indicate that such changes are needed to improve student achievement. | 1<br>Program changes are never made. | 2<br>Program changes are made in the absence of data. | |
| 7. Evaluation of effectiveness is a dynamic, responsive, *ongoing process* that is reviewed periodically. | 1<br>No process is used to evaluate effectiveness. | 2<br>Evaluation of effectiveness only takes place annually, but the team does not make program changes based on data. | |

| | | |
|---|---|---|
| 3<br>Responsibilities for collection, evaluation, and interpretation of data are shared by some team members. | 4<br>Responsibilities for collection, evaluation, and interpretation of data are shared by most team members. | 5<br>Responsibilities for collection, evaluation, and interpretation of data are consistently shared by team members. |
| 3<br>Team identifies specific student behaviors related to IEP goals, but inconsistently collects data. | 4<br>Team identifies specific student behaviors related to IEP goals, and generally collects data. | 5<br>Team identifies specific student behaviors related to IEP goals, and consistently collects data on changes in those behaviors. |
| 3<br>Evaluation of effectiveness is not consistent or is based on limited data about student performance. | 4<br>Evaluation of effectiveness is generally based on quantitative and qualitative data about student performance from a few sources. | 5<br>Effectiveness is consistently evaluated using both quantitative and qualitative data about student's performance obtained from a variety of sources. |
| 3<br>Effectiveness is evaluated during structured activities across environments and a few naturally occurring opportunities. | 4<br>Effectiveness is generally evaluated during naturally occurring opportunities and structured activities in multiple environments. | 5<br>Effectiveness is consistently evaluated during naturally occurring opportunities and structured activities in multiple environments. |
| 3<br>Data are superficially analyzed.. | 4<br>Data are sufficiently analyzed most of the time. | 5<br>Data are sufficiently analyzed all of the time. |
| 3<br>Program changes are loosely linked to student performance data. | 4<br>Program changes are generally linked to student performance data. | 5<br>Program changes are consistently linked to student performance data. |
| 3<br>Evaluation of effectiveness only takes place annually and the team uses the data to make annual program changes | 4<br>Evaluation of effectiveness takes place on an on-going basis and team generally uses the data to make program changes. | 5<br>Evaluation of effectiveness takes place on an on-going basis and the team consistently uses the data to make program changes. |

# Quality Indicators for Assistive Technology in *Transition*

| QUALITY INDICATOR | UNACCEPTABLE | |
|---|---|---|
| 1. *Transition plans address the AT needs* of the student, including roles and training needs of team members, subsequent steps in AT use, and follow-up after transition takes place. | 1<br>Transition plans do not address AT needs. | 2<br>Transition plans rarely address AT needs, critical roles, steps, or follow-up. |
| 2. Transition *planning empowers the student* using AT to participate in the transition planning at a level appropriate to age and ability. | 1<br>Student is not present. | 2<br>Student may be present but does not participate or input is ignored. |
| 3. *Advocacy related to AT use is recognized as critical* and planned for by the teams involved in transition. | 1<br>No one advocates for AT use or the development of student's self-determination skills. | 2<br>Advocacy rarely occurs for AT use or the development of student self-determination skills. |
| 4. *AT requirements in the receiving environment* are identified during the transition planning process. | 1<br>AT requirements in the receiving environment are not identified. | 2<br>AT requirements in the receiving environment are rarely identified. |
| 5. Transition planning for students using AT proceeds according to an *individualized timeline*. | 1<br>Individualized timelines are not developed to support transition planning for students using AT. | 2<br>Individualized timelines are developed, but do not support transition planning for students using AT. |
| 6. Transition plans address specific *equipment, training, and funding* issues, such as transfer or acquisition of AT, manuals, and support documents. | 1<br>The plans do not address AT equipment, training, and funding issues. | 2<br>The plans rarely address AT equipment, training, and/or funding issues. |

| | | |
|---|---|---|
| 3<br>Transition plans sometimes address AT needs but may not include critical roles, steps, or follow-up. | 4<br>Transition plans always address AT needs and usually include critical roles, steps, or follow-up. | 5<br>Transition plans consistently address AT needs and all team members are involved and knowledgeable about critical roles, steps, and follow-up. |
| 3<br>Student sometimes participates and some student input is considered. | 4<br>Student participates and student input is generally reflected in the transition plan. | 5<br>Student is a full participant and student input is consistently reflected in the transition plan. |
| 3<br>Advocacy sometimes occurs for AT use and the development of student self-determination skills. | 4<br>Advocacy usually occurs for AT use and the development of student self-determination skills. | 5<br>Advocacy consistently occurs for AT use and the development of student self-determination skills. |
| 3<br>AT requirements in the receiving environment are identified, some participants are involved and some requirements are addressed. | 4<br>AT requirements in the receiving environment are identified, most participants are involved and most requirements are addressed. | 5<br>AT requirements in the receiving environment are consistently identified by all participants. |
| 3<br>Individualized timelines are sometimes developed and support transition planning for students using AT. | 4<br>Individualized timelines are generally developed and support transition planning for students using AT. | 5<br>Individualized timelines are consistently developed and support transition planning for students using AT. |
| 3<br>The plans sometimes address AT equipment, training, or funding issues. | 4<br>The plans usually address AT equipment, training, and funding issues. | 5<br>The plans consistently address AT equipment, training, and funding issues. |

# Quality Indicators for *Administrative Support* of Assistive Technology

| QUALITY INDICATOR | UNACCEPTABLE | | |
|---|---|---|---|
| **1. The education agency has *written procedural guidelines* that ensure equitable access to AT devices and services for students with disabilities, if required for a free, appropriate, public education (FAPE).** | 1<br>No written procedural guidelines are in place. | 2<br>Written procedural guidelines for few components of AT service delivery (e.g., assessment or consideration) are in place. | |
| **2. The education agency *broadly disseminates* clearly defined procedures for accessing and providing AT services, and supports the implementation of those guidelines.** | 1<br>No procedures disseminated and no plan to disseminate. | 2<br>A plan for dissemination exists, but has not been implemented. | |
| **3. The education agency includes appropriate AT responsibilities in *written descriptions of job requirements* for each position in which activities impact AT services.** | 1<br>No job requirements relating to AT are written. | 2<br>Job requirements related to AT are written only for a few specific personnel who provide AT services. | |
| **4. The education agency employs *personnel with the competencies* needed to support quality AT services within their primary areas of responsibility at all levels of the organization.** | 1<br>AT competencies are not considered in hiring, assigning, or evaluating personnel. | 2<br>AT competencies are recognized as an added value in an employee but are not sought. | |
| **5. The education agency includes *AT in the technology planning and budgeting process.*** | 1<br>There is no planning and budgeting process for AT. | 2<br>AT planning and budgeting is a special education function that is not included in the agency-wide technology planning and budgeting process. | |
| **6. The education agency provides access to *ongoing learning opportunities about AT* for staff, family, and students.** | 1<br>No learning opportunities related to AT are provided. | 2<br>Learning opportunities related to AT are provided on a crisis-basis only. Learning opportunities may not be available to all who need them. | |
| **7. The education agency uses a *systematic process to evaluate* all components of the agency-wide AT program.** | 1<br>The agency-wide AT program is not evaluated. | 2<br>Varying procedures are used to evaluate some components of the agency-wide AT program. | |

| | | |
|---|---|---|
| 3<br>Written procedural guidelines that address several components of AT service delivery are in place. | 4<br>Written procedural guidelines that address most components of AT service delivery are in place. | 5<br>Comprehensive written procedural guidelines that address all components of AT service delivery are in place. |
| 3<br>Procedures are disseminated to a few staff who work directly with AT. | 4<br>Procedures are disseminated to most agency personnel and generally used. | 5<br>Procedures are disseminated to all agency personnel and consistently used. |
| 3<br>Job requirements related to AT are written for most personnel who provide AT services but are not clearly aligned to job responsibilities. | 4<br>Job requirements related to AT are written for most personnel who provide AT services and are generally aligned to job responsibilities. | 5<br>Job requirements related to AT are written for all personnel who provide AT services and are clearly aligned to job responsibilities. |
| 3<br>AT competencies are recognized and sought for specific personnel. | 4<br>AT competencies are generally valued and used in hiring, assigning, and evaluating personnel. | 5<br>AT competencies are consistently valued and used in hiring, assigning, and evaluating personnel. |
| 3<br>AT is sometimes included in the agency-wide technology planning and budgeting process, but is inadequate to meet AT needs throughout the agency. | 4<br>AT is generally included in agency-wide technology planning and budgeting process in a way that meets most AT needs throughout the agency. | 5<br>AT is included in the agency-wide technology planning and budgeting process in a way that meets AT needs throughout the agency. |
| 3<br>Learning opportunities related to AT are provided to some individuals on a pre-defined schedule. | 4<br>Learning opportunities related to AT are provided on a pre-defined schedule to most individuals with some follow-up opportunities. | 5<br>Learning opportunities related to AT are provided on an ongoing basis to address the changing needs of students with disabilities, their families, and the staff who serve them. |
| 3<br>A systematic procedure is inconsistently used to evaluate a few components of the agency-wide AT program. | 4<br>A systematic procedure is generally used to evaluate most components of the agency-wide AT program. | 5<br>A systematic procedure is consistently used throughout the agency to evaluate all components of the agency-wide AT program. |

# Quality Indicators for *Professional Development and Training* in Assistive Technology

| QUALITY INDICATOR | UNACCEPTABLE | | |
|---|---|---|---|
| **1. Comprehensive AT professional development and training** *support the understanding that AT devices and services enable students to accomplish IEP goals and objectives and make progress in the general curriculum.* | 1<br>There is no professional development and training in the use of AT. | 2<br>Professional development and training address only technical aspects of AT tools and/or are not related to use for academic achievement. | |
| **2. The education agency has an AT professional development and training plan that** *identifies the audiences, purposes, activities, expected results, evaluation measures, and funding for* **AT professional development and training.** | 1<br>There is no plan for AT professional development and training. | 2<br>The plan includes unrelated activities done on a sporadic basis for a limited audience. | |
| **3. AT professional development and training address and are** *aligned with other local, state, and national professional development initiatives.* | 1<br>Professional development and training do not consider other initiatives. | 2<br>Professional development and training rarely align with other initiatives. | |
| **4. AT professional development and** *training include ongoing learning opportunities that utilize local, regional, and/or national resources.* | 1<br>There are no professional development and training opportunities. | 2<br>Professional development and training occur infrequently. | |
| **5. Professional development and training in AT follow** *research-based models for adult learning* **that include multiple formats and are delivered at multiple skill levels.** | 1<br>Professional development and training never consider adult learning. | 2<br>Professional development and training rarely consider models for adult learning strategies. | |
| **6. The effectiveness of AT professional development and training is** *evaluated by measuring changes* **in practice that result in improved student performance.** | 1<br>Changes in practice are not measured. | 2<br>Changes in practice are rarely measured. | |

| | | |
|---|---|---|
| 3<br>Some professional development and training include strategies for use of AT devices and services to facilitate academic achievement. | 4<br>Most professional development and training include strategies for use of AT devices and services to facilitate academic achievement. | 5<br>All professional development and training include strategies for use of AT devices and services to facilitate academic achievement. |
| 3<br>The plan includes some elements (e.g., variety of activities, purpose, levels) for some audiences. | 4<br>The plan includes most elements of a comprehensive plan for most audiences. | 5<br>The comprehensive AT professional development plan encompasses all elements, audiences, and levels. |
| 3<br>Professional development and training sometimes align with other initiatives. | 4<br>Professional development and training generally align with other initiatives. | 5<br>Professional development and training consistently align with other initiatives as appropriate. |
| 3<br>Professional development and training are sometimes provided. | 4<br>Professional development and training are generally provided. | 5<br>Professional development and training opportunities are provided on a comprehensive, repetitive, and continuous schedule, utilizing appropriate local, regional, and national resources. |
| 3<br>Professional development and training sometimes consider research-based adult learning strategies. | 4<br>Professional development and training generally consider research-based adult learning strategies. | 5<br>Professional development and training consistently consider research-based adult learning strategies. |
| 3<br>Changes in practice are measured using a variety of measures but may not be related to student performance. | 4<br>Changes in practice are usually measured using a variety of reliable measures linked to improved student performance. | 5<br>Changes in practice are consistently measured using a variety of reliable measures linked to improved student performance. |

# Self-Evaluation Matrices Summary Sheet

Afer completing the Quality Indicators matrices, record the self-rating numbers on this summary sheet. Circle the variation number to the right of each indicator. Then connect the circles to create a depiction of strengths and areas of concern.

Completed by: _____

District/School: _____

Date: _____

| AREA: CONSIDERATION OF AT NEEDS | | | | | | |
|---|---|---|---|---|---|---|
| **INDICATOR** | | **SELF-RATING #** | | | | |
| **1.** Assistive technology devices and services are *considered for all students with disabilities* regardless of type or severity of disability. | 1 | 2 | 3 | 4 | 5 | |
| **2.** During the development of the individualized educational program, every IEP team consistently uses a *collaborative decision-making process* that supports systematic consideration of each student's possible need for assistive technology devices and services. | 1 | 2 | 3 | 4 | 5 | |
| **3.** IEP team members have the *collective knowledge and skills* needed to make informed assistive technology decisions and seek assistance when needed. | 1 | 2 | 3 | 4 | 5 | |
| **4.** Decisions regarding the need for assistive technology devices and services *are based on the student's IEP goals and objectives, access to curricular and extracurricular activities, and progress in the general education curriculum.* | 1 | 2 | 3 | 4 | 5 | |
| **5.** The IEP team *gathers and analyzes* data about the student, customary environments, educational goals, and tasks when considering a student's need for assistive technology devices and services. | 1 | 2 | 3 | 4 | 5 | |
| **6.** When assistive technology is needed, the IEP team *explores a range* of assistive technology devices, services, and other supports that address identified needs. | 1 | 2 | 3 | 4 | 5 | |
| **7.** The assistive technology consideration process and *results are documented in the IEP* and include a rationale for the decision and supporting evidence. | 1 | 2 | 3 | 4 | 5 | |

| AREA: ASSESSMENT OF AT NEEDS | |
|---|---|
| INDICATOR | SELF-RATING # |
| **1.** *Procedures* for all aspects of assistive technology assessment are clearly defined and consistently applied. | 1   2   3   4   5 |
| **2.** Assistive technology assessments are conducted by a *team with the collective knowledge and skills* needed to determine possible assistive technology solutions that address the needs and abilities of the student, demands of the customary environments, educational goals, and related activities. | 1   2   3   4   5 |
| **3.** All assistive technology assessments include a functional assessment in the student's *customary environments*, such as the classroom, lunchroom, playground, home, community setting, or work place. | 1   2   3   4   5 |
| **4.** Assistive technology assessments, including needed trials, are completed within *reasonable timelines*. | 1   2   3   4   5 |
| **5.** Recommendations from assistive technology assessments are *based on data* about the student, environments, and tasks. | 1   2   3   4   5 |
| **6.** The assessment provides the IEP team with clearly *documented recommendations* that guide decisions about the selection, acquisition, and use of assistive technology devices and services. | 1   2   3   4   5 |
| **7.** Assistive technology needs are *reassessed* any time changes in the student, the environments, and/or the tasks result in the student's needs not being met with current devices and/or services. | 1   2   3   4   5 |

| AREA: DOCUMENTATION IN THE IEP | |
|---|---|
| INDICATOR | SELF-RATING # |
| **1.** The education agency has *guidelines for documenting* assistive technology needs in the IEP and requires their consistent application. | 1  2  3  4  5 |
| **2.** All *services* that the IEP team determines are needed to support the selection, acquisition, and use of assistive technology devices are designated in the IEP. | 1  2  3  4  5 |
| **3.** The IEP illustrates that assistive technology is a *tool to support achievement of goals* and progress in the general curriculum by establishing a clear relationship between student needs, assistive technology devices and services, and the student's goals and objectives. | 1  2  3  4  5 |
| **4.** IEP content regarding assistive technology use is written in language that describes how assistive technology contributes to achievement of *measurable and observable outcomes*. | 1  2  3  4  5 |
| **5.** Assistive technology is included in the IEP in a manner that provides a *clear and complete description* of the devices and services to be provided and used to address student needs and achieve expected results. | 1  2  3  4  5 |

| AREA: AT IMPLEMENTATION | | | | | |
|---|---|---|---|---|---|
| INDICATOR | SELF-RATING # | | | | |
| **1.** Assistive technology implementation proceeds according to a *collaboratively developed plan.* | 1 | 2 | 3 | 4 | 5 |
| **2.** Assistive technology is *integrated* into the curriculum and daily activities of the student across environments. | 1 | 2 | 3 | 4 | 5 |
| **3.** Persons supporting the student across all environments in which the assistive technology is expected to be used *share responsibility* for implementation of the plan. | 1 | 2 | 3 | 4 | 5 |
| **4.** Persons supporting the student provide opportunities for the student to use a *variety of strategies—including assistive technology*—and to learn which strategies are most effective for particular circumstances and tasks. | 1 | 2 | 3 | 4 | 5 |
| **5.** *Learning opportunities* for the student, family, and staff are an integral part of implementation. | 1 | 2 | 3 | 4 | 5 |
| **6.** Assistive technology implementation is initially based on assessment *data* and is adjusted based on performance data. | 1 | 2 | 3 | 4 | 5 |
| **7.** Assistive technology implementation includes *management and maintenance of equipment* and materials. | 1 | 2 | 3 | 4 | 5 |

| AREA: EVALUATION OF EFFECTIVENESS | |
|---|---|
| INDICATOR | SELF-RATING # |
| **1.** Team members share *clearly defined responsibilities* to ensure that data are collected, evaluated, and interpreted by capable and credible team members. | 1  2  3  4  5 |
| **2.** Data are collected on specific student achievement that have been identified by the team and are *related to one or more goals*. | 1  2  3  4  5 |
| **3.** Evaluation of effectiveness includes the *quantitative and qualitative measurement of changes* in the student's performance and achievement. | 1  2  3  4  5 |
| **4.** Effectiveness is evaluated *across environments* during naturally occurring and structured activities. | 1  2  3  4  5 |
| **5.** Data are collected to provide teams with a means for *analyzing student achievement and identifying supports and barriers* that influence assistive technology use to determine what changes, if any, are needed. | 1  2  3  4  5 |
| **6.** *Changes are made* in the student's assistive technology services and educational program when evaluation data indicate that such changes are needed to improve student achievement. | 1  2  3  4  5 |
| **7.** Evaluation of effectiveness is a dynamic, responsive, *ongoing process* that is reviewed periodically. | 1  2  3  4  5 |

| AREA: ASSISTIVE TECHNOLOGY TRANSITION | | | | | |
|---|---|---|---|---|---|
| INDICATOR | SELF-RATING # | | | | |
| **1.** *Transition plans address assistive technology needs* of the student, including roles and training needs of team members, subsequent steps in assistive technology use, and follow-up after transition takes place. | 1 | 2 | 3 | 4 | 5 |
| **2.** Transition *planning empowers the student* using assistive technology to participate in the transition planning at a level appropriate to age and ability. | 1 | 2 | 3 | 4 | 5 |
| **3.** *Advocacy related to assistive technology use is recognized as critical* and planned for by the teams involved in transition. | 1 | 2 | 3 | 4 | 5 |
| **4.** *AT requirements in the receiving environment* are identified during the transition planning process. | 1 | 2 | 3 | 4 | 5 |
| **5.** Transition planning for students using assistive technology proceeds according to an *individualized timeline.* | 1 | 2 | 3 | 4 | 5 |
| **6.** Transition plans address specific *equipment, training, and funding issues,* such as transfer or acquisition of assistive technology, manuals, and support documents. | 1 | 2 | 3 | 4 | 5 |

| AREA: ADMINISTRATIVE SUPPORT | | | | | | |
|---|---|---|---|---|---|---|
| INDICATOR | SELF-RATING # | | | | | |
| **1.** The education agency has *written procedural guidelines* that ensure equitable access to assistive technology devices and services for students with disabilities, if required for a free, appropriate, public education (FAPE). | 1 | 2 | 3 | 4 | 5 | |
| **2.** The education agency *broadly disseminates* clearly defined procedures for accessing and providing assistive technology services, and supports the implementation of those guidelines. | 1 | 2 | 3 | 4 | 5 | |
| **3.** The education agency includes appropriate assistive technology responsibilities in *written descriptions of job requirements* for each position in which activities impact assistive technology services. | 1 | 2 | 3 | 4 | 5 | |
| **4.** The education agency employs *personnel with the competencies* needed to support quality assistive technology services within their primary areas of responsibility at all levels of the organization. | 1 | 2 | 3 | 4 | 5 | |
| **5.** The education agency includes *assistive technology in the technology planning and budgeting process.* | 1 | 2 | 3 | 4 | 5 | |
| **6.** The education agency provides access to *ongoing learning opportunities about assistive technology* for staff, family, and students. | 1 | 2 | 3 | 4 | 5 | |
| **7.** The education agency uses a *systematic process to evaluate* all components of the agency-wide assistive technology program. | 1 | 2 | 3 | 4 | 5 | |

| AREA: PROFESSIONAL DEVELOPMENT AND TRAINING FOR AT | | | | | |
|---|---|---|---|---|---|
| INDICATOR | SELF-RATING # | | | | |
| **1.** Comprehensive assistive technology professional development and training *support the understanding that assistive technology devices and services enable students to accomplish IEP goals and objectives and make progress in the general curriculum.* | 1 | 2 | 3 | 4 | 5 |
| **2.** The education agency has an AT professional development and training *plan that identifies the audiences, purposes, activities, expected results, evaluation measures, and funding* for assistive technology professional development and training. | 1 | 2 | 3 | 4 | 5 |
| **3.** The content of comprehensive AT professional development and training *addresses all aspects of the selection, acquisition, and use* of assistive technology. | 1 | 2 | 3 | 4 | 5 |
| **4.** AT professional development and training address and are *aligned with other local, state, and national professional development initiatives.* | 1 | 2 | 3 | 4 | 5 |
| **5.** Assistive technology professional development and *training include ongoing learning opportunities that utilize local, regional, and/or national resources.* | 1 | 2 | 3 | 4 | 5 |
| **6.** Professional development and training in assistive technology follow *research-based models for adult learning* that include multiple formats and are delivered at multiple skill levels. | 1 | 2 | 3 | 4 | 5 |
| **7.** The effectiveness of assistive technology professional development and training is *evaluated by measuring changes* in practice that result in improved student performance. | 1 | 2 | 3 | 4 | 5 |

# QIAT Planning Documents

# QIAT Planning Document: Consideration of the Need for AT

Student: _____

Student ID: _____ Birthdate: _____

School: _____

Participants: _____

Date: _____

*IEP teams may use this form to guide discussion and determine if assistive technology devices and/or services are necessary for the student to make progress in IEP goals and curricular tasks.*

| INSTRUCTIONAL AREA | COMPLETES TASKS WITH ACCOMMODATIONS/ MODIFICATIONS AND/OR ASSISTIVE TECHNOLOGY | | CONSIDERATION OUTCOMES—DOCUMENT OUTCOME IN THE IEP |
|---|---|---|---|
| **Column A**<br>❏ Initial IEP<br>❏ Annual IEP<br><br>Based on the student's previous performance or IEP goals and objectives, check the curricular area(s) or tasks in which the student is not making progress.<br>❏ Reading<br>❏ Written Expression<br>❏ Handwriting<br>❏ Computer Access<br>❏ Oral Communication<br>❏ Math<br>❏ Activities of Daily Living<br>❏ Behavior<br>❏ Transition<br>❏ Other<br>❏ Student is making adequate progress<br>Go to column C.<br>❏ Student is not making adequate progress<br>Go to column B I. | **Column B I**<br>What accommodations and/ or modifications have been tried?<br>1)<br>2)<br>3)<br>Results of above:<br>1)<br>2)<br>3)<br>Circle the above accommodations and modifications currently being used.<br>❏ Student is making adequate progress with current accommodations/modifications. Go to Column C.<br>❏ Student is not making adequate progress with current accommodations or modifications.<br>List other accommodations or modifications to explore:<br><br><br>❏ No accommodations and modifications have been tried.<br>Go to column B II. | **Column B II**<br>What assistive technology has been tried?<br>1)<br>2)<br>3)<br>Results of above:<br>1)<br>2)<br>3)<br>Circle the above assistive technology tools that are currently being used.<br>❏ Student is making adequate progress with current assistive technology. Go to Column C.<br>❏ Student is not making adequate progress with current assistive technology.<br>List features of assistive technology needed:<br><br><br>❏ No assistive technologies have been tried.<br>Go to column C. | **Column C**<br>❏ Student independently accomplishes tasks in all instructional areas. No assistive technology is required.<br>❏ Student accomplishes tasks in all instructional areas with current accommodations and modifications. No assistive technology is required.<br>❏ Student accomplishes tasks in all instructional areas with currently available assistive technology. Assistive technology is required.<br>❏ Student does not successfully accomplish tasks in all instructional areas. Additional solutions including assistive technology may be required. (Document the nature of the assistance that is needed and follow agency procedures.) Take following action:<br>_____<br>_____<br>_____ |

# Assistive Technology Assessment Process Planner

Student Name: _____     Planning Date: _____

| Referral for AT assessment is made by any member of the student's team when classroom strategies and tools do not meet the student's needs. | | |
|---|---|---|
| | **By Date** | **Person** |
| **AT assessment** is completed by a collaborative team sharing responsibilities | | |
| Determine team members | | |
| **Create a written AT assessment plan** including: | | |
| Determine the assessment question(s) | | |
| Identify expected results & outcomes (*e.g., Student will be able to____*) | | |
| Determine what will be measured (e.g., speed, quantity, quality, rate, accuracy, endurance) | | |
| Assign responsibilities | | |
| Set a timeline | | |
| **Gather information** from multiple sources including previous information (e.g., educational reports, assessments, background interviews, and other records) | | |
| Student's strengths | | |
| Student's needs | | |
| Environmental expectations | | |
| Tasks (e.g., required curricular work, testing, homework, projects, in-class work, materials, statewide testing, & other school functions) | | |
| Current levels of performance for identified tasks (baseline data) | | |
| Barriers to participation & independence | | |
| **Analyze information to identify tools & strategies for the trials** | | |
| Determine the features needed | | |
| Choose tools with appropriate features | | |
| Determine source of trials from demos, loaners, & rental programs | | |
| Set timelines | | |
| Prepare data collection recording method (measurable determined above) | | |
| **Conduct the trials with identified tools** | | |
| Have student use tools in customary environment for identified tasks | | |
| Collect data | | |

*(continued)*

| Referral for AT assessment is made by any member of the student's team when classroom strategies and tools do not meet the student's needs. | By Date | Person |
|---|---|---|
| **Analyze Data** | | |
| Report the results of the trials | | |
| Revisit the assessment question(s) to determine the outcomes | | |
| Determine the most appropriate tool(s) & strategies or if additional trials are necessary | | |
| **Document recommendations in written form following district assistive technology procedural guidelines** | | |
| Summarize student performance while using AT tools, including tools that were and were not successful | | |
| Document appropriate tools and potential impact on student achievement | | |
| If needed, include specific language for procurement of AT, and possible funding sources (Refer to Quality Indicator for Administrative Support for AT) | | |
| **Document required tools & strategies in student's plan (e.g., IEP, 504 Plan) (Refer to Quality Indicator for Documentation in the IEP)** | | |
| Develop implementation plan | | |
| Instructional/access areas which were explored during the trial | | |
| Summary of specific skills assessed | | |
| Written action plan including team member roles & responsibilities (refer to Quality Indicator for AT Implementation) | | |
| **Reassess as needs change** | | |
| Monitor the student abilities, environment, tasks, and barriers as well as effectiveness of current AT on an ongoing basis | | |

# Assistive Technology in the IEP Planner

The following questions guide IEP team discussion for considering and documenting AT in the IEP.

| QUESTIONS FOR IEP TEAMS: | DOCUMENT IN IEP SECTION: |
|---|---|
| Does the student currently use AT devices to participate and make progress in the general education curriculum?<br><br>▪ For what tasks is AT used?<br>▪ Is AT effective in completing these tasks?<br>▪ In what environments is AT used?<br>▪ Are AT services currently being provided?<br>▪ Are there additional tasks for which AT might be effective? | Present Levels of Academic Achievement and Functional Performance |
| Does the student need AT devices and/or services to accomplish annual goals?<br><br>▪ How will AT support progress toward annual goals?<br>▪ In what environments will AT be used?<br>▪ Do goals need to be developed that address acquisition of technology related skills? | Measurable Annual Goals (Functional and Academic) |
| Does the student need AT devices and/or services to accomplish benchmarks and/or short-term objectives?<br><br>▪ How will AT support progress toward benchmarks and/or short-term objectives?<br>▪ In what environments will AT be used?<br>▪ Do benchmarks and/or short-term goals need to be developed that address acquisition of technology related skills? | Short-term Objectives or Benchmarks |
| Does the student need AT devices and/or services to participate and progress in the curriculum or to benefit from specially designed instruction?<br><br>▪ Does the student need AT to remove barriers to participation in the general education curriculum?<br>▪ Does the student need AT to complete educationally relevant tasks? | Consideration of Special Factors |
| Does the student need AT devices and/or services as part of related services to enable the student to benefit from special education?<br><br>▪ Will the provision of AT devices or services become part of the services of a current service provider?<br>▪ Will an additional service provider provide the AT services? | Related Services |
| Does the student need AT devices and/or services as part of supplementary aids and services to support participation in general education classes or other education related settings to enable him or her to be educated with children without disabilities? | Supplementary Aids and Services |
| Do the school personnel working with the student need any AT-related training or supports?<br><br>▪ Do school personnel need training to develop and/or implement the student's AT?<br>▪ Do school personnel need technical assistance and support to develop and/or implement the student's AT? | Program Modifications or Supports for School Personnel |

*(continued)*

| QUESTIONS FOR IEP TEAMS: | DOCUMENT IN IEP SECTION: |
|---|---|
| Does the student need AT to participate in state-wide and district assessments?<br>▨ Is the identified AT a component of the student's typical instruction and/or classroom assessments?<br>▨ Is the use of identified AT allowed in the assessment?<br>▨ Is the identified AT available within or compatible with the assessment?<br>▨ Can the identified AT be used without invalidating the test construct? | Accommodations for Participation in State and District-wide Assessments |
| Does the student need AT devices and/or services as a part of transition to post-school environments?<br><br>Does the student need AT devices and/or services to accomplish measurable goals related to:<br>▨ Post-secondary education<br>▨ Vocational education<br>▨ Employment<br>▨ Adult services<br>▨ Independent living<br>▨ Community participation<br><br>Have AT service providers been identified for post-school environments and invited to participate? | Transition Services |

# Implementation of Assistive Technology Planner

Teams may use this form to guide discussion in the development of an implementation plan that is well thought-out with input from all stakeholders (team members). Best practices suggest that all components below should be considered when developing the AT implementation plan.

| KEY ELEMENTS OF AN AT IMPLEMENTATION PLAN |
| --- |
| Who will collaborate in the development of the implementation plan? |
| What specific goals and tasks will be addressed in the plan? |
| What aspects of the student's performance are expected to change (e.g., reduced time, increased accuracy, quantity, quality, engagement)? |
| How will AT be integrated into the curriculum and daily activities across environments? |
| What tools and strategies will be used to accomplish identified tasks? |
| What evidence/data will be needed to determine which tools and strategies are most effective for particular environments and tasks? |
| How will performance evidence/data be measured and collected? |
| When will the performance evidence/data be reviewed to determine what changes, if any, are needed in the implementation plan? |
| What do team members need to do for successful implementation to take place? |
| Which team members (e.g., staff, family, supporters, student) will share responsibility for each action that needs to be taken? |
| What initial and ongoing learning opportunities will be provided for all team members, including the student? |
| How will equipment and materials be managed and maintained? |

# Plan for Evaluation of Effectiveness of AT Use

Student's Name: _____

Student ID: _____    Grade: _____    Date: _____

School Agency: _____

Team members present: _____

The intent of this document is to guide planning about how the use of assistive technology will be evaluated. Completion of this document will help the team to create a shared vision of the process for data collection.

IEP Goal: _____

| | |
|---|---|
| Step 1: What is the present level of performance (baseline data) on this goal? | Describe: |
| Step 2: What changes are expected as a result of implementation? (e.g., Student will be able to _____.) | Describe: |
| Step 3: What aspects will change?<br>❑ Quality     ❑ Independence<br>❑ Quantity/productivity     ❑ Spontaneity<br>❑ Frequency     ❑ Duration<br>❑ Participation     ❑ _____ | Describe: |
| Step 4: What obstacles may inhibit success?<br>❑ Physical access     ❑ Skill<br>❑ Opportunity     ❑ Attitude<br>❑ Instruction/practice     ❑ Medical<br>❑ Student preference     ❑ _____ | Describe: |
| Step 5: How will the occurrence of obstacles be reflected in the data? | Describe: |

Step 6: What format will be used to collect the data?

❑ Report (self, other)　　❑ Audio/video recording

❑ Work samples　　❑ _____

❑ Observation

Describe:

Step 7: What is the data collection plan?

Environment(s): _____

Activity: _____

Frequency: _____

Person(s) responsible: _____

　　Data Collection _____

　　Data Analysis _____

　　Changes in Response to Analysis _____

Review date(s): _____

# Transition Planning Worksheet for AT Users

Student: _____ Age: _____

Indicate Transition:

❏ Early Childhood to School          ❏ Program to Program

❏ School to School                   ❏ School to Post-secondary

Persons completing this worksheet: _____

| NAME OF PROGRAM AND/OR SCHOOL | |
|---|---|
| Current Placement & Services: | Future Setting & Services: |

| NAME THE PRIMARY POINT OF CONTACT (E.G., SERVICES COORDINATOR, SUPERVISOR) WITH CONTACT INFORMATION (E.G., PHONE NUMBER, EMAIL ADDRESS). | |
|---|---|
| Current Setting: | Future Setting: |

| SERVICES NEEDED IN FUTURE SETTING (E.G., OT, PT, SPEECH/LANGUAGE, TRANSPORTATION, MEDICAL) | PERSON | DATE |
|---|---|---|
| | | |

*(continued)*

| GENERAL TRANSITION TASKS TO BE COMPLETED | PERSON | DATE |
|---|---|---|
| ▨ Staff members from current setting observe in future setting | | |
| ▨ Student/family visit future setting | | |
| ▨ Staff from both settings meet to plan | | |
| ▨ Arrange enrollment in needed non-school services (e.g., DD, VR) | | |
| Other: _____ | | |

| DEVICE SPECIFIC TASKS TO BE COMPLETED<br>NAME/TYPE OF AT USED: _____ | PERSON | DATE |
|---|---|---|
| ▨ Arrange transfer of technology including manuals, service records | | |
| ▨ Create artifacts to demonstrate current level of use and independence (e.g., video recording, work samples) | | |
| ▨ Identify any new technology that may be needed in future setting | | |
| ▨ Identify sources of funding for new technology | | |
| ▨ Identify person(s) to do troubleshooting in future setting | | |
| Other:_____ | | |

---

**AT SKILLS TO INCREASE STUDENT INDEPENDENCE**
**(TO BE INCLUDED IN IEP AS NECESSARY)**

Device-specific use/operational skills: Knowing how to operate the technology

Functional Use Skills: Using AT to accomplish meaningful tasks across settings

Strategic Skills: Choosing the right tool for a specific task

Social Skills: Using technology effectively and appropriately around other people

**AT SKILLS TO INCREASE STUDENT SELF DETERMINATION**
**(TO BE INCLUDED IN IEP AS NECESSARY)**

Choice-making:

Decision-making:

Problem-solving:

Goal-setting/attainment:

Self-regulation/self-management:

Self-advocacy/leadership:

Transition planning teams should consider how the student's current or future AT use will impact success in each of these transition areas.

❑ **Instruction**—Is instruction needed to prepare the student for new settings? Is the current AT appropriate? Will additional devices or services be needed for new settings?

❑ **Related Services**—Is there a need for additional related services to prepare the student for post-secondary life? Are the current related services supporting AT use needed in future settings? Who will provide these? How can the student/family connect with necessary services?

❑ **Community Experiences**—What opportunities need to be provided for the student to use AT in community experiences to prepare for post-secondary life, including socialization, recreation, banking, transportation, etc.?

❑ **Employment**—If AT will be used as part of the student's employability, what services and strategies need to be considered? What activities using AT are needed to develop work-related skills, including job seeking and retention skills, career exploration, and paid employment?

❑ **Post-school Adult Living**—What activities will be needed to prepare the student to use his AT in developing independence in adult living, including accessing medical services, registering to vote, accessing transportation, and paying rent and other bills?

❑ **Daily Living Skills**—What activities will be needed to prepare the student to use her AT in developing independence in daily living, such as cooking, dressing, shopping, maintaining health and hygiene, housekeeping, etc.?

❑ **Functional Vocational Evaluation**—How is the use of AT incorporated into the vocational evaluation? Do the evaluation results indicate a need for continued use of AT or the use of new AT?

# Administrators' Planner for Effective Technology Supervision and Leadership

Principals and administrative leaders are powerful change agents. Research shows that perceived pressure from principals and other administrators to use technology is one of the most powerful factors in increasing technology use for teaching and learning (O'Dwyer, Russell, & Bebell, 2004). This planner can be used to support and guide administrators in their work as they identify effective technology use, including assistive technology (AT), and mentor teachers and staff. Suggestions for use include staff discussion of service quality, goal-setting, supervision, continuous improvement efforts, monitoring, and progress assessment.

| EFFECTIVE TECHNOLOGY LEADERSHIP FOR PRINCIPALS AND OTHER ADMINISTRATORS | YES | NO |
|---|---|---|
| Principals and teachers have clearly defined, shared expectations of the importance of implementing technology, including AT, in teaching and learning. | | |
| Administrators' expectations for technology use including AT are communicated throughout the school year in a variety of ways. | | |
| Administrators ensure that teachers have equitable access to current technologies, software, appropriate technical support, and the Internet. | | |
| Reward structures (e.g., recognition, opportunities to share, credits toward salary advancement) are in place to support technology in teaching and learning. | | |
| Administrators ensure that principals and teachers know how to access resources to support students who need additional technology assistance. | | |
| **EFFECTIVE TECHNOLOGY PRACTICE FOR TEACHERS** | | |
| Teachers are skilled in the use of technology for preparing and delivering instruction. | | |
| Teachers access professional development opportunities to support technology use in teaching and learning. | | |
| Teachers ensure that technology is available and operational and seek technical assistance in a timely manner. | | |
| Teachers utilize innovative ideas for using technology resources to support standards-based instruction. | | |
| Teachers facilitate appropriate student use of technology-based resources using a variety of applications. | | |
| Teachers regularly measure the effectiveness of technology for learning. | | |
| Teachers proactively incorporate technology into teaching and learning activities to support diverse learners. | | |
| Teachers ensure that students have the opportunity to use the technology, including assistive technology, written into their IEPs. | | |
| Teachers routinely include specific evidence about technology use when reporting student progress to parents. | | |

(continued)

| EFFECTIVE TECHNOLOGY USE BY STUDENTS | YES | NO |
|---|---|---|
| Students regularly use technology, including assistive technology, as required to participate in learning activities, complete assignments, and interact with peers. | | |
| Students who experience difficulty with reading use technology to access information, acquire knowledge, and demonstrate skills. | | |
| Students who experience difficulty with writing use technology to demonstrate knowledge and skills. | | |
| Students who experience difficulty with physical or sensory access to classroom materials use technology to access the curriculum and demonstrate knowledge and skills. | | |
| Students who experience difficulty with math use technology to access information, acquire knowledge, and demonstrate skills. | | |
| Students who experience difficulty with oral communication use technology to support communication efforts. | | |

# Encouraging Effective Technology Use in Schools

One of an administrator's responsibilities is to manage the technology that is currently used. However, it is important to point out that when considering AT for an individual student, a wide range of options should be considered in addition to what is available in the district.

A school leader can encourage appropriate and effective use of technology by:

1. Involving staff in the creation of a school-wide technology plan that includes AT.

2. Leading staff in becoming familiar with the educational and assistive technology available at their school.

3. Encouraging staff to become familiar with resources to support technology use at school, district, and statewide levels.

4. Periodically assessing the technology training needs of staff at your school.

5. Planning professional development about teaching with technology.

6. Using Universal Design for Learning strategies to support the needs of diverse learners.

   • Advocating for technology that supports accessibility for diverse learners.

   • Promoting the use of technology-based learning activities in line with curriculum objectives.

7. Recognizing effective technology use (e.g., highlight effective practices at staff meetings, bulletin board postings, peer sharing, and newsletter articles).

8. Creating a database of all assistive and educational technology used in the building in order to:

- Obtain information about what the district has committed to provide to meet individual student needs.

- Monitor building-wide usage.

- Plan for future needs.

9. Monitoring AT consideration at IEP meetings to ensure that AT is considered for every student receiving special education.

10. Making a master list of assistive technology included in each IEP. Prior to a teacher observation, check the master list to determine which students should have technology available and operational in that class.

11. Ensuring timely technical support and repairs to support continuous student achievement.

## References

O'Dwyer, L. M., Russell, M. & Bebell, D. J. (2004, September 14). Identifying teacher, school and district characteristics associated with elementary teachers' use of technology: A multilevel perspective. *Education Policy Analysis Archives,* 12(48).

International Society for Technology in Education (2003). *National educational technology standards for teachers.* Eugene, OR: Author. Retrieved from *http://www.iste .org/standards/ISTE-standards/standards-for-teachers.*

# Assistive Technology Professional Development and Training Planner

Topic: _____  Date of Training: _____

School/Agency: _____  Planning Team Members: _____

| | |
|---|---|
| **Audience:** | **Describe Evidence of Need:** |
| **Purpose of Training:** | **Brief Overview of Content:** |

**Level of Training:**

❑ Awareness  ❑ Application

❑ Knowledge  ❑ Mastery

**Focus of Training:**

❑ Devices

❑ Services

**Content Learning Objectives:**

**Format(s) for Training:**

❑ Face-to-face  ❑ Online learning module

❑ Ongoing class  ❑ Blog or wiki

❑ Online workshop  ❑ Podcast

❑ Online credit course  ❑ Video training

❑ Webinar  ❑ Community of Practice

**Describe:**

**Formats for Follow-up:**

❑ Coaching  ❑ Social media

❑ Mentoring  ❑ Professional Learning Community

❑ Email/phone support

**Describe:**

**Expected Results for Students:**

*(continued)*

---

Evaluation Measures:

---

Resources Needed:

❏ Training coordination

❏ Instructor

❏ Funding source

❏ Training site (face-to-face or electronic)

❏ Registration, enrollment

❏ Electronic communications

Describe:

---

# References

Alper, S., & Raharinirina, S. (2006). Assistive technology for individuals with disabilities: A review and synthesis of the literature. *Journal of Special Education Technology, 21*(2), 47–64.

Amado, A. N., and McBride, M. (2001), *Increasing person-centered thinking: Improving the quality of person-centered planning: A manual for person-centered planning facilitators.* Minneapolis, MN: University of Minnesota, Institute on Community Integration. Retrieved October 30, 2014 from *rtc.umn,edu/docs/pcpmanual1.pdf.*

Americans With Disabilities Act of 1990, Pub. L. No. 101-336, 104 Stat. 328 (1990).

Ashton, T., Lee, Y., & Vega, L. A. (2005). Assistive technology: Perceived knowledge, attitudes, and challenges of AT use in special education. *Journal of Special Education Technology, 20*(2), 60–63.

Ashton, T., & Wahl, L. (2004). Assistive technology: Surveying special education staff on AT awareness, use, and training. *Journal of Special Education Technology,* 19(2), 57–58.

Bagnato, S. J., Neisworth, J. T., & Pretti-Frontczak, K. (2010). *Linking authentic assessment and early childhood intervention: Best measures for best practices* (2nd ed.). Baltimore, MD: Brookes Publishing.

Bouck, E.C. (2010). Technology and students with disabilities: Does it solve all the problems. In F. E. Obiakor, J. P. Bakken, & A. F. Rotatori (Eds.) *Current Issues and Trends in Special Education: Research, Technology, and Teacher Preparation* (Advances in Special Education, Vol. 20), 91–104. Bingley, England, UK: Emerald Group.

Bowser, G., Korsten, J., Reed, P., & Zabala, J. (1999). Quality indicators for effective assistive technology services. *TAM Connector, 11*(5), 1–5.

Bowser, G., & Reed, P. (1995). Education TECH points for assistive technology planning. *Journal of Special Education Technology, 12*(4), 325–338.

Bowser, G. & Reed, P. (2004). *A school administrator's desktop guide to assistive technology.* Arlington, VA: Technology and Media Division of the Council for Exceptional Children.

Bowser, G., & Reed, P. (2011). The ABC's of effective AT consideration. Winchester, OR: Coalition for Assistive Technology in Oregon. *www.educationtechpoints.org*.

Bowser, G. & Reed, P. (2012). *Education tech points: A framework for assistive technology planning* (2nd ed.). Winchester, OR: Coalition for Assistive Technology in Oregon.

Bray, M., Brown, A., & Green, T. D. (2004). *Technology and the diverse learners.* Thousand Oaks, CA: Corwin Press.

Breslin-Larson, J., Smith, M., Fields, J. L. S., & Hill, K. (2004). Quality indicators in action. *Closing the Gap, 23*(3), 1–2.

Carl, D. F., Mataya, C. K., & Zabala, J. S. (1994). *What's the big IDEA?: Legal and practical aspects of assistive technology in school settings.* Professional development conducted at Closing the Gap Conference on Technology in Special Education and Rehabilitation, Minneapolis, MN.

Castellani, J., Reed, P., Zabala, J., Dwyer, J., McPherson, S., & Rein, J., (2004). *Considering the need for assistive technology within the individualized education program.* Arlington, VA: Technology and Media Division of the Council for Exceptional Children.

Cheliotes, L. G., and Reilly, M. F. (2010). *Coaching conversations: Transforming your school one conversation at a time.* Thousand Oaks, CA: Corwin.

Collaborative for Technology Standards for School Administrators. (2001). Technology standards for school administrators. Naperville, IL: North Central Regional Technology in Education Consortium. Downloaded December 13, 2014 from *www.kyepsb.net/documents/EduPrep/tssa.pdf*.

Dalton, E. (2002). Assistive technology in education: A review of policies, standards, and curriculum integration from 1997 through 2000 involving assistive technology and the Individuals with Disabilities Education Act. *Issues in Teaching and Learning, 1*(1).

DeCoste, D. (2006). *Assistive technology assessment: Written productivity profiles.* Volo, IL: Don Johnston, Inc.

DeCoste, D., & Wilson, L. B. (2012). *Protocol for accommodations in reading.* Volo, IL: Don Johnston, Inc., Retrieved August 2, 2014 from *www.donjohnston.com/products/par/index.html*.

Delaney, E. (1999). *Curriculum and intervention strategies* [PowerPoint Presentation]. Presented at University of Illinois, Chicago. Retrieved June 10, 2014 from *www.uic.edu/classes/sped/sped508/aug30.ppt*.

Dell, A. G., Newton, D. A., & Petroff, J. G. (2008). *Assistive technology in the classroom: Enhancing the school experiences of students with disabilities.* Upper Saddle River, NJ: Pearson Prentice Hall.

Dimmitt, S., Hodapp, J., Judas, C., Munn, C., & Rachow, C. (2006). Iowa Text Reader Project impacts student achievement. *Closing the Gap, 24*(6), 12–13.

Edyburn, D. L. (2004). Rethinking assistive technology. *Special Education Technology Practice, 5*(4), 16–23.

Edyburn, D. L. (2005). Special education technology networks of practice. *Journal of Special Education Technology, 20*(3), 67–69.

Edyburn, D. L. (2007). Assistive technology team tools. *Special Education Technology Practice, 9*(2), 16–20.

Elbro, C., Rasmussen, I., & Spelling, B. (1996). Teaching reading to disabled readers with language disorders: A controlled evaluation of synthetic speech feedback. *Scandinavian Journal of Psychology, 37,* 140–155.

Erickson, K., Hanser, G., Hatch, P., & Sanders, E. (2009). *Research-based practices for creating access to the general curriculum in reading and literacy for students with significant intellectual disabilities.* Chapel Hill, NC: Center for Literacy and Disability Studies.

Fried-Oken, M., Bersani, H., Anctil, T., & Bowser, G. (1998). *TechTransmitter.* Portland, OR: Oregon Health Sciences University.

Fixsen, D. L., Naoom, S. F., Blase, K. A., Friedman, R. M. & Wallace, F. (2005). Implementation research: A synthesis of the literature (FHMI Publication 231). Tampa, FL: The National Implementation Research Network, University of South Florida. Retrieved June 10, 2015 from *http://ctndisseminationlibrary.org/PDF/ nirnmonograph.pdf.*

Fullan, M. (2003). *Change forces with a vengeance.* New York, NY: RoutledgeFalmer.

Gersten, R., & Edyburn, D. L. (2007). Enhancing the evidence base of special education technology research: Defining special education research quality indicators. *Journal of Special Education Technology, 22*(3), 3–18.

Hall, G. E., and Hord, S. M. (1987). *Change in schools: Facilitating the process.* Ithaca, NY: State University of New York Press.

Hargrove, R. (2000). *Masterful coaching fieldbook.* San Francisco, CA: Jossey-Bass/Pfeiffer.

Hitchcock, C., Khalsa, A., Malouf, D. B., Parette, P., Zabala, J. S., & Edyburn, D. L. (2005). Forum: The future of assistive technology. *Threshold: Exploring the Future of Education, 2*(4), 10–14.

Heur, M. B., Parette, H. P., & Scherer, M. (2004). Effects of acculturation on assistive technology service delivery. *Journal of Special Education Technology, 19*(2), 31–41.

Hodapp, J., & Rachow, C. (2010). Impact of Text-to-Speech Software on Access to Print: A Longitudinal Study. In Seok, S., Meyen, E. L., & DaCosta, B. (Eds.). *Human cognition and assistive technology: Design, accessibility, and transdisciplinary perspectives* (pp. 119–219). Hershey, PA: Medical Information Science Reference. doi:10.4018/978-1-61520-817-3.ch014.

Hutinger, P., Johanson, J., & Stoneburner, R. (1996). Assistive applications in educational programs of children with multiple disabilities: A case study report on the state of practice. *Journal of Special Education Technology, 13*(1), 16–35.

Individuals with Disabilities Education Act of 1990 (IDEA), P.L. 101–476.

Individuals with Disabilities Education Act of 1997 (IDEA), P.L. 105–17.

Individuals with Disabilities Education Improvement Act of 2004 (IDEA), P.L. 108-446. 20 U.S.C. § 1401 et seq.; 34 C.F.R. § 300.1 et seq.

International Society for Technology in Education (2003). *National educational technology standards for teachers.* Eugene, OR: Author. Retrieved from *http://www.iste. org/standards/ISTE-standards/standards-for-teachers.*

Joint Committee on Standards. (1994). *The program evaluation standards* (2nd ed.). Thousand Oaks, CA: Sage Publications, Inc.

Joyce, B., & Showers, B. (2002). *Student achievement through staff development* (3rd ed.). Alexandria, VA: Association for Supervision and Curriculum Development.

Killion, J. (2009). Coaches roles, responsibilities, and reach. In J. Knight (Ed.) *Coaching approaches & perspectives.* Thousand Oaks, CA: Corwin Press.

Korsten, J., Foss, T., & Berry, L., (2007). *Every move counts, clicks and chats: emc3.* Lee's Summit, MO: EMC Communications, Inc.

Langley, G. L., Nolan, K. M., Nolan, T. W., Norman, C. L., Provost, L. P. (2009). *The improvement guide: A practical approach to enhancing organizational performance* (2nd ed,). San Francisco, CA: Jossey Bass.

Maccini, P., & Gagnon, J. (2005). Math graphic organizers for students with disabilities. Washington, DC: American Institutes for Research, The Access Center: Improving Outcomes for All Students K-8. Downloaded from *http://digilib.gmu. edu:8080/jspui/handle/1920/283.*

Marsters, A. E. (2011). An exploratory study of the assistive technology knowledge, skills, and needs among special education teachers and related services personnel. Unpublished doctoral dissertation.

Martin, S. (2013). Personal communication, October 16, 2013.

McCormick, L. K., Steckler, A. B., & McLeroy, K. R. (1995). Diffusion of innovations in schools: A study of adoption and implementation of school-based tobacco prevention curricula. *American Journal of Health Promotion, 9*(3), 210–219.

Millar, D., Schlosser, R. W., & Light, J. C. (2006). The impact of augmentative and alternative communication intervention on the speech production of individuals with developmental disabilities: A research review. *Journal of Speech, Language, and Hearing Research, 49*(2), 248–264.

O'Dwyer, L. M., Russell, M., & Bebell, D. J. (2004, September 14). Identifying teacher, school and district characteristics associated with elementary teachers' use of technology: A multilevel perspective. *Education Policy Analysis Archives, 12*(48).

Olson, R. K., & Wise, B. (1992). Reading on the computer with orthographic and speech feedback. *Reading and Writing: An Interdisciplinary Journal, 4*(2), 107–144. doi:10.1007/BF01027488.

Olson, R. K., Wise, B., Ring, J., & Johnson, M. (1997). Computer-based remedial training in phoneme awareness and phonological decoding: Effects on the post-training development of word recognition. *Scientific Studies of Reading, 1*(3), 235–253. doi:10.1207/s1532799xssr0103_4.

Ostensjo S., Carlberg E. B., Vollestad, N. K. (2005). The use and impact of assistive devices and other environmental modifications on everyday activities and care in young children with cerebral palsy. *Disability and Rehabilitation 27*(14), 849–861.

Paine, S. C., Bellamy, G. T., & Wilcox, B. L. (Eds.). (1984). *Human services that work: From innovation to standard practice.* Baltimore, MD: Brookes Publishing.

Panzano, P. C., Roth, D., Crane-Ross, D., Massatti, R., Carstens, C., Seffrin, B., and Chaney-Jones, S. (2005). The Innovation Diffusion and Adoption Research Project (IDARP): Moving from the diffusion of research results to promoting the adoption of evidence-based innovations in the Ohio mental health system. In D. Roth & W. J. Lutz (Eds.), *New Research in Mental Health, (16)*, 78–89. Columbus, OH: Ohio Department of Mental Health.

Pavitt, C., & Curtis, E. (2001). *Small group discussion: A theoretical approach, 3rd Edition.* Retrieved July 30, 2014 from *www.uky.edu/~drlane/teams/Pavitt.*

Poole, M. S. (1990). Procedures for managing meetings: Social and technological innovation. In R. A. Swanson & B. O. Knapp (Eds.), *Innovative meeting management* (pp. 53–109). Austin, TX: 3M Meeting Management Institute.

Raskind, M. H. & Bryant, B. R. (2002). *Functional evaluation of assistive technology (FEAT).* Port Chester, NY: National Professional Resources, Inc. *www.nprinc.com/assist_tech/feat.htm.*

Reed, P., & Bowser, G. (2005). Assistive technology in the IEP. In D.L. Edyburn, K. Higgins, & R. Boone (Eds.), *The handbook of special education technology research and practice* (pp. 61–77). Whitefish Bay, WI: Knowledge by Design, Inc.

Reed, P. & Bowser, G. (2012). Consultation, collaboration, and coaching: Essential techniques for integrating assistive technology use in schools and early intervention programs. *Journal of Occupational Therapy, Schools, & Early Intervention, 5,* 15–30.

Reed, P., Bowser, G., & Korsten, J. (2002). *How do you know it? How can you show it?* Oshkosh, WI: Wisconsin Assistive Technology Initiative. Retrieved September 17, 2014 from *http://dpi.wi.gov/files/sped/pdf/at-know-it-show-it.pdf.*

Rehabilitation Act of 1973, Section 504, PL 93-112, 29 U.S.C. § 794, 1977.

Rose, D. H. & Meyer, A. (2002). *Teaching every student in the digital age: Universal design for learning.* Alexandria, VA: Association for Supervision and Curriculum Development.

Rowland, C. (2004). *Communication matrix.* Portland, OR: Oregon Health Sciences University. Retrieved August 10, 2014 from *www.communicationmatrix.org.*

Schrag, J. (1990). OSEP policy letter. Washington, D.C.: U.S. Office of Education.

Sitko, M.C., Laine, C.J., & Sitko, C.J. (2005). Writing tools: Technology and strategies for struggling writers. In D. Edyburn, K. Higgins, and R. Boone (Eds.) *Handbook of Special Education Technology Research and Practice* (pp. 571–598). Whitefish Bay, WI: Knowledge by Design, Inc.

Strangman, N., & Dalton, B. (2005). Technology for struggling readers: A review of the research. In D. Edyburn, K. Higgins, & R. Boone (Eds.), *Handbook of special education technology research and practice* (pp. 545–569). Whitefish Bay, WI: Knowledge by Design, Inc.

Stumbo, N. J., Martin, J. K., & Hedrick, B. N. (2009). Assistive technology: Impact on education, employment, and independence in individuals with physical disabilities. *Journal of Vocational Rehabilitation, 30*(2), 99–110.

Sturm, J. M., Nelson, N. W., Staskowski, M., & Cali, K. (November, 2010). *Outcome measures for beginning writers with disabilities.* Mini-seminar presented at the American Speech-Language-Hearing Convention, Philadelphia, PA.

Technology-Related Assistance for Individuals with Disabilities Act. (1988). PL 100-407, Title 29, U.S.C. § 2201.

Todis, B., & Walker, H. M. (1993). User perspectives on assistive technology in educational settings. *Focus on Exceptional Children, 26*(3), 1–16.

Todis, B. (1996). Assistive technology in educational settings. *Journal of Special Education Technology, 13*(2), 49–61.

U.S. Department of Justice and U.S. Department of Education. (2014a). Dear Colleague Letter from the Acting Assistant Attorney General for Civil Rights, U.S. Department of Justice, the Acting Assistant Secretary Office of Special Education and Rehabilitative Services, U.S. Department of Education, and the Assistant Secretary, Office for Civil Rights, U.S. Department of Education on effective communication-November 12, 2014. Retrieved December 8, 2014, from *www2.ed.gov/about/offices/list/ocr/letters/colleague-effective-communication-201411.pdf*.

U.S. Department of Justice and U.S. Department of Education. (2014b). Frequently asked questions on effective communication for students with hearing, vision, or speech disabilities in public elementary and secondary schools. Retrieved December 8, 2014, from *www2.ed.gov/about/offices/list/ocr/docs/dcl-faqs-effective-communication-201411.pdf*.

Wallace, F., Blase, K., Fixsen, D., & Naoom, S. (2008). *Implementing the findings of research: Bridging the gap between knowledge and practice.* Alexandria, VA: Educational Research Service.

Warshauer, M. (2007). A teacher's place in the digital divide. *Yearbook of the National Society for the Study of Education, 106*(2), 147–166.

Watson, A. H., Ito, M., Smith, R. O., & Andersen, L. T. (2010). Effect of assistive technology in a public school setting. *American Journal of Occupational Therapy, 64*(1), 18–29.

Wehmeyer, M. L., & Field, S. L. (2007). *Self-determination: Instructional and assessment strategies.* Thousand Oaks, CA: Corwin Press.

Wilcox, J. M., Dugan, L. M., Campbell, P. H., & Guimond, A. (2006). Recommended practices and parent perspectives regarding AT use in early intervention. *Journal of Special Education Technology, 4*(21), 7–15.

Wilcox, J. M., Guimond, A., Campbell, P. H., & Weintraub Moore, H. (2006). Provider perspectives on the use of assistive technology for infants and toddlers with disabilities. *Topics in Early Childhood Special Education, 26*(1), 33–49.

Winter, S. G., & Szulanksi, G. (2001). Replication as strategy. *Organization Science, 12*(6), 730–743.

Wisconsin Assistive Technology Initiative. (2009). *WATI assessment forms packet.* Milton, WI: Author. Retrieved August 1, 2014 from *sped.dpi.wi.gov/sped_at-wati-resources*.

Wojcik, B. (2011). *Voices from the field: Issues and lessons from the QIAT listserv.* Unpublished doctoral dissertation, Illinois State University, Normal, IL.

Zabala, J. (1999). *SETT Scaffolds.* Retrieved August 4, 2014 from *www.joyzabala.com/Documents.html.*

Zabala, J. S., Bowser, G., Blunt, M., Carl, D. F., Davis, S., Deterding, C., Foss, T., Korsten, J., Hamman, T., Hartsell, K., Marfilius, S. W., McCloskey-Dale, S., Nettleton, S. D., & Reed, P. (2000). Quality indicators for assistive technology services. *Journal of Special Education Technology, 15*(4), 25–36.

Zabala, J. S. (2007). *Development and evaluation of quality indicators for assistive technology services.* University of Kentucky Doctoral Dissertations. Paper 517. Retrieved May 5, 2015 from *http://uknowledge.uky.edu/gradschool_diss/517.*

Zabala, J. S., & Carl, D. F. (2005). Quality indicators for assistive technology services in schools. In D. L. Edyburn, K. Higgins, & R. Boone (Eds.), *The handbook of special education technology research and practice* (pp. 179–207). Whitefish Bay, WI: Knowledge by Design, Inc.

# About the Authors

## The QIAT Leadership Team

### Gayl Bowser

Gayl Bowser, M.S. in Education, currently works as an independent consultant and is an adjunct faculty member at the University of Wyoming. Her work focuses on the creation of service systems that encourage the integration of technology into educational programs for students with disabilities. Formerly the coordinator of the Oregon Technology Access Program (OTAP) and the State of Oregon's specialist in assistive technology, Gayl currently provides assistive technology consultation, training, and technical assistance throughout the United States and internationally. Gayl has co-authored numerous publications about assistive technology services including *Education Tech Points: A Framework for Assistive Technology* and *Assistive Technology Pointers for Parents.*

### Diana Foster Carl

Diana Foster Carl has a B.A. and M.A. in Psychology and is a Licensed Specialist in School Psychology in Texas. She has more than 35 years of experience in various capacities in public education, including leadership roles in national, state, and regional organizations. Currently, Diana contracts with CAST as the special projects coordinator for the National Center on Accessible Educational Materials for Learning (the AEM Center). Diana is a former director of special education services at Region 4 Education Service Center in Houston, Texas, where she was lead facilitator of the Texas Assistive Technology Network for 12 years. Diana's daughter has cerebral palsy and uses a power wheelchair for mobility.

### Terry Vernon Foss

Terry Vernon Foss has an M.Ed. with an emphasis in Special Education. Terry has been a special educator for more than 35 years in classrooms for students with autism and with severe and profound disabilities including speech, intellectual, and motor impairments. For the last 20+ years, she has been an assistive technology specialist for the Shawnee Mission School District in Kansas. Terry is a coauthor of *Every Move Counts* and *Every Move Counts Clicks and Chats.*

## Kelly S. Fonner

Kelly Fonner has a B.S. in Special Education and an M.S. in Educational Technology with an emphasis in Rehabilitation/Special Education Technology. She has done continuing education in Adult Education and Special Education Technology. Kelly has been a teacher, para-educator, instructional media specialist, and assistive technology specialist. She is currently self-employed as a consultant in assistive and educational technology. She has worked for a statewide AT project and has been an instructor in university courses on AT. Since 1986 she has presented to schools, conferences, and families in 46 states and internationally on a wide range of topics in AT. Kelly is also the daughter of a person with an acquired physical disability, the sister-in-law of a woman with cerebral palsy, and the cousin of individuals with a teenager with Aspergers.

## Jane Edgar Korsten

Jane Edgar Korsten holds a B.S. in Elementary Education and an M.A. in Speech Pathology and Audiology. She currently works as an independent consultant, a speech pathologist, and AT resource for individuals of all ages. She has worked in public schools, supported settings for adults, and had a private practice developing alternate communication systems for individuals who are non-verbal. She was the principal investigator on an Innovative Research Grant funded through the National Institutes of Health which led to the development of Every Move Counts, a sensory based approach to communication. Jane is a coauthor of *Every Move Counts, Every Move Counts Clicks and Chats,* and *How Do You Know It? How Do You Show It?*

## Kathleen M. Lalk

Kathleen M. Lalk has a B.S. in Recreation Therapy and an M.S. in Educational Technology. For more than 20 years, she has served as an assistive technology specialist for Special School District in St. Louis County, Missouri. Her work includes support of students with disabilities, their families, and their educational team in the consideration, implementation, and evaluation of the use of assistive technology. She is also a consumer support provider for Missouri Assistive Technology.

## Joan Breslin Larson

Joan Breslin Larson holds an M.Ed. in Adult Education. Joan is the supervisor for low incidence disabilities and special education workforce at the Minnesota Department of Education. She is also a consultant to other state organizations and schools on systems issues in AT. Joan has worked in assistive technology for over 25 years as an independent consultant, in school settings, and at a state education agency. Joan has family members with disabilities, including a child who had an IEP and others with acquired disabilities.

## Scott Marfilius

Scott Marfilius has an M.A. in Education (Curriculum and Instruction). Scott has worked with individuals with disabilities for more than 33 years, and for the past 29 years has been involved in implementing assistive technology services at various levels. Scott assists teams and individuals in assessing students' AT needs. Scott also works with universities and has assisted in reorganizing postsecondary curriculum to infuse technology throughout the teacher-preparation experience. He also consults with individuals and businesses to determine adaptations that are needed in workplace settings. Scott's focus areas in assistive technology include computer access and technologies that assist those with cognitive and learning disabilities.

## Susan R. McCloskey

Susan R. McCloskey, MS, CCC-SLP, is a speech language pathologist who worked for the PA Assistive Technology Center/PaTTAN in Pennsylvania and is now chairperson of the Volusia Adaptive Assistive Technology Team (VAATT) in Daytona Beach, FL. She is a past steering committee member for ASHA's Division 12: Augmentative and Alternative Communication. Susan has consulted nationwide with teams whose focus has been to integrate assistive technology into the classroom. She has been a trainer of environmental communication teaching (ECT) since 1989. She is currently involved in implementing the SCERTS project, focused on students on the autism spectrum in her district and lives in Ponce Inlet, FL.

## Penny R. Reed

Penny R. Reed has an M.S. and Ph.D. in Special Education and a B.S. in Elementary Education. Dr. Reed has been a teacher, consultant, and administrator in the field of special education and assistive technology. She regularly provides consultation and training on a variety of topics related to assistive technology assessment and service delivery with a special focus on helping school districts improve their delivery of assistive technology services. She is the author and coauthor of numerous publications about assistive technology services, including *Education Tech Points: A Framework for Assistive Technology*.

## Joy Smiley Zabala

Joy Smiley Zabala, Ed.D., holds degrees in Elementary and Early Childhood Education and Special Education Personnel Preparation. Currently she is the Director of Technical Assistance for CAST and the National Center on Accessible Educational Materials for Learning. She is an experienced general and special educator who has worked for more than 30 years with educators, families, and students across the US and abroad to expand the use of assistive and accessible technologies, accessible materials, and Universal Design for Learning for the participation and achievement of all learners across the lifespan. Dr. Zabala is the developer of the SETT Framework, a past president of the Technology and Media Division of the Council for Exceptional Children, and serves as a faculty member for the Center on Technology and Disability.

# Index